Nothing

n My Mind

Nothing on My Mind

BERKELEY, LSD,
TWO ZEN MASTERS,
AND A LIFE ON THE
DHARMA TRAIL

Erik Fraser Storlie

SHAMBHALA
Boston & London
1996

SHAMBHALA PUBLICATIONS, INC.
HORTICULTURAL HALL
300 Massachusetts Avenue
Boston, Massachusetts 02115

9 8 7 6 5 4 3 2 1

First Edition

Printed in the United States of America

⊛ This edition is printed on acid-free paper that meets the
American National Standards Institute Z39.48 Standard.

Distributed in the United States by Random House, Inc.,
and in Canada by Random House of Canada Ltd

Library of Congress Cataloging-in-Publication Data
Storlie, Erik.
    Nothing on my mind: an intimate account of American Zen/Erik
Storlie.—1st ed.
        p. cm.
    ISBN 1-57062-183-7 (alk. paper)
    1. Zen Buddhism—United States.   2. Spiritual life—Zen Buddhism.
3. Storlie, Erik.   I. Title.
BQ9262.9.U6S76   1996
294.3'927'092—dc20   96-16432
    [B]   CIP

When even just one person, at one time, sits in zazen, he becomes, imperceptibly, one with each and all of the myriad things, and permeates completely all time, so that within the limitless universe, throughout past, future, and present, he is performing the eternal and ceaseless work of guiding beings to enlightenment. . . . This is not limited to the practice of sitting alone; the sound that issues from the striking of emptiness is an endless and wondrous voice that resounds before and after the fall of the hammer.

—DOGEN, *Bendowa*

We are the mirror as well as the face in it.
We are tasting the taste this minute
of eternity. We are pain
and what cures pain. We are
the sweet, cold water and the jar that pours.

—RUMI

I play my song eating, eating the peyote, waiting to see the flower, the beautiful flower in the center there of the fire. I play to the four winds, offering all my will, all my affections, all my strength. I went to bathe in the sea, to learn how to sing, to learn how to play. Waves come and go, waves come and go. I ate of them. I ate the foam. Who now knows better how to sing? Who now knows better how to play? I ate the foam of the sea, the pure foam of the sea.

What does one see in the fire? You do not speak of it, not to the companions, not to you, not to anyone does one reveal what one has seen. One makes a garland of peyote to hang on the horns of the deer, of our elder brother.

—*Songs sung during*
the Huichol Indian
peyote quest

Dainin Katagiri Roshi,

Teacher

And dear friend,

Wherever you wander

Or don't wander,

Know that this is for you.

Contents

Preface

IF READERS ARE CURIOUS ABOUT THE MAKING OF this book, I should tell them it is not fiction, nor is it quite fact. All the incidents described happened to me. But it is memory—memory of events that go back over thirty years—and memory in the service of a narrative.

In the first half of the book, the Berkeley half, I have freely telescoped or expanded events and, at times, drawn together traits of several people I knew and placed them in one character. Or placed the traits of one person in several. No actual names have been used. I sincerely beg pardon of all old friends and acquaintances who find here fragments of themselves. Please forgive these liberties. No offense is intended.

In the second half, the zen half, I have not altered events and people in this way. My experiences with Suzuki Roshi and Katagiri Roshi I have described to the best of my ability and memory. I have, nonetheless, reconstructed situations and conversations that I could not remember in precise detail. Occasionally I have gathered trenchant remarks that I remember from over the years into one place. The reader whose first purpose is to study these two zen masters must read with the knowledge that everything here is filtered through my memory—and through my follies, weaknesses, and attachments. The names given in this latter half are real.

I hope this book will encourage American forms of meditation practice—forms freed from the trappings of any specific culture, whether of a Japan or a Tibet or an India. This is a delicate matter, but I look for an American practice that does not forget our own ancestors: the Native American living in intimacy with the earth, the Puritan fiercely devoted to God, the Transcendentalist seeking spirit in all things, the African-American transforming and transmuting Christianity. The East gives us the Sanskrit *dhyana*, the Chinese *ch'an*, the Japanese *zen*—upright sitting in firm, awake, one-pointed awareness. What American form can array this miraculous consciousness with which all are gifted?

I want to thank some of those friends who, in helping with this writing, have helped me weave together two painfully separated strands of my life: the student, teacher, and lover of words in the tradition of the Greeks—and the student of the wordless. I owe a great debt to William E. Coles. Bill was my instructor in Freshman English when I was seventeen and he, only several years older, the youngest member of the English Department at the University of Minnesota. Since then, he has ever pressed me to write good English. About ten years ago he gave me a method for doing my writing. Over scores of telephone calls, it has led to this book. The method is pure zen.

I also thank Robert Bly. He read and criticized the book and made valuable suggestions. More important, at many of the Minnesota Fall Men's Conferences and other gatherings, he has helped modulate my prairie Norwegian, Zen Buddhist way of being. His gift is the companionship of other men with dance, drum, song, and spirit—a taste of the joy that in more dour traditions must wait until death.

I am grateful to Robert Pirsig. He read the book, made valuable comments, and offered encouragement. His *Zen and the Art of Motorcycle Maintenance* and *Lila* were and are inspirations to write about the movement of Eastern modes of consciousness into America.

My agent Scott Edelstein has been solidly behind this project. In his readings and re-readings, he has been midwife. My editor Peter Turner has offered quiet, perceptive, and firm criticism. Edward M. Griffin read an early draft and told me things I did not want, but needed, to hear. Alan Trachtenberg was kind enough to read, comment, and encourage. Shohaku Okumura Sensei gave valuable advice on the English wording of a key Dogen passage and, most important, further instruction in zazen.

I am grateful for permission to use material from *The Psychedelic Experience* by Timothy Leary, Ralph Metzner, and Richard Alpert. I owe them a great debt for their courageous pursuit of Aldous Huxley's seminal insight that the psychedelic experience opens up meditative states of consciousness. I am thankful for the kind persmission granted to quote Rumi #1652 from *Open Secret: Versions of Rumi*. I acknowledge the use of quotations from Dogen from the beautiful translations by Norman Waddell and Masao Abe, and the use of Huichol songs from the film *To Find Our Life*.

Nothing
on My Mind

1

The Crag

I'M SITTING ON THE TOP OF A LOW, NAMELESS mountain in foothills that cup the northwest edge of the Flute Reed Basin. I'm sitting at seven thousand feet and looking off miles over basins and valleys toward the ten- and eleven-thousand-foot peaks of the Bitterroot and Flute Reed River ranges. I'm sitting with legs crossed in the full lotus position, back and neck upright, hands resting in my lap on the upturned soles of my feet.

I'm sitting on three black chunks of rock, each sheared along a single flat plane. Thirty years ago I fit them into a level seat just large enough for one person with legs crossed in the lotus position. This seat perches on the highest point of the mountain, a spur of ridgeline—a jumbled outcrop spared by the glacier ten thousand years ago. I call it the Crag.

It's sunny, the sky brilliant, a late morning in early October. I'll meditate till sundown. My gaze drops at a forty-five degree angle down to a soft focus on the rocks before me, eyelids following so my eyes are half closed. The round, sun-drenched pool of my visual field is fluid, the shapes, textures, and colors of the black rocks before me drifting subtly beneath my gaze. Sometimes, distracted by small, vivid patches of crusty green lichen clinging to the dark rock, I shut my eyes and watch the muted red velvet behind my eyelids.

I'm alert, marking the posture of my body and the posture of my mind. This is Zen Master Dogen's *zazen*—sitting meditation. A voice in my head whispers his command, "Settle into a steady, immobile sitting position. Think of not-thinking."

Noticing that my shoulders slump a bit, I straighten up, then sway gently from side to side in a steadily decreasing arc, centering my head, neck, and back.

The voice reminds me, "Yes, keep your back and neck erect—buoyant and easy. Let your vertebrae be a graceful S-curve of balanced golden coins.

"Rest your left hand, palm upward and slightly cupped, gently atop the palm of the right hand—just so.

"Ground your right hand firmly on the soles of your feet and touch your thumb tips together—lightly, lightly. A spark of consciousness jumps between those tips—electricity between the two halves of the body, east and west of a dark continent, meat and bone and muscle and nerve.

"Now, cupped in your hands, feel a vast, invisible universe concentrated in your very palms, smooth and round like a hen's egg, yet radiating out, out, in every direction."

My chest relaxes and drops, my breath slows down, flowing in, flowing out, flowing in, slowly, slowly expanding my belly into the shape of a pot. Effortlessly, the mind watches breath. As cloud thoughts dissolve in a vast blue sky, I remember the yogi's words, "Let mind be before thought!"

Subtle currents vibrate from my toes up through my feet and legs, through stomach, chest, arms, and hands to fingertips, from fingertips back to toes—a circle completed by my hands nestling on the soles of my feet. The spark tingles between my thumb tips. Dogen's words again steal through my mind: "Once its heart is grasped, you are like the dragon when he gains the water, like the tiger when he enters the mountain."

My slow breath moves in and out, in and out, ecstatic shivers lapping from the top of my head to the base of my spine. My head, chest, and belly are spacious hollow vessels, pooling, drenched with luscious mind stuff. For many long, golden minutes no thoughts arise.

I sit under open sky, a mote spun up into the vast basin and come to rest on solid rock. Warm breezes purl over the Crag, punctuated with birdsong carried up from the steep slopes of pine and fir that fall down and away.

But then, pleased with this emptiness, a voice in my head sings congratulations: "Erik, you've done it. Thirty years sitting in zazen has finally paid off. It's bliss. The Buddha said this vibrant, empty consciousness would arise after the cessation of thought."

On the heels of proud thoughts, doubts rush in. A scornful voice mocks, "Come on, now. You call this emptiness? This pitiful drop in the bucket? Since when did the Buddha settle for an occasional peak experience in the mountains? Or confuse some maverick practice of zen sitting with enlightenment itself?"

Then the voice, contemptuous, turns to my past: "And since when did the old zen masters in China and Japan write useless doctoral dissertations? Or hang about for years teaching college English? Or have a divorce and girlfriend troubles? God, God, a life filled with loose ends—unwoven strands."

Now, sitting on the Crag, my mind clouds with memory. I no longer mark the sun heightening toward noon, beating hot on my left shoulder, the wind drying the sweat on the small of my back, the basins and valleys spread out at my lap.

Strands of my life, one by one, float up like incense and curl through my mind—a path unfolding that leads step by step to just this moment, just this jagged outcrop, just these three rough black rocks on the Crag.

2

My Ditch

IT'S EARLIER, THAT SAME OCTOBER MORNING. I'M in a ditch with pick and shovel, the sun barely up and frost covering the meadow grasses. The ditch runs back up behind my cabin to an old gravity-feed well. I've lived thirty summers in this ramshackle two-story log building, once part of a Depression-era gold-mining speculation on Flute Reed Creek. It failed, leaving the creek upended and the cabin derelict on the land. It sits at the end of miles of gravel road—no power, no water, no sewer, no phone, no neighbors. When I look out the front windows, across ten miles of basin to the Flute Reed peaks, only a distant fence line betrays the work of human hands. Behind me, beyond the Crag, the uninhabited mountains of the far west roll for hundreds of miles to the north.

This is my third morning in the ditch. I'm digging out a section of rotten iron pipe laid fifty years ago between the cabin and the well. The well lies in lodgepole pine a hundred yards behind the cabin up a gentle slope—a slope that in the mile to the north rises more and more steeply a thousand vertical feet through open sage, then back into pine, then up onto long ridgelines crested with great Douglas fir, then at last up to the Crag.

For days after I open the well, the pipe spouts stinking, sulfurous, rusty red water. As it begins to run clear, I use it for dishes and a solar shower. The shower water runs through coils of black plastic pipe thrown out on a gentle sage-covered hillside a hundred feet east of the cabin. The pipe then empties into a coffee can punched with holes and wired to a pole suspended between two lodgepole pines. I shower here in the open air at the bottom of the slope on the edge of the forest. At noon on a hot, sunny day, the water is scalding. By sundown it's icy. Whenever it's just right, I shower. Afterward, my skin smells of sulfur and old iron.

I don't care. I love my shower. But this summer, my kids, thirteen and sixteen, balked at using it. I'm ditching so I can replace the old iron with plastic.

The work is good. I dig with pick and shovel, up to my hips in dirt. Hot, sweating already in the chill morning air, happy in the animal force of my back and arms, I swing the pick. It arcs high overhead. Exhaling in a grunt, I smash the point into the tough glacial matrix of hardpan clay and gravel. Stooping, I lever boulders free of their beds. I straighten, and on the return stroke, the wooden handle slides smoothly through the circle of my right thumb and fingers, the iron head swinging back massive and low, ready to be caught by the up-thrust. Inhaling the cool moisture of broken earth drifting up to meet the smell of pine needles, I sense the delicate fulcrums of wrist and elbow, shoulder and knee, hip and vertebra.

Yes, the work is good. But it's beautiful this morning—cloudless blue over mountains ten miles distant where steep hanging snowfields shimmer in angling sunlight. Why not a day of zazen up on the Crag? Yes, why not? I throw down the pick.

Back at the cabin, the coffeepot on the wood stove still hot, I fill up my white ceramic cup and drink another cup of coffee, make peanut butter and jelly sandwiches, then pack sandwiches, water bottle, apple, chocolate bar, sunscreen, binoculars, and down vest into my day pack. Grabbing a broad-brimmed hat, I step out the front door of the cabin and walk east toward my shower and the edge of the forest. It descends down foothills to touch open sage and meadow and the back and sides of the cabin.

I stand for a moment in the shadow of the trees, then turn to gaze at the mountains. Still chilled with morning air sweeping down the slopes, the meadow grasses at my feet are thick with frost. My boots, warm from the stove, bead with moisture. My toes are suddenly cool.

The treetops at the forest's edge cast a jagged line of shadow before me across the ground. The angling sunlight creeps imperceptibly toward my boots, closer and closer, carving the meadow frost into an echo of the Flute Reed peaks.

I sit down on the ground to watch. The grass gives up its cold and wet to my jeans, and I shiver. As the mountains of frost near my boots, I see forests of tiny white fingers on each blade of grass burn away and gather suddenly into transparent droplets clinging on green.

I stand and walk north up into the trees, then follow my ditch a few hundred feet to the raw cut I've just left for another day. I pick the shovel out of the damp grass and lean it against a lodgepole pine. Struck by a shaft of sunlight that finds its way through the forest canopy, sprinkles of drying sand tumble from the top of the last shovelful I threw only minutes ago. The work beckons. It can wait till tomorrow.

I follow the ditch through sage and meadow up to the open well. It's eight feet deep, cribbed in with rotting pine poles. A few wild roses cling to the gravelly brim, the blossoms now turned to hips. Chewing one slowly, savoring the tartness, I lie down at the lip, elbows on the rotting top pole, and stare down into the cold, shadowed waters. A slight, cool breeze wafting from the treetops starts a convulsive shudder up my spine, and the shaking of my forearms loosens gravel that kerplunks down into the well.

Bigfoot! Just as I lie here now, he lay. Twenty-five years ago, digging in the bottom of the well at sundown, my brother felt eyes upon him and looked up. A huge red gorilla face stared down, filling the opening of the well.

My brother glanced away, then back up. It was gone. He climbed out of the well and ran the hundred yards down to the cabin, where I was cooking dinner. Strangely, he found that I, too, was in a state of panic. For the last half hour, working in the kitchen, waves of nameless fear had poured over me. Abandoning supper on the table, we drove into town and drank beer after beer, returning finally to the cabin only after the bar closed.

Since then, in hundreds of comings and goings past the well, I always remember. Today, again, my eyes search out into the dark spaces between tree trunks for that tall, shadowy form, that huge red face.

Nothing. Of course, nothing.

"Well," I think to myself, "I'll never know. There are wilderness routes unbroken from here clear to the Northwest Territories and Alaska. But he'd still have to be damn clever to stay so well out of sight."

A dead squirrel floats in the well, its dusky red-brown fur puffed out from its body. Did it fall out of the pine overhead or lose its grip as it tried to bury pine cones in holes by the edge? The well is a death trap for squirrels. I dip it out with a coffee can nailed to a long stick kept here for this purpose.

Leaving the well, walking up into open slopes of sage, I'm out of the shadow. The sun is already warm. The sage, crushed underfoot, is pungent. Then I'm up into lodgepole pine and, higher, into virgin Douglas fir.

For an hour I wander the steep foothills, circling on and off the old mining road that worms partway up the mountain. I stop below the lowest of two tunnels and sit on the fan of broken rock that spews from the opening and sprawls down the slope—debris dumped from the mine. Pulling out my binoculars, I scan the Flute Reeds, then east to the Bitterroots, then down into the great basin that lies between the ranges, then back up to the Flute Reeds. Peak after peak shimmers before me in the glass. Lovingly, I remember cirques and lakes beneath them.

I linger on a pass on the horizon ten miles distant—a V in the black cliffs with a delicate finger of snow reaching up almost to the cleft. I've never been over it. For years I've planned a crossing. "You better do it soon," I think to myself. "How many more years will you still be agile in the mountains?"

I stand. My feet slide on the steep fan of shattered waste rock. Years ago, I helped create this pile with Roscoe, my only neighbor, an un-shaven, unsavory old man with a shock of short white hair. We met over thirty years ago, and on that day he held me at gunpoint, enraged at my encroachment on his mountain. We made our peace over whis-key, and from then on I saw him every summer.

He would come up from Utah in a battered pickup, hauling a ram-shackle trailer that he'd perch on the side of the mountain, then work his hardrock claims above. And each summer he'd tell me he was about to hit the widening in his vein of silver ore.

"Just a few more feet into this devil mountain," he'd say. We'd drill, place charges, light fuses, and then run fast down the steep slide rock to take cover behind a boulder.

He'd count the blasts as the mountain shook. "One, two, three . . . Hey, where's that last bastard? Ah, there it is!"

Then we'd shovel the heavy rock into a wheelbarrow, wheel it to the mouth of the tunnel, and dump it, stinking with spent explosive, down the slope.

At sundown, back at the trailer, we'd drink beer and build a fire outside the trailer door. He'd fetch steaks of poached venison from a meat bag hung far back in the shade of the pines.

Throwing it in the fry pan, he'd wink, "Nothing like that good old mountain mutton!"

We'd sit outside in folding chairs and eat—then drink some more, watching the fire die down and stars spread canopies out over the mountaintops. Then Roscoe would spin out dreams of silver and girls and easy street. By this time of year, he'd always be gone, heading out before snow could catch him.

I kick at the rock and smile toward clumps of brilliant yellow aspen scattered on the hills across the valley, a rare red tree flaring like an autumn torch. Patches of heather, a darker red, splash the green-gray sage. Beyond, rising above creeks and bottomlands, I see the distant tumble of the Flute Reed peaks.

"Yeah," I think to myself, "this is what Roscoe really came here for. Like me. Not just to grub for silver. Not just to look for easy street. He never made a dime on those damn prospect holes."

I'm jarred back to awareness at the Crag by two hawks. My eyes have been cast down, my gaze coming to rest in soft focus on the patch of rock several feet below the elevation of my seat and about ten feet in front of me. Flying between me and the sun, the hawks throw their shadows directly before me, momentarily darkening my gaze. Now I notice the graininess of the rock shimmering in the sunlight, and variations in the lichen—some green, some gray, some a startling orange.

Growing curious, I glance up to find the hawks soaring only a hundred feet above my head. In some mutual agreement, they wheel suddenly, then drop away a thousand feet and disappear in trees far below me on a low, distant hillside to the north. Excited, I rummage in my day pack for the binoculars and scan the horizon. No hawks. I give up, then notice they're already back, now drifting high overhead.

The sun, heightening toward noon, is hot. I'm thirsty. I strip off my long-sleeved shirt, pull the water jug out of my day pack, and drink. The water, which was cold this morning, is now lukewarm. I stretch out my legs, lean against a smooth upthrust rock, and scan again for the hawks.

It takes several minutes to locate them. They're distant, to the west, two spots against the blue sky. They play, soaring in closer and closer to each other, then apart, then together again until merged in one speck of brown moving against the sky. Suddenly the speck drops toward the basin floor, then they're apart again, soaring up in different directions. I feel the swooping fall and sudden steep climb in my stomach and chest. In heartbeats, they cover distances that take me laborious hours through sage, timber, and rockslide.

After drinking half my liter of water, I'm ready to return to my seat. This time I'll be alert, attentive, one-pointed—aware of awareness itself. The trained mind, say the Tibetans, sticks to itself like bread dough.

I massage a liberal dose of sunscreen on my bare arms and face to protect my freckled Scots-Norwegian skin. I sit down, cross my legs, and gently pull my attention back to the Crag, to the blue sky overhead, to the beginning of a familiar ache just below my left shoulder

9

blade. My head must be drooping a bit forward. I sway gently forward and back, then from side to side, bringing my head and neck into alignment.

I return to the breath, breathing in, breathing out, expanding my belly into the shape of a pot. I watch carefully the empty space between the ceasing of the out-breath and the beginning of the in-breath, the ceasing of the in-breath and the beginning of the out-breath. I count heartbeats in these spaces, holding the emptiness for three counts—three pulsations that surge up and recede in my chest, spreading out to fingertips and toes.

"My version of an old yogic practice," I think. "So strange that all this began with Huxley and Wasson and with Leary's acid manual inspired by the *Tibetan Book of the Dead*. What if I'd never gone to Berkeley?

"Oops. Thinking thoughts again. Okay, Erik, count!"

The voice in my head counts "One," as I slowly inhale, then slowly exhale. "Two" (slow inhale, slow exhale). "Three" (slow inhale, slow exhale). "Four" (slow inhale, slow exhale).

"Uh-oh." Now I'm remembering the Mixer's Bar in the run-down Seven Corners neighborhood in Minneapolis. It's the fall of 1961. I hear the Friday afternoon rush hour traffic creeping from the University of Minnesota over the long bridge that spans the Mississippi River. The university lies on the east bank. Here on the west bank begins a skid row. My elbows are on the long, scarred mahogany bar, installed when Seven Corners was the heart of a vibrant commercial district. My foot rests on the brass rail, there's a double shot of the cheapest bourbon with a beer back foaming before me, and comrades stream in to begin drinking in earnest.

Then it's the Berkeley campus. I see in my mind's eye the vista from the campanile across the bay to the Golden Gate Bridge, remembering the sound of bells after riding the old elevator to the very top of the tower on an afternoon softened with bay breezes.

I count more fiercely. "Five" (slow inhale, slow exhale). "Six" (slow inhale, slow exhale). Thoughts crowd in. My breath, inexorable, scatters them like ninepins. "Seven" (slow inhale, slow exhale). Stubborn thoughts begin to form again, tenacious, insistent, demanding attention. I tense my body and force my breath and attention through them—the breath a great ocean liner forging ahead in shining mind stuff, tossing the mind waves back from the prow, scattering them back into the sea.

"Seven" (inhale, exhale).

I'm getting really foggy. I know it. I'm doing three things at once now—counting breaths and thinking thoughts and worrying about thinking thoughts. My mind shouts, "Stop it! Concentrate!" I straighten my spine and force muscular tension into my arms and legs and diaphragm. "It's time for eight. Or—no—did you finish seven?"

Now I can't stop the remembering—and then the count is gone.

3

Berkeley—the Sixties

It's Berkeley, the fall of 1962. I'm almost twenty-two, beginning my first semester in the graduate program in English here, eager for a specialty in Middle English. I live in a basement efficiency apartment near Lake Merritt in downtown Oakland—a long bus ride to the Berkeley campus, but all I can afford. My folks send me one hundred dollars a month to cover everything but tuition and books. The rich kids have the lovely apartments on palm-studded streets that plunge down the Berkeley hills into the campus and on to the bay.

At first I'm lonely. I know only Miscorski—an old drinking buddy, a math major from Minnesota who moved here two years ago with his B.A. in math. He earns a princely salary working for the emerging computer industry. On weekends he and his girl take regular pity on me and invite me to dinner at her house or to restaurants in North Beach and Jack London Square. We eat fine meals and drink stupendous quantities of beer and wine. Miscorski pays the bill. I leave the tip.

Then, one afternoon after classes, heading for the bus down Telegraph, I bump into Rosenfeld, an old drinking buddy from the hip Seven Corners scene in Minneapolis. There he is, standing at Ludwig's Fountain—huge, an immense stomach, hairy arms and chest, balding, a full, wide brown beard, horn-rimmed glasses, a great Jewish bear. At twenty-five he looks forty. I didn't even know he was out here—and he tells me of other Minneapolis friends who are on their way to the Bay Area.

I'm delighted. In Minneapolis Rosenfeld sold books in oddball bookstores—he calls himself a "bookman"—and he proudly tells me he's working at a used bookstore that just opened in North Beach. In his off hours and after closing at night, he hangs out. I imagine Rosenfeld rolling his good-natured bulk up and down the streets of North Beach, greeting everyone at the bars and coffeehouses.

Rosenfeld takes me home to meet his girlfriend, Samantha, and her two little kids. They're renting a house down on the flats about a mile from campus. They offer me their spare bedroom for thirty dollars a month and babysitting on Wednesday nights. The room is so tiny the bed touches three walls and there's no room for an armchair.

I jump at the chance. No more long bus rides into Oakland to a damp, dingy, lonely basement apartment, with a few hot buttered rums before bedtime at one of the downtown Oakland bars, empty except for maybe an old man drinking a beer.

Rosenfeld brews beer in plastic garbage cans. He owns an espresso machine. Friday nights he gives parties where friends gather for espresso, home brew, poetry reading, and folksinging. At my first soirée, Rosenfeld introduces me to Lisa, a young woman conservatively dressed in a skirt and blouse, her long, blond hair caught up in a severe bun. She works as a secretary on Telegraph Avenue and takes night classes in business. She sits on the floor in the corner of the living room, where she's been quietly listening to an earnest young man playing a guitar and singing. As she stands up, I notice nylons and shapely legs. She greets me with a solemn smile and a slow, firm handshake.

I settle into a routine of going to classes and studying late at the library. As a graduate student, I get my own work space in the Humanities Reading Room, its walls crammed with texts necessary to the scholar in English language and literature.

Rosenfeld is concerned about my diminished life as a graduate student. As we stroll one crisp fall afternoon through Berkeley toward the campus to browse in bookstores, he smokes marijuana in a briar pipe, chuckling, delighted that the bourgeoisie and the Berkeley cops are too dumb to catch on.

"You're not in Minneapolis anymore," he says, waving his hands urgently. Abruptly, he stops on the sidewalk and turns to tap my shoulder with the stem of his pipe. "You're in the Bay Area, man, home of the gold rush, Mark Twain, earthquakes, Jack London, North Beach, and the beats. Did you come here to be a professor or a poet?" Clenching his pipe between his teeth, he eyes me meaningfully. "Grass opens the doors. Remember your Bible, 'Knock and it shall be opened.' "

This is all new to me. In Minneapolis, we drank. Every Friday and Saturday afternoon, and weekdays too, the East Hennepin Bar and, across the Mississippi, the Mixers at Seven Corners filled with an amorphous crowd of students, professors, poets, artists, musicians, truck drivers, mechanics, petty criminals, street people, and beatniks. Endless, intense discussions of art, politics, and the meaning of life became long, roaring drunks that spilled over into all-night parties.

Here were the poet Jim Wright, the singer Dylan, and the strange Korean medical doctor with a Ph.D., a prestigious researcher on staff at the university, who like clockwork, once every weekend, wearing dark slacks, a white dress shirt, and a black bow tie, joined us and drank himself into insensibility.

We were liberated, free, a little band of embattled beings standing against American corruption, the drab wasteland of the burgeoning suburbs, and midwestern bluenose conformity. We were an avant-garde lifting the banners of art and intellect and libertine ecstasy on the glass-littered pavement of those seven old corners where the university merged with skid row.

As we resume walking, Rosenfeld expounds. "Listen, man. Grass is holy. Grass opens the doors of perception. Yeah, booze is okay now and then, but it makes you dumb. Really dumb. Head-busting hangovers—Christ, look at you last Saturday morning after getting drunk again with Miscorski? Sick for two days! Lisa comes by and you can't even go out with her. Do I have to tell you this? You're smart. You're a graduate student!"

I make no response. I can't quite imagine not drinking on Friday and Saturday nights. But marijuana is alluring, evoking visions of jazz musicians and artists, of Greenwich Village and liberated negroes with berets and pointed goatees.

"Grass expands consciousness," Rosenfeld continues. "You know, man, I smoke a pipe and sit down and I write poetry—one, two, three poems in an afternoon—it's lubrication, it's oil. It just happens, they flow out of me. Grass short-circuits dead parts of the brain—parts killed by your parents, by the fucking schools, by General Eisenhower.

"Do your profs at Berkeley know about any of this? Bullshit!" Rosenfeld pauses meaningfully, then goes on, "No way! You know that. It's a game. They don't give a shit about *you* writing anything. Or a real poet like Ferlinghetti, or Ginsberg, or Kerouac—forget it, the dumb fucks won't read the real stuff. They don't even really give a shit about the greats like Shakespeare or Auden either—all they care about is what some other big-name prof geek is writing *about* Shakespeare or Auden, and what they can write to pimp *that* geek and get a better job. It's all career bullshit. You know it, man. It's true. You can't deny it."

I don't deny it. Still, I don't have a draft scam. And I can't quite imagine not being in school.

"Listen. Tonight I'm going to meet the man at the bookstore. I'll split a lid with you. Twenty for the lid—that's only ten bucks apiece. I know you've got that much bread. You know, if you had to, it'd be cool even if you were a little late on the rent. Just don't tell Samantha I said so. Let Miscorski buy your beers this weekend."

"What's a lid?" I ask.

"Why, it's an ounce of grass, man. You dig? People call it that because they measure it off in the top of a tobacco can."

"Well, maybe," I say. "I tried it once with Lon and his girl in Minneapolis. Yeah, it was pretty cool! But that's a lot of money."

"A lot of money!" roars Rosenfeld. "A lot of money! How much do you spend drinking booze with Miscorski—even when he picks up most of the tab with those death dollars he makes programming rocket trajectories?"

"Hey," I protest, "that's not what he's really working on. It's something to do with some big system for an assembly line."

Rosenfeld slows our walk and rolls the alliteration of "death dollars" on his tongue a few times.

"Not bad. I can use that." He picks up the pace again.

"Anyway, where do those drunks leave you by Sunday morning? The booze is killing your good times with Lisa. And when are *you* going to write some poetry? I see the Storlie biography now: he learned at the feet of the geek profs of Berkeley—and then became one." Rosenfeld stops short on the sidewalk, his briar clenched between his teeth, and stares at me knowingly.

"You can spare the bread, man. It's not that much. What's really important here?"

"Well," I say, "I don't have that much *money*, as I still prefer to call it. My folks send me a hundred dollars a month and you get thirty. I'm not too flush."

"Don't argue. I'll bring it home after work tonight. We'll test it out. But don't worry, it'll be fine weed, mighty fine. We'll read Ginsberg and Auden—and before dawn we'll write one epic poem apiece!"

That night we don't write any epic poems. Rosenfeld and Samantha get the kids to bed, then holler at me to come downstairs. They sit on the living room couch and I sit opposite in an old overstuffed armchair. Rosenfeld fills his briar with the green tobacco. He fires it up and passes it to me. I puff tentatively.

"No, man, no. Pull it in your lungs. Deep." I inhale—and choke on the thick, spicy smoke. "No, man, easy. Just a thin stream. Let a little air come in on the sides of your lips along with the toke."

In half an hour the old armchair is a magic carpet. I curl up luxuriously and lean back into the cushions. Rosenfeld and Samantha, smiling broadly, float across from me on the couch. Samantha picks up a towel from the laundry basket on the floor next to her and wraps it around her head. "I'm a Gypsy. Sir, would you like your fortune told today?"

"Yeah, sure," I murmur.

"Soon you will write all your papers. You will become full professor. You will not go into the marines. And your destiny is riches. Even now, a wealthy and beautiful blonde awaits you outside in her sports car. Her mansion is on Knob Hill. She will drive you to classes every morning."

Rosenfeld and I can't stop laughing. Then Samantha can't stop. We laugh until our sides and cheeks ache so badly we avoid each other's gaze.

Hesitant, amazed, I reach down for the tin containing this dry, green, crumbly plant and bring it to my nose. I inhale slowly, deeply, and my eyes close as the pungent smell carries me into fields of summer grass unrolling endlessly toward a horizon.

Rosenfeld puts Coltrane on the record player. My eyes won't stay open now, yet I'm pure attention. Every note hangs in space, a silver bell, shimmering. My mind moves with the melody, a crystal receptor. Note after note, instant after instant flows by, dissolving in a stream of time. The record stops. All I can say to Rosenfeld and Samantha is, "Wow, too much. This stuff is beautiful. The music—and the grass."

Rosenfeld and Samantha lean back on the couch holding hands. They nod and smile like happy children.

And now, with a shudder of infinite relief, I hear a voice deep in my head saying, "Thank God! There really is another way. Another way out of middle-American drabness and despair. Another path to truth and beauty.

"We've been doing it all wrong. A whole generation of poets, artists, and professors. An avant-garde that worshiped alcohol.

"Now I can tell them that you don't have to drink all night and puke your guts out. You don't have to spend three days sick and shaking. Here in this humble plant lie sweet ecstasy and the meaning of life."

It's four months later, the end of January, the beginning of spring semester, a sunny, cool day—but it feels balmy after three weeks back in subzero Minnesota for Christmas break.

As I walk by Ludwig's Fountain, someone in tattered jeans, a work shirt, and a wispy beard rants about socialist reform. A smell of grilling hamburgers wafts from the hole-in-the-wall fast food joint on Telegraph Avenue just across Bancroft. Then I'm in Professor Herling's office in the English Department.

"Terribly sorry, Mr. Storlie, but your grade in the Renaissance class *did* suffer when your annotated bibliography omitted Hubble's recent article. The Hubble article is, at the moment anyway, definitive. There are other lapses as well, but that was perhaps the most serious. Hubble holds the Renaissance Chair at Yale, as you know."

I don't, but nod in agreement.

"Your examination of this year's bibliography volume of *Current English Studies* was clearly inadequate—the article is cited there."

"I guess I did look through it rather too quickly," I reply. Actually, I neglected *Current English Studies* altogether—though I stared at it balefully one night at closing time in the Humanities Reading Room, then went drinking with some other grad students at Robbie's on Telegraph.

"Yes," says Herling, "Dick Hubble's article *was* overlooked by PMLA this year. Unusual, but these things happen. That's precisely the kind of thing that keeps us sharp."

"Well," I say, "I know I should have found the Hubble article. And I know it's not an excuse, but I was under tremendous pressure in my Jonson course and the Gawain seminar. And, really, in view of the A on my term paper, and considering how damaging a B is in the program, are you sure that's all you can give me?"

"Very sure, Mr. Storlie. Or I wouldn't have assigned the B. We demand thorough, independent scholarship. That's the gauntlet we throw down here—and, I might add, the one you chose to pick up! You're here, after all, Mr. Storlie, for scholarship! You're here to train!"

Walking out of the building and down along the path leading to the eucalyptus grove, I snarl to myself, "Fuck, yes, I'm here for scholarship. And I picked up the gauntlet. Stupid me—an idiot midwesterner."

Then, more reasonably, I think, "Well, face it, it was no help that the weekend before the project was due you and Lisa were drunk two nights with Miscorski and his girl in Jack London Square. And then, after the bars closed Saturday night, you just had to jump out of Miscorski's VW and hop a slow freight rolling toward downtown Oakland. Great way to end a date. Lisa hasn't spoken to you since.

"But Professor Herling says I've got to get serious. Herling's training at Duke led him to exhaustive researches into Milton's attitude toward virginity. What are you training me for, Dr. Herling? Is the Herling training better than a late-night train ride through the Oakland switchyards—or seafood and wine in North Beach with Lisa and Miscorski and his girl?

"Do you train me for graduate colloquiums? Like the one where you read from your article 'The Virgin, the Lamp, the Chalice Broken: Miltonic Truth or Consequences in *Paradise Lost, Paradise Regained*, and the Three "Disputed" Poems'?"

And the term paper assignment! I couldn't believe it:

Write a 5,000 word essay that fulfills this pattern:
$$X \text{ Milton} + Y$$
where X = an aspect of Milton's thought or a particular Miltonic work
and Y = an aspect of the seventeenth century.

O shriveled Herling, O desiccated Herling, O exoskeleton of a Renaissance man! Did I come here to convert poetry into logical positivism or some phony fractured mathematical formula?

Later, I write home that I'm going to quit school and join the army or become a math major, like Miscorski! My father, who himself taught college English for years, reasons with me by letter.

Dear Erik,

I wonder if your Mr. Herling's specification is necessarily as dreary as you assume. He may be in his cross-eyed way trying to get the fact- and form-grubbing graduate students to use their brains to discover something new. Teachers sometimes become pretty desperate. It looks to me as though he is merely saying to take something of Milton that is important and to set that alongside something of importance in seventeenth-century literature and discover a meaning that is interesting or significant. He may have a forlorn hope that something creative may come of his formula. The "X Milton + Y" is a figure of speech, and could be an opening for the imagination.

I think I understand your problem. It is built into the choice you made. I do not have a solution. If you choose English literature as your field of study, *all* English literature is your burden, even what Mr. Herling includes in his course. But there must be more to the department than you have yet seen. Give yourself time to explore.

We want you to have every chance to do top-rank work. It is not only necessary to you professionally, but now, with the war threat, top-rank work is necessary to give you the chance to stay in school. So we have to make provision.

Dad

So I stick with it. I make last-ditch, last-minute efforts to survive classes. I don't want to lose my draft deferment or shame my parents.

But after each night in the library, I walk home along a Telegraph Avenue that day by day becomes more bizarre, fascinating, alive, hopping—a sea change happening to America right here before my eyes.

It's an evening in late February. Rain has poured down for a week, gushing down streets, geysers of water popping manhole covers lower down in the hills. Rosenfeld's friend Sammy drops by. Sammy's a slight, blond, easygoing kid from somewhere out east, an undergraduate at San Francisco State College. Sammy smokes a lot of grass, hangs around the bookstore with Rosenfeld. I'm up in my room struggling to write a paper on *Walden*. It's almost midnight when Rosenfeld shouts up the stairs, "Get your ass down here, Storlie. We're in the kitchen." I set my work aside and walk down the stairs.

"What's up? Hi, Sammy," I say.

"What's up," says Rosenfeld, "is cactus. Sammy's got cactus. And he thinks you need it bad."

I look curiously at Sammy, who shakes his head deprecatingly, smiles broadly, and opens a brown paper bag, dumping out a heap of shriveled, brown disks onto the Formica top of the kitchen table. Each disk has a fuzzy center.

"Cactus," I say. "What's cactus?"

"Peyote, man. Peyote," says Rosenfeld. "Think of Aldous Huxley. Think of Havelock Ellis. Don't you read real books? The Indians use it to get high and talk to the spirits. We can talk to the spirits. It's something else. True, Sammy?"

"It *is* something else," Sammy says. "The whole world gets these incredible glowing, pulsing colors. I took it last week and spent an hour just hanging out in the supermarket, digging the fruits and vegetables. The Chinese lady couldn't figure me, but she knows I'm weird anyway."

"Well," I ask, "what do we do with this stuff?"

"Oh, you can just chew it up. But it'll be easier if we cut it into little pieces, get rid of the fuzz, and rinse it down with something."

"Okay, sounds cool," I say, thinking that there's no way I'll get the *Walden* paper done tonight anyway.

Rosenfeld produces his briar and we solemnly smoke a preliminary bowl of dope together, the seeds occasionally snapping and producing greasy smoke.

"Jeez," says Sammy, "you could at least clean the stuff."

"Wasteful," says Rosenfeld. "Waste not, want not. *Poor Richard's Almanac*. That's Ben Franklin, in case you didn't know."

Rosenfeld gives us knives and we get to work dressing out the peyote. He makes up some frozen pineapple juice. We wash down small palmfuls of bitter, pill-sized chunks.

After an hour nothing has happened. In two hours we're giddy and silly, but it's 2:30 A.M. and there's still not much effect.

By four in the morning I'm tired and go up to bed.

I lie down and shut my eyes and find myself in high space orbit, looking lazily down at a distant planet. Then I'm falling, caught by gravity, falling faster and faster toward the surface. I'm about to hit—I clench my teeth, ball my hands into fists, and squeeze my eyes shut waiting for the impact—but the planet is a round, yellow-gray peyote button. Its wrinkly surface gracefully opens like a flower—and now I'm falling endlessly into the center of the peyote planet.

My eyes pop open in the darkened room. "Wow," I whisper to myself. I get up and go downstairs to find Rosenfeld and Sammy lying stretched out on the living room rug.

"This is something else," I say, gingerly letting myself down onto the couch. "What's going on with you guys?"

"It's really very, very hard to say," says Rosenfeld. "But it has something to do with colors when you close your eyes. Sammy just said he was seeing rainbows."

"I was," says Sammy. "But that's gone. Now I'm seeing—well, I can't really explain. But it's ugly. You don't even want to know."

Sammy gets up slowly, walks around the living room, peeks out a window past the curtain. Rosenfeld and I remain silent, absorbed.

Sammy turns from the window. "Hey, I really need to get out of the house. A drive over the Bay Bridge to North Beach would be cool—we can wake up Joy and Elton."

"Naw, screw it, Sammy," says Rosenfeld, sitting up and loading his briar. "We're here, it's five in the morning. Everything's cool. Here, take a hit."

"No, man, really, I just want to take a drive. It's already almost light."

"No way," says Rosenfeld, "I'm tired and I've got to be at the bookstore at noon. Besides, Samantha'll get up and wonder where the hell we've gone."

Sammy sits down on a chair across from me and stares down at the rug, silent. Then abruptly he gets up, pulls on his shoes, and starts methodically tightening and tying the laces.

"Hey, man, it's cool," I say. "We can just hang out here for another few hours, then maybe take a drive over the Bay Bridge and groove on North Beach."

Sammy won't look at us. His shoes are on and he's hunting for his jacket.

"Okay, okay," says Rosenfeld. "Jesus Christ, a ride across the bridge'll be cool. Far out. Let's go."

Once in the car—an old Chevrolet convertible Rosenfeld and I bought together for sixty dollars—Sammy relaxes. As we soar along the freeway, coasting the bay on our right, we start to giggle at the various abstract driftwood sculptures erected by artist freaks in the mud flats at the edge of the bay.

"Look at that one," shouts Sammy. "Must be Dr. Freud's dick." We dissolve in giggles.

"Or yours," roars Rosenfeld. "No, way too big for that!"

"Think so?" smirks Sammy. "It's always the big fat kids in the locker room who've got little eensey weensey ones."

"Ha!" says Rosenfeld cheerfully. "Don't get personal or I'll show you what a little one can do."

"Fat chance," says Sammy. "Samantha tells me the equipment works maybe once a month, if she's lucky."

"Hey," I shout, waving a finger out the open window at a vaguely vulvular, ten-foot-high structure made from driftwood, lumber, and old tires. "That one's Lisa's pussy. Big enough for a truck. She's been modeling on the beach again."

As we approach the toll plaza, Rosenfeld suddenly shifts his weight in his seat, then sits up straight, both hands gripping the wheel. He commands, "Okay, you guys, stop smiling. Unless this son of a bitch is a hip spade, he'll see these smiles at five in the morning and turn us in. Everyone knows a head. Cool it, please."

Rosenfeld slows the car, and Sammy and I subside into smirks. Rosenfeld hands out quarters, and we're off again.

In North Beach, we park the car and swagger up and down the early morning streets like sailors on leave. Only a few Chinese shopkeepers are out, readying shops for the day.

As we walk by the silent, darkened Old Spaghetti Factory, Rosenfeld shouts, "God, the Old Spaghetti Factory. They actually call it that. They actually manufacture spaghetti in there. Spaghetti like pale, underground worms. Too much—*too* much—I just can't take it, man. Oodles and noodles of spaghetti factory with even a truck in front named after their very own name."

Rosenfeld doubles up in laughter, stamping each foot on the sidewalk. We join him, helplessly, looking into each other's joyful, silly faces—then become embarrassed as a solemn middle-aged Chinese man in a suit and briefcase walks by, eyeing us balefully. Then once again, staring at his receding gray back, we dissolve into helpless giggles.

It's fall of 1963. Not willing to stay in my cramped room at Rosenfeld's another year, I've moved to a studio apartment in East Oakland. It means a long walk to classes or taking the bus. But maybe away from the scene at Rosenfeld's I'll be better able to concentrate on my studies.

It's late morning and I'm still in bed. The alarm went off at 7:30, but somehow—again—I couldn't force myself into the routine of getting up. I've been missing all my classes for weeks. Unable to sleep longer, doubts pry into and disturb my mind. "Maybe, after all, there is a price for smoking grass every day. Maybe this magical plant is not, finally, what it seems?"

Footsteps crunch on the gravel sidewalk outside. There's a hammering on the door. Then Rosenfeld's voice.

"Storlie, open the door. Kennedy's been shot."

Depressed, uncomprehending, I say nothing.

"I know you're in there. It's no bullshit. Let me in and we'll turn on the radio."

Again, I say nothing. It doesn't matter to me if Kennedy's been shot. Nothing matters to me. I just want to be left alone, to sleep.

"Come on, Storlie, it's really true."

There's a long pause, then Rosenfeld's voice, "Oh, fuck you."

The footsteps crunch slowly back up the sidewalk and fade away.

It's late February, the middle of the 1964 spring semester. It's eight in the evening. I'm in the apartment trying to pull together useful quotations for a paper on Caxton. My mind resists, refusing to focus. I write and rewrite the same page over and over again.

I hear footsteps outside my window. There's a knock on the door, then Rosenfeld sings out, "Storlie, open the door. Joel's got a little present for you."

Joel is a new friend of Rosenfeld's from North Beach. Joel came into the bookstore a few months ago looking for a used copy of Camus's *Myth of Sisyphus*. Rosenfeld and I are awed by his rebellion. He refuses to work and lives on some frantic beatnik edge, stealing food from supermarkets, cadging drinks at the bars, crashing with different people in different pads in Berkeley and North Beach. Short, slight, stooped, with bedraggled hair and a navy pea jacket, he cultivates the Jean-Paul Sartre look with round, steel-rimmed glasses—haunted, furtive, all-knowing, chain-smoking.

I breathe a sigh of relief and head for the door. Tomorrow I'll pull this paper together.

"Hey, what's happening, man?" I say.

"Stuff," says Joel, with a wry smile. "Let's go in and sit down."

We sit down around my blond Formica coffee table on a couch and two chairs upholstered in plastic. Joel pulls out a small bottle of clear liquid. "Crystal," he announces. "A gram of pure crystal meth dissolved in water. This is righteous, righteous stuff. You tried it before? You want?"

"Sure," I say. "Rosenfeld gave me some before at his place. We stayed up all night reading poems. I read a hundred pages of Auden. And Rosenfeld wrote at least fifty more pages of his magnum opus."

"Some of my best work," Rosenfeld responds happily.

I look quizzically at Rosenfeld. "But that stuff was pharmaceutical shit in sealed glass vials."

"So?" says Joel. "This shit is the same stuff. No one's fucked with this. You worried? You some kind of control freak?"

"So, how do we do it?" I ask.

"We could shoot it," Joel says, "but that's a hassle. I've got cotton wads. Just dip 'em and stick 'em under your tongue. The big veins under there carry the shit right to the brain. You got some reefer?"

"Sure, man," I say. "It's dynamite. Rosenfeld's been scoring it from some dude from L.A."

"Yeah," says Rosenfeld. "It is *far out*. It's genuine one-toke weed."

Hours go by as we tuck cotton balls under our tongues, smoke joints, and talk endlessly—faster and faster—interminable, hyper talk.

Intensely, Joel explains again and again, "The only meaning, man, is that there's no meaning anywhere in this fucking universe."

At first I protest. This sounds like the endless nihilism of barroom conversations at the Mixer's Bar on Seven Corners. This is the old despair, no longer necessary or useful.

"Listen, man," I argue, "the drugs are keys—keys that unlock the mind. Every different kind of grass, every hash, gives its own special trip. Cactus, coke, meth—each one opens some new groovy door in your head. This is just the beginning of something huge. Dig it, man, just dig it."

Then Rosenfeld chimes in. "Storlie's right, man. You're just bumming yourself out. A little grass, a little meth can trigger your artistic powers. You're a thinker, a philosopher, man."

Joel laughs scornfully, bitterly.

"No, man," Rosenfeld persists. "I mean it, you really are. We all are. All you have to do to get with it is start writing your own stuff. We can't let this dead capitalist country take us down with it!"

But finally we can't listen to each other. We each wait for our chance to talk again—poised, vultures at a carcass—desperate to relieve a pent-up agony with words.

Toward dawn, Rosenfeld and I sit immobilized—Rosenfeld on the couch, me in a chair. Joel, fidgeting, paces the small room and begins to rummage through things on my desktop. He picks up a little framed picture of the family cat sent by my mother. "Oh, Storlie, this *is* sweet. Tell us about this. Storlie, there must be a cat in your life!"

"Oh," I say, stiffening. "No big deal. My mother sent it out here."

"Of course," says Joel, in syrupy tones. "Your mother thought you'd get lonely in your student garret. So she sends family cat pictures—along with a nice check for the rent. What *do* you get a month to be a grad student, Storlie? Take a look at this, Rosenfeld. Storlie has a cat in his life. *This* cat must be very important to *that* cool cat."

Joel waves the picture at me, then hands it to Rosenfeld, whose bulk is slumped on the couch, legs crossed, one foot jouncing, fingers twiddling in his lap. Rosenfeld looks at it quietly and, without looking at either of us, sets it down on the coffee table.

Silent, heart pounding, I feel an icy sweat break out over my body.

"Well, so Storlie doesn't want to talk anymore," Joel says, sitting back down and picking up the picture. "Wow, what a groovy kitty. What a very groovy kitty. Is it a boy or a girl kitty? What's its name? You're afraid to live with a real pussy-cunt, so you've got to settle for kitty cats. C'mon, Storlie, cat got your tongue?

"Hey Rosenfeld, man, you asleep too? Fat chance. No one's asleep in *this* room. Open your eyes. We got to find out from Storlie about the cat in his life. Storlie, look at the picture." Joel holds it up in front of my face. "Let's *groove* on the kitty. Let's *groove* on the pretty cat's whiskers. Look at those long, silky, pretty whiskers. Wow! Oh, wow! Too much, man, too much! C'mon, Storlie, say 'wow, far out' some more! Be hip, man!"

Rosenfeld stares at Joel and says, "It's almost morning, man. Leave it alone. I'm beat." He rolls back on the couch and turns his back to the room.

"Well, Storlie, I guess it's just you and me now. How about another cotton?"

"Why not?" I say, now angry, resolved, thinking, "I can take anything this bastard can take."

Joel passes the little bottle. I dip in my cotton and place it—cold, bitter—under my tongue.

"It's been a long, long night, man," says Joel. "Let's do some more of that boss reefer."

"Sure, man," I say, and roll a joint.

Rosenfeld lies on the couch, still facing the wall, unmoving, withdrawn. We know his mind is racing too, but there's no more talk. Joel and I smoke. Then, sitting on my chair, hurt, furious, I stare steadily at the floor, the late-night silence of the apartment broken occasionally by the buzzing of the old, noisy refrigerator.

A squeaking sound intrudes. I glance up and freeze. It's Joel. He's staring at me, leaning back in his chair, tipping it slightly back, feet splayed out in front of him flat on the floor. He's cranking his hips rhythmically up and down, up and down, thrusting forward an erection inside his pants.

He smiles, licking his lips. A husky, contracted voice says, "Hey, man, let's go! Or you too square? Don't you know what hip folks really do?"

With dead eyes, I stare back, holding his gaze until it breaks.

He looks away, muttering, "Aw, fuck you, man. It's getting light out. I'm gonna go get a paper." Then he's out the door.

Exhausted, I lie down on the floor and shut my eyes. Every muscle in my body is a knot, my skull an agony of shifting pain. I hear Rosenfeld sit up, move around, and suddenly, silently, with a click of the door, he's gone too.

I climb wearily into bed, a dim light rising behind the curtains. Sleep, oh, God, sleep, if only I could sleep! My mind races in endless, exhausting circles—then into forbidden corners.

"Storlie, you're a failure. You can't finish your papers, can't get your ass out of bed before noon. You're skipping all your classes. When you did show up at American Lit last week, everyone's eyes followed you with disgust and pity—they know what's going on. They know. And you can't face it. You're not superior to the Master's Program in English at the University of California, Berkeley—that's an act, a cover for your second-rate mind spawned in a second-rate town at a second-rate midwestern university. You can't compete. You don't cut it here.

"You lie around this dump and smoke dope. It's easier to get stoned than make love to a woman. When'll Lisa figure that one out? You're really just scared of chicks, aren't you? Scared they'll see through you, scared they'll find someone else and leave.

"And all the doping—just a macho cover—acting tough when you're scared shitless. You're hiding—hiding from the profs. You're still a scared little shrimp like in grade school—big nose, chubby—hiding out in your room reading books when the neighborhood kids play too rough."

Now I'm pacing, pacing back and forth in the small apartment.

Suddenly paranoid, I think, "The landlady'll hear me pacing. She'll know I'm stoned again. The old bitch'll call the university. Christ, she'll call the cops!

"Hey, hey, cool it. That's ridiculous. Sit down and relax. Or lie down in bed. Try to sleep again.

"Yeah, sure. Dream on! You'll just lie there again and thrash and twist and sweat.

"What if she does call the cops? Christ, they'll find the grass—and the meth. I've got to get rid of it. But that's dynamite grass, it's the best shit you've ever had. You know what they'll all say! 'Well, Storlie finally blew his mind. He freaked out. He's so paranoid he can't turn on anymore.' "

Hours of pacing, trying to sleep, pacing, sitting down, standing up again. The morning goes by. No way can I go out to class or the library.

Then it's afternoon. The meth is relentless.

"Oh, God, if it would only end," I groan to myself, and stretch out again on the bed.

Now all I feel is my heart. It hammers, exploding in my chest.

Suddenly I grow icy.

"I know what's going to happen," I say to myself. "My heart's going to rupture. I'll die. The folks'll have to come here to pick up the body. They'll be humiliated, heartbroken. It's all my fault.

"I've got to get out of here."

In panic, I walk out onto my little stoop in the chill light of a late winter afternoon. It's been twenty hours since we got stoned. A tall eucalyptus in a neighbor's yard rustles in steady breezes coming in off the bay. I sit down on the stoop.

The hammering in my chest drowns out everything.

"My heart's going to stop. I'll die!

"Get inside! Call a doctor, an ambulance! How about the university hospital?"

I reach for the phone.

"No, no, don't call, you can't go in there. They'll call the narcs.

"Who gives a fuck, you're dying, you idiot. *Do something!"*

Somehow I walk from East Oakland to the campus. Now for the hospital. Heart smashing in my chest, ears pounding, riding a wave of panic, I enter the front doors. Asking for a doctor, refusing to answer questions, I stand shakily in front of a frightened-looking girl at the reception desk.

It's a late Friday afternoon. For a few weeks I've avoided Rosenfeld and worked to catch up with classes and papers. I get back from the library with more materials for the Caxton paper and Rosenfeld appears at the door, eager for more of the one-toke dynamite. I really don't want to turn on right now. What if I plunge back into that huge, crushing paranoia? But things are beginning to come together with school. I don't want to let Rosenfeld think anything's wrong—maybe nothing's wrong! Anyway, it's a Friday night.

I roll up a slim joint. Neither of us mentions Joel. We toke up, put on Indonesian music, all gongs and bells that go on in endless crescendo and decrescendo. He stretches out on the couch. I lie down on the living room rug, ready to ride the magic carpet.

Muscles all over my body tighten, hands clench into fists, the back of my neck turns rigid, contracts, forcing my head back into the rug. Bells and gongs rattle in my head and I observe, deep inside my brain, a tall metal tower, smooth, rounded at the top like a gigantic cypress knee. Suddenly, a tremor like a lightning bolt whipping through my body, I see a triphammer smash the tower into four quadrants, each splitting, peeling apart from the others—splintered fibers tearing from each other with a wrenching sound of agony.

I sit bolt upright, groaning. "Oh, man."

Rosenfeld slowly opens his eyes, raising his large, bearded face and peering down from the couch. "Storlie, man, what the fuck's happening? You okay?"

"Oh, sure, man. Sure."

It's May, three months later, a Berkeley spring evening. Joy, Elton, Right Hand, and I are sitting, slowly drinking doppios in the balcony at the Café Mediterranean on Telegraph Avenue. We stare at each others' pupils with knowing amusement. Even in the dim light, they're pinpoints, the effect of heroin we injected some hours earlier.

Joy and Elton are fixtures on Telegraph and in North Beach. I met Joy one afternoon as she wafted up and down Telegraph wearing a brightly colored, flowing dress and trailing long, very pale blond hair. She hailed me cheerfully as I walked home one afternoon from the library, we struck up a conversation, and soon she, Elton, and I were companions. As teenagers, Joy, Elton, and Right Hand grew up in the East Bay, running with a crowd on the edge of juvenile delinquency.

Right Hand is small, seems wizened, though he's only twenty-five. He's recently back from Vietnam, his left arm missing, the shirt sleeve neatly tucked away inside itself. He lives with his blue-collar family in Oakland, has no work, and takes the bus every day to Telegraph Avenue to hang out with hippies who are into smack. After I first met him, Joy confided that his arm was hopelessly shattered by machine gun fire, but that he would never talk about it. Envious, impressed, she told me he'd brought an ounce of pure heroin home with him from Vietnam and, for his first month back in Oakland, never left the house. He sat in his room injecting a vein in his leg.

Joy drains the last of her double espresso and lazily eyes a young woman in Gypsy robes below us on the main floor making a noisy entrance into the Mediterranean. Behind her follow three large, fine-looking dogs, a small girl child, and a toddler of indeterminate sex. For the last hour, the woman has been sitting on the sidewalk outside the door in fading evening light, the children and dogs frolicking about her. Now the toddler is fussy. She takes a table at the front window, pulls up her blouse, and nurses it.

We talk this evening in quiet undertones about needles, about techniques to protect veins and hide tracks. Joy was recently busted. As a condition of probation, she's monitored every week in some drug program. Joy and Elton ask me to sign for diabetic needles at a nearby drugstore. They've become too well known to get them themselves. Reluctantly, I agree.

"Hey," Joy says, "how about that Sammy killing himself last week? Slit his wrists in a bathtub full of hot water. I've tried that myself, but I didn't want it to work bad enough." She smiles coolly and turns her wrists toward us, displaying thin white scars on even whiter skin. "I did that at twenty-one when my dear professor father freaked that I'd been kicked out of grad school in my first semester. Skipped all my classes. Fucked at least half the guys on the avenue. Humiliating to the family. Blew father's cool! Very unlike him. He stomped and shouted all over the house."

Joy mimics a deep, booming voice. " 'Little selfish bitch. After all the opportunities we've provided for you!' Mother just locked herself in the master bedroom. Great view of the bay from there. They always told the relatives back east about that view."

"But what about Sammy?" I ask. "He never seemed down to me. Rosenfeld says he was in the bookstore just the day before. They drank some beers next door."

"I dunno," Joy says. "Doesn't really figure, does it?"

"Didn't know the dude," says Right Hand, continuing to stare toward the front picture windows.

"Me neither," murmurs Elton.

"I guess his old man had to come out from New York and collect the body," I say. "Jeez!"

"Fuck the old man," says Joy. "Let's go back to your place and do up the rest of those papers. You can swing by the drugstore on the way there."

We leave the Mediterranean. An occasional star shines through fog moving in from the bay high overhead. We detour by a drugstore, where I go in alone and sign for diabetic needles. Then we walk down to my new place on Grove Street. Lisa invited me to move in with her in March. After a few months she left, taking her furniture with her. As we walk in, it echoes vacantly.

The four of us sit down at a scarred wooden table in the dimly lit middle room. I pull from a built-in buffet drawer a little white tin Band-aid box containing paraphernalia and the two papers we'd scored that morning.

Right Hand accepts help injecting himself. He'd rather not shoot the veins in his leg. He waits patiently, not asking. We're solicitous of Right Hand. We feel bad about his arm. We always fix him. I massage the vein at the elbow of his right arm and reassure him, "Hey, man, it's no trouble at all, really, you know that."

Since Joy's being monitored, Elton struggles to inject a vein in her leg—it rolls under the skin and he can't hit it. Frantic, she screams curses at him. Finally he gets it, and she apologizes for freaking out.

It's my turn. In a spoon half-filled with water, I cook the brownish Mexican heroin over a match and drop in a tiny wad of cotton, through which the needle smoothly sucks up the fix. I tie off and ball my fist, then with a sharp, aching sting enter the vein just inside my left elbow. Fascinated, I watch blood burst up through the needle into the clear brownish fluid balancing in the eyedropper—a tiny red mushroom signaling contact with pulsing, living blood. I squeeze the bulb until a little burble of air tells me the fix is all in. Finally, I pull up a pulsing red column into the eyedropper to wash out any remnant of heroin, squeeze the bulb again, and watch the red column disappear back into the vein—stomach pulsing now with butterflies as the warm, liquid relief of a rush cascades through legs and arms and feet and hands and brain.

As the night goes by, we keep fixing until the papers are clean, puking quietly and without discomfort in the bathroom. Then we sit in the darkened living room and watch TV. For an hour after the night's programming is over, we still sit quietly and watch the blank dance on the screen.

Then, after everyone walks out into the chilly late spring night, I go to my bedroom and pull another paper from my sock drawer. "No use sharing everything," I think. "Got plenty here for a little nightcap for myself!"

The next morning I get up late, too late to bother with classes. The thought of breakfast is sickening. There's no milk in the refrigerator anyway. I look to see what traces are left in the papers. Nothing. Not even in the paper I got from my sock drawer. At least I can do up the cottons.

I pick up the little white Band-aid stash box and find the eyedropper syringe submerged and stuck to the bottom in thick gouts of black, clotted blood.

"My God! Where did it come from?" I ask myself. "How many times did I fix again after they left? Did I nod with a needle stuck in my arm? What am I doing! I could've killed myself!"

I get up from the table and walk into the front room, facing Grove Street. Except for one old wooden chair, it's empty. My footsteps on the bare floor echo around the edges of the room, mocking me with Lisa's departure.

I stand there in the dim room, indecisive. Morning traffic rattles by. The sounds reverberate and die. I want to score another gram of heroin in its delicate, intricately folded paper. But suddenly I know that if I do, something, for me, will be finished.

"What's happened—to me, to my friends? We were poets, artists, intellectuals, an avant-garde. Alcohol lifted us from dull despair. Then drugs gave us a dozen keys to the psyche, opened doors that no one even dreamed were there.

"But we're not exploring the frontiers of the mind anymore. We're not psychonauts—not the modern counterparts of Columbus and Magellan. We're petty criminals!"

Slumping down on the old straight-backed chair, elbows resting on the front window ledge, I stare out the window. I rest my forehead on my hands and shut my eyes. Traffic shushes by, shushes by.

An image begins to form itself in my mind. A figure, wrapped in swirls of black cloud, deep in space, its hand doing one thing only— injecting the vein inside the elbow of an arm. Over and over, the figure injects the vein.

Then, at last, the hand stops injecting. Alone in that deep, remote space, I rest.

It's all right. I'll smash this pattern. Panic? Paranoia? Depression? I can bear anything. I can bear everything this brutal, bullying mind dishes out.

These memories of pain jolt me back to awareness—back to the Crag—and shame fills my body. Shaking my head, shuddering, I groan in an undertone that's spun off to the north by the breezes. Pores open on my back—hot, prickly. My belly trembles, my pulse races. Leaning forward, I stretch, reaching my hands to grip edges of black rock in front of me. My shirt sticks and clings along the backbone.

A voice in my head moans, "I don't want to remember all this! It's over with. Why should I have to? How can things thirty years old still hurt so bad?"

Unsteadily, I rise to my bare feet. Losing my balance as I step off my seat onto the sharp, jumbled boulders, I flail my arms and left leg, suddenly scraping the arch of my left foot on the flinty, broken edge of an upthrust rock.

Holding the foot, I scream out into the empty spaces, "Pull yourself together, Erik, for Christ's sake."

I lean back against a boulder and examine the torn place, watching it quickly fill with drops of blood.

Savagely, I pull on my wool socks—first the right, then the left—gratified as the coarse, clinging weave scours and stings the wound.

"Slow down now, slow down," I whisper to myself.

I take a few deep breaths, sigh, and sink down to pull on and lace my boots. Carefully, I walk down into the sage to pee. Standing, I swing my arms from side to side for several minutes, then rotate them like twin propellers. Finally, I run back and forth a few hundred feet in the grass at the foot of the Crag.

I come to a stop. A voice asks, "Did that young man simply want to wipe himself out? Couldn't he find a better path? What loss, what waste!

"Oh, yes, what waste. But where would you be now without your passion and intensity?

"You came through. You made it. You're alive. You're fifty-four. You've got the privilege of zen, of the mind stuff, of the Crag right now, right here, today. Everything shines before you—the wind, the rocks, the grasses, the ancient trees, the dark mountains swirling down to embrace the valleys and bottomlands.

"Remember Dogen's words: 'All the universe is one bright pearl.'

"You see it, too. 'That stalk of grass, this tree, is not a stalk of grass, is not a tree; the mountains and rivers of this world are not the mountains and rivers of this world. They are the bright pearl.'

"And where would you be now without that agony and low despair? A niche in the academy? Full White Male Professor of Deconstructive Literary Analysis? They'd say, 'He's a medievalist, did his work at Berkeley, trying really hard to be relevant now. Kind of sweet.'

"So thank your gods for this obscure, nameless mountaintop, for zazen, for the bright pearl shining in every fir twig, grass blade, and stone. 'Your whole body is a radiant light. Your whole body is Mind in its totality. When it is your whole body, your whole body knows no hindrance. Everywhere is round, round, turning over and over.' "

Slowly, I climb back up to take my seat. My heart and breathing have slowed. I unlace my boots, remove them, and carefully peel off my left sock. There's a sharp sting as the wool fabric peels soft clotted blood off the wound on the sole of my foot. I pick it out of the wool knit with my fingernail and flick it into the rocks.

At the center of a patch of reddened, scraped skin, the beginning of the scab remains, sticky and dark brown, beading with fresh drops of blood where raw flesh is again exposed. I tenderly squeeze and massage my foot, watching the red drops begin to thicken and get dark.

"What in the world is it," asks the voice in my head, "what in this body is it that so quickly moves to heal a clumsy scrape? Ah, of course. It's the bright pearl. Yes, oh, yes. One bright pearl is its name."

4

Lysergic Acid Diethylamide-25

IT'S THE SPRING OF 1964. I'VE COMPLETED MOST of my course work and am teaching at St. Mary's College, a four-year Catholic men's school a dozen miles inland from Berkeley. An old friend from Minneapolis is teaching there. He convinced John Logan, a poet who chairs the humanities department, to hire me.

And I convince Celeste to move in with me at Grove Street. She is a black girlfriend from Kansas City. We met one summer in high school at a Unitarian church camp in the midwest. As undergraduates, we visited each others' hometowns several times. After Lisa moved out, I wrote Celeste enthusiastically about the wonders of Berkeley. She came for a visit—and stayed.

Other old friends from Minneapolis are arriving, too—gathering, drawn to this scene that now the whole country hears and wonders about.

Acid has arrived in Berkeley, and Telegraph Avenue is erupting in rainbow colors. No more black Sartrean turtlenecks. No more existential leather jackets and nihilistic motorcycle denim. Now, a bedraggled beatnik slouching with baleful eyes down Telegraph Avenue endures friendly but impatient stares from the multitude. He is accosted by Montrose, a swarthy man sporting a neat black Vandyke and shod in Elizabethan boots with flaring tops. Montrose wraps himself in a flamboyant robe sewn from a dozen brilliant fabrics. He wears a wide-brimmed hat trailing an ecstatic golden plume.

"Why so down, man?" he asks, soothingly. "You can get with it. I know you can. You've got to groove, man. Life is a flower, a gorgeous huge flower. I'm smelling it, right here, right now. For real. Can you dig it, too? And right here, right now, I'm ready to change your world." Montrose leans forward, stares intently into the other's eyes, and plucks his sleeve. "I've got something that will blow your mind, pop your cork, bring a smile to those sad, sad lips. For real, man. For real. Just say the word."

Everybody's talking about this stuff. It's the drug that tops all drugs. It's incredible—and scary. Old-time hard-nosed beatniks take it and bathe, shave their beards, barber themselves, and in a frenzy clean out their pads, sheepishly emerging onto Telegraph Avenue the next morning, trying to explain themselves to staring comrades.

And dedicated Berkeley engineering students suddenly shuck slacks and white shirts with plastic pocket protectors filled with ballpoint pens, skip classes, and appear cautiously at evening in coffeehouses wearing jeans and torn T-shirts, hair unkempt, wondering about the action, ready to talk the meaning of life.

Celeste, Right Hand, and I take our first acid trip one afternoon at Grove Street. I'm beyond debating whether to do it or not. "I've tried everything else," I think. "I'm not stuck on anything. Let's just see. It won't beat me!"

To our surprise, Joy and Elton refuse to join us. They tried it a week ago and had to hospitalize themselves.

"Someone fucked up on that batch," Joy grumbles somewhat defensively. But they get us two vials of a mysterious blue liquid. We carefully divide them in the kitchen among three glasses of plain tap water and drink them off.

A bit edgy in the dingy apartment, we wander into the front yard and sit idly on the tailgate of my old green Studebaker wagon, parked at the curb. Celeste carries a single red rose she plucked from a vase in the dining room. We kick our legs back and forth—smiling, giggling, poking each other. In wonder, we stare all around, pointing out gleaming pebbles suspended in the concrete beneath us, taking turns handling and seeing and smelling the single red rose.

As afternoon rush hour traffic builds and cars slow down, we're suddenly self-conscious—two white boy beatniks on either side of one black girl beatnik, all three sitting in a row on a Studebaker tailgate, kicking their heels back and forth, back and forth.

My aged landlady, nervous and disapproving since Lisa left, now upset with Celeste's arrival, huffs by in a halo of white hair and carries her grocery bag into the house without a word.

"Celeste, Right Hand," I say in a voice of mock alarm. "We're not watching them anymore. They're watching us. Let's get out of here."

"Cool, dude," says Right Hand.

"Fine with me," says Celeste.

We jump in the old wagon and I drive randomly around the neighborhood. Right Hand's in the back seat, functioning like a compass. Whenever the car points in the direction of the Berkeley police station, he moans, "No no, man, not that way, we'll be busted. I'm a fuzz detector, I can *feel* the cops. Turn, turn." Celeste and I dissolve in laughter, trying to reassure him. "Forget it," Celeste says in a soothing voice, "we're not holding, we're just innocent little hippies out for an afternoon drive."

Half laughing and half serious, Right Hand cries out again at the next turn toward the station. "No, man, no, I feel 'em, they're just three blocks down. Please, man, please, any direction but that."

I begin to drive uphill at each intersection, and soon we're climbing out of the Berkeley flats into the hills, our heads bobbing like balloons on wiggly stalks as we zoom around twisting curves and up steep, roller-coaster streets. Soon we're in Tilden Park, the hills falling off into the bay behind us.

Driving by a grove of eucalyptus, Celeste shouts enthusiastically, "Oh, man, I mean *men*, look at that huge tree. I'm in love. Erik, stop, stop, I've got to go see it." I stop and we slowly, carefully climb out and step into the grove.

Inhaling pungent smells of leaf scatter and earth deep into our lungs, we pace reverently to the great tree. Gently, Celeste and I place both hands on the smooth, scaling bark. Right Hand strokes it with his right hand. Smiling, eyes alight, we hold our tree, then sit down in the leaves at its base.

I lie at full length on my back and, entranced, stare up at the leaf canopy above us—a living cathedral bower swaying in the breezes. Celeste stands over me, then straddles me, one foot on each side, and slowly bends her knees to sit comfortably on my stomach.

"Erik, look at you," she says, smiling, reverent, staring down into my face. "You're a god."

I smile back, admiring her, loving her black eyes, the glowing nut brown of her face, her glossy hair intricate in black curls and kinks, each harboring a flash of diamond.

"Oh," I murmur, "Your hair! Your hair! It's . . ."

"What? What about it?" she breaks in, face suddenly clouding.

"Nothing." I say. "Nothing at all. It's just beautiful."

Suddenly Right Hand groans, his voice a strained whisper, "Oh, fuck, no, man, no! No! *No!*" He's staring at a squad car that's just pulled up behind the Studebaker. An officer, blue-uniformed, opens the passenger's door and climbs out.

We struggle up to our feet. Celeste smiles broadly toward the squad car. Right Hand grabs my left arm with his right hand, hissing, "You left the goddamn car in the middle of the parkway—we're busted for *sure!*"

Heart pounding, I look at Right Hand and Celeste and whisper, "Be cool, be cool, be *cool!* For God's sake, we can handle this. We're not holding. Just look normal as hell." For an instant, Celeste's beaming face freezes into a scowl. Then a series of snorts burst through her nostrils, turning into irrepressible giggles. "Celeste, Celeste, be cool!" I whisper urgently. "Be cool! You guys just stay up here and I'll go down there."

Drawing myself up, brusquely walking down through the scattered leaves to the parkway and the Studebaker, I observe the two cops. There's a tall one; he's out of the squad car, looking over the Studebaker. The other, the driver, is on the radio. I'm astonished to find myself calm, amused.

"What's the problem, officer?"

"Whaddaya think? You can't park in the middle of the street. Let's see your license."

"Sure. No problem." I fish for my license, noticing my fingers vibrating with a microtremor. I worry for an instant, then conclude that no normal eye can register it.

Handing him the license, I say sincerely, "I'm really sorry, officer. We got curious about that huge eucalyptus up there. My girlfriend's new to the area. I teach at St. Mary's College. And my friend there missing his arm is just back from Vietnam. Had a pretty bad time. I was just driving my friends back the long way around through the park for a view of the bay."

The man curls his lip, eyes me with disgust, and looks at his partner, who's now out of the car.

"Car okay?" he asks.

"Checks out."

"Okay, just get this thing moving."

"Sorry, officer. Thanks a lot for your patience." I beckon Right Hand and Celeste to get in, pursing my lips, scowling at Celeste, trying to get her to wipe the wide grin off her face.

Once we're in the car, pulling away slowly with the cop car behind us, Celeste collapses into stifled snorts and giggles. "Those c-c-c-c-creatures," she stammers. "Imagine spending your life in a blue suit hassling people who have simply fallen in love with a tree."

I start laughing quietly, the squad car still on our tail.

Right Hand breaks out furiously, "Holy Christ, you two, shut the fuck up and for once pay attention to the road. I know these Berkeley cops. Jesus, take a right up here, get us the hell away from that fuzz."

"Okay, man, okay, I'm cool." I pull off the parkway into a golf course parking lot. Taking a vacant spot in the crowded lot, I announce, "Well, here we are. Let's play."

Right Hand groans. "Oh, man, I just want to be home, even if it means walking through the living room past the old man and his fucking TV. We *can't* go in there. Look at us. Maybe *you* think you belong in a country club! C'mon, man, let's get going."

But Celeste and I are half out of the car. "Hurry up, Right Hand," she smiles, "or we'll leave you here alone to talk to the parking lot attendant."

With Right Hand trailing disconsolately, Celeste and I walk serenely across the parking lot into the clubhouse. Suddenly parched, we feed quarters into a Coke machine that sits by the front picture window overlooking the course. In minutes the three of us guzzle four cans of Coke.

"Oh, delicious," says Celeste. Then, choking with giggles, she points out the window. "Look, I see strange animals out there wearing funny clothes and hats and hitting little white balls back and forth with sticks. This is weird. This is very, very weird. Anyway, let's go home now."

An hour later, Celeste and I drop a subdued Right Hand at his house in Oakland and return to park the Studebaker at Grove Street. Then we walk up to Telegraph Avenue, excited, eager to catch the late afternoon action.

The street crowds with men and women, mostly young, in wild, natural hair and extravagant costumes. An old, gaily painted van disgorges hippies, in from some country retreat. On the way to the Café Mediterranean for a cold drink, passing the laundromat, Celeste looks in the picture window and sees a young, lanky black guy, high school age, sitting on the floor against some washing machines, absorbed in playing a twelve-string guitar.

"Let's go hear him," she says, a broad, happy smile on her face.

"Groovy," I say.

We walk in through the open door. The air is suddenly hot, the room filled with the sounds of washers churning and buttons and zippers ticking on the revolving drums of dryers. A young couple, normal-looking college types, are washing and drying laundry at the rear of the establishment. We sit down on the concrete under a row of washers opposite the guitarist. Now cool air flows in over us from the street.

The guitarist doesn't look up. He pretends not to notice his audience, but we feel his excitement. His playing falters for a few seconds, becoming precise and self-conscious.

Celeste turns to me, whispering in my ear, "Oh, look how dark his skin is, how glossy. My people are so beautiful!"

I murmur assent, brushing my lips on her cheek. He glances up furtively and sees we're taken with him, and he's inside his music again. The twelve-string becomes intense and resonant, pouring out notes, filling us with sound that aches with longing and joy.

We listen, swept away for long minutes.

Then the couple passes between us on their way out the front door, the man carrying white laundry that swells up from the basket like fresh-baked bread. Brought back to the hard, concrete floor of the laundromat, to ourselves, we look at each other, smiling, shaking our heads in disbelief. Is it just us?

The guitarist pauses and looks up, shyly smiling. Embarrassed, we smile back and nod to him, murmuring our thanks, and slip out the door.

"Let's skip the Med," I say. "It'll be mobbed. How about a walk up into the hills?"

"Oh, yeah," Celeste says. "That's a really good idea."

We start walking up into the hills, block after block, following our feet. As we get further up, the streets steepen, and we stop again and again, turning to view the city, where a few lights begin to wink on. A golden sun drops into the bay.

Hand in hand, we walk slowly, lingering to admire houses whose window eyes smile back at us. Colors inside glow, backlit like stained glass. We feel reverence, as if pacing through a church.

Every few minutes we come to a standstill, eyes roving over fences, into front yards and side yards, feasting on strange tropical trees, entranced by colors glowing through intricate webs of grasses, flowers, and shrubs.

I'm elated, exhilarated, blown free of despair. What's been wrong with me? All I ever wanted was this undeniable, unutterable beauty—beauty in the tiny, intricate patterns of pebble and sand crystallized in the concrete beneath our feet. Beauty beckoning with the fingers of leaves on shrubs standing in ordinary Berkeley front yards. Beauty in modest flowers standing up in side yards speaking soundless, gentle hellos.

It's late summer. I'm in the back of a transport truck with five Mazatec Indians and two old friends from Minneapolis, bouncing up mountain roads that wind to a little village called Huatla de Jiménez. The Indians are returning home after a day at the big market in a larger town nearby. Lon Pilgrim, Frank Farmer, and I are on a Grail quest. For help, we seek the Mazatec *curandera* Maria Sabina.

Lon has been studying a fast-growing literature on drugs and mysticism. He's read Aldous Huxley's *Doors of Perception*, which describes the mescaline intoxication and concludes that it triggers enlightenment experience. He's read Alan Watts. He subscribes to Timothy Leary's *Psychedelic Review*.

And he's read about Gordon Wasson's journey in the late 1950s, only a few short years ago, to this Mexican village. The conservative New York banker and mycologist, studying linguistic and anthropological evidence, had a hunch. And the Indians gave him what they had hidden for over four centuries from the tormenting, torturing conquistadores and their priests. He received the gift of a communion. He received the mushroom, *teonanacatl*, the "flesh of the gods."

Maria guided Wasson on this solemn mushroom journey. He described it as a pure ecstasy, a true agape. It changed his life, and he repeated it several times before returning to the north.

Lon, Farmer, and I want to know this experience that so moved the old banker. We too want to find Maria. We too want to taste this agape.

I've known Farmer since childhood. We grew up together in Sunday schools and youth groups in the Minneapolis First Unitarian Society. He's of medium build and deeply tanned from the Mexican sun. His blond hair unkempt, he sports the beginnings of a scruffy goatee and mustache, but they don't hide his cheerful good looks.

Lon we've known since high school and from the Seven Corners drinking scene as undergraduates. He's patrician, tall and thin, with long, flowing brown hair and beard. In robes he'd resemble an intent, cloistered, medieval monk—but we're all in ragged jeans and dirty work shirts. We haul worn backpacks stuffed with sleeping bags and a few extra clothes.

Huatla de Jiménez is perched in the mountains. The gentler slopes are cultivated in corn, the fields coming down to the backs of small huts whose open front doors face dirt paths.

Unfortunately, news of Maria has spread. The village has filled with hippies this summer. Within an hour of our arrival we're stopped in the market by the sheriff and a deputy. Lon talks to them in Spanish, then explains to us that we must follow them to the courthouse. We troop through the market and up a nearby street to a squat stucco building. Inside we're brought before a man who appears to be the local magistrate. He sits behind a low wooden desk and eyes us lazily. The sheriff, deputy, and now a half dozen curious men from the street stand and look on.

The magistrate and Lon speak in Spanish, then Lon explains to us that the magistrate has suggested that it would be a great courtesy on our part if each of us would help the village of Hautla de Jiminez by making a contribution to the fund they have newly begun for the building of a school for the children. The magistrate, Lon explains, hopes that each of us could donate twenty American dollars to show our appreciation of the hospitality that the citizens of Huatla de Jiminez will surely extend to us.

Lon, Farmer, and I huddle in consternation. The magistrate, sheriff, deputy, and onlookers watch us intently.

"New school, indeed," I mutter.

"Yeah, I dig," whispers Lon. "But we've got to do something. And listen to me. Don't show any disrespect or impatience. This isn't the USA!"

"But what can we do?" Farmer asks. "That'll take almost half the bread we've got left to get out of here, let alone back to the States."

"Well," Lon says, "we may have to wire for more back in Mexico City. But we've got to do something. I'll sign a ten-dollar traveler's check and offer it for all of us. That's at least something. Actually, it's quite a bit. God knows what Maria will want for the ceremony."

Deferentially, Lon turns and addresses the magistrate. We learn later that Lon thanks him for his concern for us and commends the village on its dedication to its children. Lon reminds the magistrate that we are young Americans on a journey to learn about their religious ways and that, though poor, we want to help. With dignity Lon reaches into his backpack and pulls out a rumpled folder of traveler's checks, signs one, and advancing to the desk, lays it before the magistrate with a bow.

The magistrate glances at it casually, then smiles and barks an order to the sheriff. Suddenly the room fills with smiles and talk. Several men break out cigars, making sure each of us has one. They are lit for us with congratulations on our generosity. Now the deputy and several of the men troop out of the courthouse with us and accompany us through the village to another stucco building by a stream. This, they explain, is a guest house where we're welcome to stay. They assure us we'll soon be contacted by those who can help us find Maria.

Exhausted now by the day of mountain roads and the uncertainties of this welcome, we roll out our bags, chat quietly, and as soon as it begins to get dark, lulled by the quiet rippling of the stream, fall quickly asleep.

The next morning we head back to the market, eager for food and directions to Maria. After a breakfast of corn tortillas, fruits, and coffee at a primitive little countertop shop, we bump into an Englishman. He too has come here curious about Maria and the mushroom ceremony.

As we chat, a young man, apparently Maria's son, appears and offers to arrange things for forty American dollars apiece. Our hearts sink again. This is impossible. But after polite, vigorous bargaining, with many expressions of our poverty and sincerity, Lon gets him down to ten American apiece. We're going to be close to broke. The young man instructs us on how to reach Maria's hut in the hills above the village and tells us to be there at sundown the next day.

Late the next afternoon, Lon, Farmer, the Englishman, and I trudge up the hill to Maria's hut. We're met by the son and a somewhat older man, apparently a brother. The brother reeks of alcohol. His eyes are sunken and red. They wave us into the interior of the hut.

We sit on thin mats on the dirt floor and wait. The room is dim, the walls made of some kind of wattle. Maria appears in a few moments wearing traditional Indian dress. She's old and wizened, with black, penetrating eyes that simultaneously convey tolerance and boredom.

She nods and speaks in Mazatec. One of the sons translates these few words of greeting into Spanish. She turns to light candles on a little altar, then leaves and returns again, bringing a dish holding small, brown mushrooms. These she sets on the altar, sits before it on a small stool, and begins to pray, invoking the names of saints over and over again.

After a time, she stops chanting and carries around the dish, giving each of us, and finally herself, several pairs of mushrooms. I chew slowly, nervously, an acrid taste on my tongue, grit from the mushrooms grinding between my teeth.

She returns to her stool and chants again. We sit listening, uneasy, for half an hour.

Suddenly Lon interrupts her, talking in English. "Maria, this stuff isn't working. What's the deal? We paid lots of money for this."

She sings out and the brothers appear in the door. Lon talks to them in Spanish, and they speak to Maria in Mazatec.

Then Lon turns to Maria. "We've got some good shit here." He pulls a joint out of his jacket pocket, lights it and inhales, then reaches it toward Maria.

The brothers watch impassively from the door. Farmer and the Englishman look worried. I'm embarrassed by Lon. I'm sure I can feel the mushrooms beginning to work.

But Maria, unperturbed, grunts and reaches out to take the joint. She inhales and passes it back to Lon, who sends it on to us. After a few minutes, she speaks to the brothers, who speak in Spanish to Lon. Lon listens, nods, and the brothers retreat.

Lon turns to us. "She says it's late in the season. The rains have stopped and the mushrooms are hard to find now. She says she'll give us some of the seed of the mushroom."

Maria disappears, then reappears rolling something between her palms that looks in the dim candlelight like gray clay. She rolls four little balls about the size of the end of a thumb and passes one to each of us.

I eat the ball—it's like eating earth—as Maria chants again before her little altar. Within a few minutes, I'm dreamy, distant—and from the corners of the hut intricate multicolored patterns begin sweeping inward, circling, and converging on me. They seem Aztec and Mayan.

Maria's chant weaves in and out of the visions, an endless recital of saint's names, soothing me. I lie back on my mat, the earth soft beneath me.

Suddenly it's late. The chant has ceased and Maria is seated on her stool in front of the altar, her face impassive, flickering in the candlelight. Occasional gusts of wind sweeping the corners of the hut carry snatches of Mexican music from a cantina far down the mountainside.

Suddenly there's a scream. "I must get out of here!"

It's the Englishman. He's risen half to his feet in the dim light, one hand supporting himself on the bare ground. His eyes are huge dark puddles that dart wildly toward the corners of the room.

"I can't take this, fellows, I simply must leave."

He rises shakily and starts for the door. Maria sings out in Mazatec and the sons appear, blocking the doorway. Lon and one of the sons talk urgently.

Then Lon says in a hurried, low voice, "We've got to stay till morning, at least. That's their agreement with the sheriff. The villagers are upset by all the gringos. Last week some guy freaked after a ceremony. They say he ran back to the village and strangled a turkey and started eating it raw." Lon puts his hands on the Englishman's shoulders and kneads them gently. "We can't go, man. You've got to stay. It'll be cool."

"I must go, I can't stand it," says the Englishman, eyes staring. "I've learned my lesson! I'll never do this again!" He struggles to his feet.

I roar with laughter. "What? You think you're at Boy Scout camp? Cool it, man!"

The Englishman tries to push past the drunk son standing in the doorway. The son reels slightly, but roughly pushes him back into the middle of the room. He sinks down on his mat and covers his face with his hands. He's quiet, but his shoulders heave and shake.

Wild-eyed, Lon, Farmer, and I look at each other. Maria sits quiet, impassive, carefully watching. Again Lon says, "It'll be cool, man. Don't worry."

I lie back, shaky, and then I'm suddenly spun free, drifting again. The dim circle of the room is a loom weaving a gorgeous, intricate Indian tapestry before my eyes in naked space—a tapestry edged with wattle walls, and earthen floor, and huddled forms, and old brown

Maria hunched before her altar where the candle dimly burns. "It's a blessing," I think. "An endless weaving." "The weaving and reweaving of life itself."

I turn my head and steal a glance at the Englishman. He's curled up on his side now, head cradled in his arms.

"Why'd you shout at him?" I ask myself. "Poor devil! What do you think you know about all this anyway?"

I peek sideways at Maria's face, little more than a shadow in the shadowy light. Her eyes are lidded, but she seems awake, observing everything.

Shutting my eyes, I drift again. I feel the mountaintop rolling down and away in cornfields, hear a dog's staccato barks in the village sleeping at the foot of the mountain.

This is Mexico. It's night. I'm on a mat in a wattle hut. Wonder rises up from the earthen floor, up through my body, into my stomach, filling my throat with an ache of sweet longing and joy. Fleas climb through my clothes, biting, tickling, as the night lengthens and cools, but I hardly notice.

Toward dawn I sleep. Then the drunk brother, bleary, wakes us with brusque commands. Maria is nowhere to be seen. He hurries us out the door, gesturing us away down the path toward the village below.

Chilled, shaken, we slowly walk down the hill. The Englishman moves off ahead, eager to leave us behind. We don't see him again. Lon, Farmer, and I slog down the path past cornfields and huts. An occasional solemn child peers at us sleepily as we walk by.

Soon we overlook the village, cupped between mountainsides. I'm suddenly transfixed by the rusting sheet iron roof of the old cathedral, burnished now by the rising sun. "Yes," I whisper to myself, "there is such beauty in this lovely world. It's everywhere."

My feet continue their walk down the steep, dusty path, but my eyes, welling with tears, caress the rusty glow, a dried blood red caught in shafts of morning light.

It's the fall of 1964. Lon and I return to Berkeley from Mexico. Farmer has headed back to Minneapolis. Lon has decided to move to the Bay

Area. "It's all happening right here," he says. "America will never be the same."

I won't teach this fall. I have one semester to prepare for and pass my M.A. orals—or I'll be drafted. Celeste and I rent a large three-bedroom upper duplex in Oakland—lots of windows, natural woodwork and built-ins, with hardwood floors recently refinished. It even has a yard with some old plantings of roses along the back fence. It's only ninety dollars a month because, along with a strip of housing several miles long, it's condemned for freeway construction. My rent check goes to the Oakland Housing Authority.

Downstairs live a blue-collar working man, his thin, faded wife, and their shy little daughter, who's about nine years old.

Celeste and I invite Striker to move in with us. He's a black friend from Minneapolis, a Golden Gloves boxer in high school who adopted the hip scene at Seven Corners. He too has heard about what's happening in the Bay Area and has just arrived in the last few weeks. We give him the middle bedroom.

Rosenfeld is a frequent visitor. He stays overnight when he's in Berkeley to make his rounds of the bookstores, looking over new inventory and talking to other bookmen.

Joy and Elton drop by, too. They're amazed at our high-class living arrangements. And we get two long-haired kittens, one orange and one gray. A family moving out down the block offers them to Celeste and she accepts immediately.

Celeste and I are excited. We've got a real house and yard. But there's not much to put in it. Miscorski's girlfriend lends us a dresser and a fine walnut coffee table. I've got an old armchair, some brick-and-board bookshelves, a floor lamp, and my mattress—odds and ends I've accumulated over two years in semifurnished rooms.

As we settle in over a few days, we're surprised that the family downstairs seems unfriendly. The wife is withdrawn, the husband cold, and the little girl apparently too shy to speak to us.

A week after we move in, we're playing music late one night when the husband begins to hammer on the water pipes. Uneasily, we ignore him, not quite understanding his message. Then the hammering stops, and we hear him shouting furiously up through the floor, "Hold it down up there, for God's sake. The kid's trying to sleep and I've got work in the morning."

Celeste gets up to turn down the volume, but Rosenfeld, enraged, screams back down, "Shut up, you goddamn redneck son of a bitch. We'll come down there and bust your ass!" I'm shocked. This is not like Rosenfeld. But Rosenfeld's a big man, and we hear no more from downstairs.

The next day a woman from the Housing Authority calls. She's heard complaints of noise and disorder. Further, the house is rented to Celeste and me, and she's aware that other parties seem to come and go at the address. She threatens eviction.

"The complaints are pure racism," I protest indignantly. "The ACLU will be delighted to hear about this case. I'll have you tied up in court for months. We'll be here until the freeway arrives." I slam down the phone.

The next week, the family below moves out. No one moves in to replace them, and miraculously we've now got the whole place to ourselves.

Lon's found a place in Berkeley now. He brings over copies of the *Psychedelic Review* and Leary, Richard Alpert, and Ralph Metzner's new book *The Psychedelic Experience*. They're in the papers now. They blew the stuffy professoriat at Harvard out of the water. But I'm getting uneasy about Lon. He's talking all the time about something called zen. He's even urging Striker and me to go to some oriental temple in San Francisco.

"This is off the deep end," I think. "I'm an atheist. And I've sure got no use for religious organizations, oriental or otherwise."

It's an afternoon in late September. Lon and I talk Striker into taking his first acid trip. Lon suggests we drop acid and spend the afternoon meditating in the empty front bedroom. Striker and I are reluctant. What's this "meditating"? We want to trip, to groove. But Lon is persistent. Celeste is cautious. "Whatever you do, you guys can do it yourselves. I'll hang out and make us some tea."

Striker is nervous. Everybody's heard about acid now, about strange trips of unbelievable power. Lon reassures him. "Hey, man, it's true, it's big stuff. But it's cool. It puts you in touch with the very deepest levels of existence."

Striker chuckles. "Yeah, man, but I'd be okay with just getting a little happy."

"Yeah, sure, that's going to happen," I say. "Anyway, people who have bad trips don't know what they're doing. They can't let go. They're control freaks."

"Well, what about Joy and Elton?" asks Celeste. "It's not as if they're straight. Look what happened to them."

"Aw, they just got way too much for the first time," I say. "A freak-out. They said they puked and saw incandescent pinwheels flying out of their mouths. Does that sound like poison? They were just at a party with strangers and wandered out into the street and panicked."

"Listen, man," says Lon, "I hear what you're saying, but remember, this stuff *is* different. This is more than just getting high. Something big is happening here. This puts you through some changes, man—real changes, good changes. Add this to the stuff that's beginning to happen up on campus. This country is not going to be the same after acid."

"That's right," I say. "It blows a lot of the bad shit out of your brain. When Celeste and I took it last spring, it was like cleaning out the basement, throwing out trash that's clogged you up for years." Gleefully, I add, "Remember what Charles Darwin said: 'I love fools' experiments. I am always making them.' "

"It even makes cops seem human," giggles Celeste.

"Listen," Striker says, subdued now, "you guys go easy on me. I don't think I'm ready for complete ego death. But let's get going, or I'll want something comfortable like beers and some weed."

In the kitchen, the three of us wash down the big capsules with hot tea, then follow Lon into the empty front room. Lon has brought three round meditation cushions, which he lines up facing the east wall. Out the west window, we look down Fifty-fifth Street as it dips toward the bay, the Golden Gate Bridge floating above the water in the distance. The sun sinks in the west and golden light illuminates the bay, the rooftops, and the walls of the room.

Lon shows us how to hold our hands in the traditional *mudra*, palms up, thumb tips lightly touching. We arrange our legs and feet in the half lotus position. He instructs us to drop our gaze down, keep our backs straight, breathe slowly, and relax. Next to his seat he sets a candle and Leary's guidebook, *The Psychedelic Experience*. He lights the candle, bows toward the cushion, and sits down. We all rotate 180 degrees to face the wall.

Then I hear Lon reading in a soft voice. It's something from Leary's book:

> O Striker, O Erik, O Lon,
> The time has come for you to seek new levels of reality.
> Your ego and the Striker, Erik, and Lon games are about to cease.
>
> You are about to be set face to face with the Clear Light.
> You are about to experience it in its reality.
> In the ego-free state, wherein all things are like the void and cloudless sky,
> And the naked spotless intellect is like a transparent vacuum;
> At this moment, know yourself and abide in that state.

Lon's voice stops. I listen to a huge emptiness in the room. Then he says, rather shyly, "Listen, you guys, if anyone gets stuck in a bad place, let me know, and I'll read one of the passages here that'll flip you out of it. Just hearing the wisdom words can direct you away from game playing toward the Clear Light." Striker and I nod, continuing to gaze down toward the baseboard.

I feel irritation. What does Striker think of all this? Does he think I'm on some kind of religious trip? I don't really want to do this, but if I don't, well, then, Lon'll be pissed and none of us will have a good time. What the hell. Go with it.

I begin to focus on my breathing. Breath after breath, I feel my stomach, a slight burning sensation beginning at the center, move slowly in and out, in and out. Then with an in-breath, cascades of shivers rise up my backbone and, with the out-breath, effervesce like champagne between the top of my brain and the bottom of my skull.

Wow! It's the kundalini energy. Lon has a book about it with Hindu pictures showing a serpent rising up the spine and transforming into the thousand-petaled lotus in the brain.

The yellow light dims outside and the traffic din softens with evening. Lon and Striker's breathing becomes louder and louder. Mine becomes louder and louder, too. Now my breath comes in uncomfortable gasps and pants.

Then I hear a low, throaty chuckle. "What's that?" I think. "Who's here? Oh, yes, Lon and Striker. Who's laughing?" Then again, a low, resonant, earthy chuckle. "Okay, Striker," I think. "You're the one who's breaking this spell, not me."

I keep sitting quietly, listening to Striker get more and more tickled by whatever's happening in his head. Finally, he says softly, "Oh, man, someone talk to me. This is too much. I'm in fifth grade at Warrington Grade School and I can see Mrs. Swanson —God, another one of those old lady Swede teachers—and is she pissed! She's just watching like a hawk to see if anyone talks. And I always do!"

Striker's off again into snorts of suppressed laughter. "Oh, man, oh, man, I feel my ego dying right now. This is it. What would all those colored folk down there on Shattuck Avenue say about me now?"

Now I'm in it too, snorting, chuckling, giggling. Finally the two of us lie on our backs on the hardwood floor, sides aching, laughing at nothing, laughing at everything, laughing at how hard we're laughing.

Rising to my elbow, weak, I reach over and poke Striker on the shoulder. "Striker, be serious. Think of the injustices of capitalism, think of the suffering poor and oppressed, think of existential despair."

Still on his back, each hand massaging the opposite biceps, kneading the rippling boxer's muscle, Striker sighs, "Okay, man, I feel it if you say it."

Then we're conscious of Lon. He still sits quietly upright in the darkening room, back straight, eyes half-lidded but open, gazing down toward the line where the floor meets the baseboard. Pointing at Lon's back with my left forefinger, I put my right forefinger across my pursed lips and quietly intone, "Shhh," shaking my head in mock solemnity. Striker cracks up and rolls over onto his stomach, helpless with laughter.

The sun is down now, the room almost dark. I begin to make ghost sounds. "Whooo. Hooo. Ooo. Aarrrggghhh! Raaahhhrrr!"

Racked with laughter, we drag a vacuum cleaner hose and tubes out of the closet and make more sounds, half forgetting Lon, who continues to sit in meditation, silent and motionless.

At last, embarrassed, we wander into the living room, where Celeste is reading a magazine.

"You guys are nuts, that's all I can say," she comments, looking up from our lone overstuffed armchair with a scowl. "Where's Lon? You better pay some attention to what he's trying to do. If you want my opinion, you guys are *way* out of your depth."

Striker and I retire to the kitchen to smoke a joint, then forget about it as we light all four stove burners and run water full blast into the kitchen sink. Engrossed, we stare as the sink fills with luminescent bubbles that gently spill over the side, then hoot with surprise when, as we reach to touch them, they're not there. "Man, it's a *hallucination* all right," Striker says.

I respond, "Wow, man, fire and water, fire and water. It's beautiful."

"Yeah," Striker says with a reverent smile. We sit down at the kitchen table and pet the two little kittens. They're electrified, long-haired fur flying up, standing out straight, tiny bodies quivering with excitement. They climb busily in and out of our laps, purring loudly.

"Celeste," I shout. "Come on in here." She comes to the door. "I hereby name these kittens Rumpters and Roar. I'm hearing those sounds in my head over and over again—it's like my mother's voice—like I'm a baby lying on my back in a bassinet, and she's talking to me."

Striker looks at me with a broad smile and comments, "Too much! Too much!"

"Please, Celeste, please," I say, "can that be their names?"

"Okay with me," she says shortly, and returns to her chair in the front room.

I pick up a Tarot deck off the table, shuffle several times, and spread the cards between us. "Pick one," I say to Striker, "but don't look at it." He picks, then slides the card in front of him. I pick and do the same. "Okay, I'll go first," I say, and flip over the card to reveal the Tower, a tall white square tower set on a steep mountaintop. It's engulfed in flames as a jagged lightning bolt blows off the roof, a crown. Two male figures, one crowned, are flying headfirst out of the tower and down into an abyss that seems to lie beneath the cliffs of the mountain.

I moan in recognition. "Oh, man," I say. "That's really it. That's me. Acid's blown me clear out of the ivory tower, out of everything in my whole life. Unbelievable!" We stare at each other in wonder, shaking our heads.

Striker hesitantly reaches for his card. "Turn it over, man," I say, intensely curious. He flips it up and we behold the Devil, a massive figure with goat legs and bird claws. Great bat wings rise off his back. Ram's horns curl from the top of his head. Standing, chained to his throne, are a naked man and woman—beautiful, but betrayed by horns and flaming tails.

Striker's face clouds and he groans with lips shut, "Umm, mmm," and looks away. "My people are all church people," he murmurs. "What *would* they say!"

It's a week later. Celeste, Striker, and I drink morning coffee in the warm kitchen. The weather has turned cold. The house, still almost empty and heated only by several wall heaters, feels vacant and drafty. Striker has a plan. Hundreds of houses purchased for the freeway project sit vacant, boarded up, some still full of furniture. Down at Little Joe's Big Ribs place on Shattuck, they say the Housing Authority bought furniture too, then resold it to Oakland salvage firms.

"Look man, we'll just cruise the neighborhood and pick things up. Fuck the salvage outfits! Who needs this stuff most? Now, that family across the street—they split yesterday with all their shit. They left a buffet and a kitchen table and chairs right there on the porch. Look at the woodwork in this place. It's a real house. We can make it real nice. Ninety a month and we can furnish it free!"

Striker and I walk across the street to check on the buffet, table, and chairs. The house is empty and locked. We carry everything across the street to 556, then hop in the Studebaker and cruise the neighborhood. A few blocks away we park in a street of large vacant houses and walk through yards, looking in windows for furniture. Two houses are left almost entirely furnished—and unlocked. Striker spots a set of matching, overstuffed living room furniture—a couch, loveseat, and two upholstered chairs with end tables. We load the couch and the tables quickly into the back of the wagon, drive home, and triumphantly carry the pieces into the living room.

Celeste is impressed. "Now, you boys are doing just fine. You are providing for the woman of the house. How *could* you have let me live here on the drafty, old floor?"

We head back for the rest of the furniture. In the other house, we find four straight-backed chairs, two more upholstered chairs, and a dresser—now Striker can have one, too. We haul all this back, and Celeste fixes peanut butter and salami sandwiches. We sit down on our new kitchen furniture and eat.

In the warmth of the kitchen, my skin starts to crawl. I set down my salami sandwich and scratch my belly, then armpits, then head. Striker's scratching too.

"What's with you two?" Celeste asks. "Born in a barn?" She looks at me closely across the table and shrieks, "Fleas! Erik, you're covered with fleas. Striker, look at his hair, he's hopping with 'em. And you too! It's the furniture."

In a scramble we carry everything out into the cold backyard. Then Striker and I head for the bathroom and jump, fully clothed, under the full force of the shower. We undress and soap and wash and soap and wash. Then I head up a few blocks to the neighborhood hardware store for insect sprays.

Hurrying out of the store with four aerosol cans in a brown paper sack, I'm surprised to bump into the family from the downstairs apartment. They're coming out of a door next to the hardware store that leads up to second-floor apartments above the commercial establishments on street level. So that's where they moved.

The man holds the door for his wife and daughter, who trudge through grimy scraps of newspaper and discarded paper cups swirled by the wind into the entry alcove. He's in the green shirt and pants of a mechanic. It's late afternoon now. He must be just back from whatever job he works. The wife looks pale and pinched. They look past me, pointedly concentrating on their exit from the door. The little girl, thinly dressed for the damp bay wind, begins to smile up at me, then looks away.

"Oh," I think, "so I'm the hero of equality that forced this child away from a house with sunny windows and a yard and grass and old rose bushes still holding a few late summer blossoms." Clutching my bag, averting my gaze, I move past them quickly.

Celeste, Striker, and I spray all the furniture and let it sit for a few hours before carrying it back in, and then we spend the rest of the afternoon arranging couches, chairs, our own rooms. We make the place cozy. It's been three years since I've lived in anything like a regular house. By late afternoon we're settled, smoking a joint and playing records. "No problem with volume now," chortles Striker, lounging in the overstuffed chair and gazing happily through the large front picture window.

Suddenly he jumps up. "Shit, man, here comes that son of a bitch from across the street. He's gotta be after his furniture."

"What should we do?" I say. "He left the stuff."

"Yeah," says Striker, hesitantly.

"Don't be ridiculous," says Celeste. "It's his stuff if he wants it."

There's loud hammering on the door.

Reluctantly I cross to the door and open it to a heavy, middle-aged black man in work clothes. "Hello," I say. "What can I do for you?"

"Do for me? Who the hell took my furniture?" He walks into the living room, eyes searching, and spots the buffet. "That's mine. Where's the kitchen set?" Striker and I look at each other.

"Well, it's here," says the man. "You boys were *seen*. Now you can help me load the stuff in my truck." We hesitate. "Right now, I mean." I steal another glance at Striker, whose brow is dark and knitted. This is Striker's turf. Striker looks worried, and I'm no Golden Gloves boxer.

"Yeah, no problem," I say. "We thought you'd just left it. Sure, we'll help you load it up."

We pull on jackets. Faintly smiling, the man carefully supervises as we haul stuff out and lift it into his truck. "Watch that tailgate, god-damn it. You already put two scratches in the buffet."

After everything's loaded, the man slowly shuts the tailgate, then turns and surveys us, hands on hips. "Listen, boys, you're young, and it's nice to see you all getting along with each other. But when you gonna learn there's no free lunch? Now, for once, just try minding what you doing!"

Back inside, Striker comments, "That son of a bitch was *mad.* I'm glad you didn't hassle him."

It's the next day, a Wednesday. Striker, Celeste, and I spend the day thoroughly cleaning the apartment and rearranging furniture. I even walk back up to the local hardware store for window cleaners, rags, and squeegees and, to Celeste and Striker's amusement, wash every window, inside and out. After finally putting away the cleaning supplies, I sit down in the living room and luxuriate as rays of golden afternoon sun slant in through the sparkling glass.

Celeste brings in some late-blooming pink roses from the backyard. She surveys the living room critically, then puts the roses in a tall water glass and sets them on a little end table in the living room.

Striker comes in from his room and begins to look through our records for some appropriate music.

"Hey, Storlie, how about some Otis Redding and a little toke?"

"Sounds just fine," I say. "But why stop there? Our house is beautiful, just like a home, and we've got nothing to do. Let's drop some acid."

"You said you had to get in some more studying for your orals," Celeste reminds me.

"Ah, I've got a few weeks yet," I say. "No big deal."

"Well, you boys go ahead," says Celeste. "I can handle any phone calls or door-to-door salesmen. After watching you guys the other day, I'm not so sure you'll be fit to talk to the general public."

"That's for sure," sighs Striker.

Just then we hear a knock on the door. It's Joy and Elton. I urge them to join us. "No, I don't think so, but thanks, man," says Elton. "We'll hang around, though, if that's cool."

"Sure, that's fine," I say. And then I add with a smirk, "But don't worry, we won't poison you. C'mon, we've got incredible stuff from that guy down in Big Sur."

"Yeah," says Striker. "Erik and Lon turned me on to it. It was cool."

"No, no," repeats Elton, an edge in his voice, "we don't happen to want to do it. Some other time."

"Man," Striker says, "it was just like the first time a bunch of us got hold of some pot. We couldn't stop laughing."

"Don't worry about us," says Joy. "We're into something else right now."

About four o'clock Striker and I each drop two caps. One was no problem, so why not two? We bounce around the apartment—adjusting this and that piece of furniture, changing records, checking the wall heaters—delighted with our house. Celeste goes to the kitchen to make some tea, and the phone rings in the dining room. It's a middle room that lies between the living room and the kitchen. We don't have furniture to put in it, so it's still largely empty.

I walk in—slowly. I'm beginning to feel unsteady on my feet, and the visual space around me begins to swirl, the volume of the room subtly expanding and contracting. Then I'm standing next to a ringing wall phone. It's John Logan from Saint Mary's. He's done with classes for the day and ready for a drink.

"John, you come right over," I urge. "We've got incredible acid. We'll turn you on to the real stuff. Man, you can forget all about your brandy." John's voice at the other end of the line, suddenly distant, nervously declines and the phone goes dead. As I place the receiver carefully back on its hanger, I see walls covered with an extravagant floral wallpaper. I'm entranced. Roses, lilies, and various luscious blossoms intertwine with leafy vines. I see into the wall. It's in three dimensions—actual, real flowers, brimming with color, their petals gently undulating in a pulsing, flowing, clear fluid.

Astounded, I call everyone into the room. "God, these flowers. You guys. Come and look! They're alive. They're incredibly beautiful. I can't believe it! Can you see it?"

Everyone troops into the dining room. Joy, Elton, and Celeste seem to be examining me more than the wallpaper. Striker seems subdued, withdrawn. His brown face, which moments ago glowed with deep, vibrant hues, is ashen, lifeless. "Hey, man, Striker, you digging this?"

"Yeah," he says flatly, "sure, it's something else."

"Well," I say, suddenly self-conscious, "let's go back in the living room and sit down, relax, put on some music, groove with this shit." I herd everyone back into the living room.

It's almost six now, and the windows are dark, the room shadowy. Celeste carries a teapot and some cups in from the kitchen. Before it's offered, with a pushing motion of his hands, Striker blurts out, "No, no man, I don't want anything at all." Rumpters, the yellow kitten, begins scratching at his pant leg, trying to climb into his lap, and he impatiently brushes it onto the floor.

"Oh, okay," says Celeste. "Tell me if you want something else." Striker says nothing. Uneasy, she chatters with Joy and Elton as she pours their tea. Their eyes keep drifting back to me. Then, abruptly, they get up, Joy saying, "Well, we've got to see a man. We're overdue. Catch you all later."

"Hey, bullshit," I say. "Let's all walk down to the ribs place on Shattuck Avenue. We can have coffee and see the action." Celeste and Striker look uncomfortable.

"Forget it, man," Striker says. "You want me to experience ego loss down *there?*"

Celeste laughs. "Why, the counter man would look at me and say, 'Little girl, what you *doin'* with these hippie boys, one black and one white? Which one belongs to *you?*' " She smiles at Striker and gently pats his shoulder.

"No, thanks," says Joy. "We're cool. We'll catch you later." And they're out the door.

Something's gone wrong. "Why won't Joy and Elton hang out with me?" I ask myself. "Where do I fit in? And why did Celeste touch Striker's shoulder just now?" The walls swim and pulsate. From the center of the rug, waves roll out to break in colored surf on a beach of hardwood floor. Striker is remote, a sharp furrow between his eyebrows. He looks like certain streets in south Minneapolis—black, surly, menacing.

Abruptly, without a word, he stands up and walks toward the front door. I stand up, too, nervous, talking fast. "Hey, man, what's wrong? Don't you like this stuff? Be cool. Can't you dig it? What's your problem?"

Then suddenly I blurt out, "Maybe you two are hiding something!"

Striker looks at me distantly, lips curling, confusion and frustration written over his face. "Hiding something? I don't get it. I'm just feeling weird, man, a little restless. Is that okay with you?"

"Bullshit," I shout. Now it's all clear. "You two are making it with each other. How could I be so stupid." My heart pounds. Waves of hurt, anger, and despair wash over me.

"Erik," says Celeste quietly, astonishment spreading over her face, "that's crazy. It's not true. I love you. I'm your woman. And Striker is our friend. It's just not true. I mean it."

"Jesus H. Christ," Striker mutters wonderingly. "Where'd this all come from? Now, just let me take my walk and things'll straighten out in a little while after everyone's cool."

Striker slips by me and heads toward the door, but I lunge past him and lean my shoulder against it, hard. "You're not going anywhere, man," I grit through my teeth.

"Just let go," he yells, turning the knob and jerking at it furiously with both hands. I feel the door budge and, bending my knees, grunting and pushing, plant my feet harder.

Suddenly we hear ripping, rending sounds, and the two top hinges tear loose from the jamb. Astonished, we both release the door and stand panting. Striker takes a step toward the now half opened door. I step into his path, grabbing his shirt at the chest, shouting, "Stay here! Talk to me!"

Explosion! I'm spinning backward, my ears filled with crashing, smashing sounds. Rumpters and Roar scatter like windblown leaves to the edges of the room. Shocked, I find myself sprawled on my back on broken glass in the corner of the darkening living room.

Celeste screams, "Striker!" Striker retires dutifully to his corner, watching me warily, while Celeste moves carefully into the space between us.

Suddenly I feel wetness on the floor. I touch my fingers together. More wet. I feel my face and hair. Everything is wet, sticky. Turning my head, I see the dark blood now pooling on the floor at my side.

"Jesus," I moan, struggling up to a sitting position, "I'm bleeding, I'm bleeding all over the place. For Christ's sake, what's going on? This is my house, you bastard. I thought we were friends. I thought I could trust you. I thought you could handle some real shit, but you're no-where, man! Just get the hell out of here."

Striker sinks down on the couch and looks at me in disbelief. He slowly raises his hands, balls his fists, and presses his knuckles into his cheeks. "Storlie, I'm sorry. You grabbed me. All I did was push you, man."

"*Push* me? You *hit* me! Fuck you. Get the hell out of here! And take your goddamned shit too. You're evicted."

Striker sits quietly, eyes staring straight ahead.

Her voice rising, panicky, Celeste says, "Erik, it's true. He only pushed you. You grabbed him."

"Okay, fucker," I shout, "move or I'm calling the cops." I stand and rush for the phone, dial 0, and ask for the police. Astonished, Celeste and Striker look at each other. "I want a squad car at five-fifty-six Fifty-fifth Street. Right now. There's been an assault here. Yeah, me. By my roommate. I'm bleeding all over the place. He's sitting right here. He won't get the hell out. I want him out of here. I want a squad car here now."

Striker looks at Celeste wonderingly. "Jesus, there's grass, acid, meth, and God knows what Rosenfeld's stashed here. I'm gone." Pulling open the front door, which hangs crazily on its bottom hinge, Striker melts into the dark street.

Celeste stands for a long moment, hands on hips, staring silently at me. Finally she offers me a slow smile. "Well, my love, my silly little white boy, you can just help clean up now. You haven't been cheated on. And you're not bleeding. Striker pushed your ass into my vase of roses and it's smashed to bits."

Subdued, shaking, I go for the mop.

After clumsy attempts to help Celeste clean up, I retreat to the bathroom. My stomach is in knots. My bowels cramp painfully. I sit on the pot and stare at the floor. The ceramic tiles groan and writhe with tension, the grout between them oozing up out of the floor—viscous, dark feces.

Nauseated, I look away and up to the hard white edge of the porcelain sink. There's a peppering of black hairs, each short and curling regularly back on itself to form spirals. Of course. They're negro hairs.

"How strange," I think. "My girlfriend is a negro. Striker is a negro. Is that why we fought?"

I rest my elbows on my knees, shut my eyes, and drop my head into the upturned palms of my hands. Endless mind stuff rolls out, forming into rivers of negro flesh sprouting black, kinky hairs.

Opening my eyes, I shake the images out of my head and reach with trembling fingers toward the roll of toilet paper. I pull off a loop and clumsily try to fold it into a square pad. It takes me several attempts. I'm five years old, alone, and I just want to cry. I peek out of the bathroom and creep unseen down the hall and quietly curl up in the blankets on the mattress on the floor of Celeste's and my room.

Two hours later, toward midnight, I'm back sitting in the living room. Celeste's gone to bed. There's a furtive knock at the door. It's Striker, saucer-eyed, pupils hugely dilated in the darkness outside.

"Hey, man, Storlie, is it cool, can I come in? I'm really sorry about it. It just happened. Did you really get hurt?"

"No, no, no, just fucked-up craziness. We've got to figure this whole thing out better. Get in here quick. This stuff is a hell of a lot more than a little toke of grass. Thank God the cops never showed up."

The next day Joy and Elton drop by to see how things went.

"I've taken a vow of silence," I announce sheepishly. "I can't be trusted to talk. I don't know what the hell happened yesterday—I can't believe some of the things that happened. But don't talk to me. I'm in exile. I'm not speaking. Ask Celeste and Striker what happened. My lips are sealed for the rest of the day."

Joy suppresses a knowing smirk as I go to the kitchen and make lunch for everyone. "What *did* happen?" I ask myself. "Lon's right. We've got to do this all differently."

After lunch, Lon drops by. We all sit down in the living room. Celeste brings in tea, then says with a teasing smile, "Hey, you guys, tell Lon about your trip yesterday." Embarrassed, Striker and I have to tell him.

Lon's face falls. "How could you guys do that? I can't believe it. It really makes me feel terrible." He sits quietly for a moment, looking first at Striker, then at me.

Embarrassed and ashamed, I stumble out a few words, "Yeah, I know, it was crazy. It's not like we were really . . ." Suddenly I can't think of anything more to say.

"You and Striker," Lon says, "have some very bad karma. 'Course, it's not just you. We all do. The whole country. There's work to do. We've got to get conscious. When are you guys going to read Leary's book? It's the road map. I'll take you over to hear Reverend Suzuki, too. He's awake! He's a Master! This is a big voyage we're on. Acid is going to change this whole country."

"Man, oh, man," Striker says, "if anything can do it, acid can. It's heavy shit. I'll go hear the reverend. That's cool. But I just think I'll leave that stuff alone for a while. A little grass keeps me pretty happy."

It's October 1, 1964. Lon calls in the afternoon. I'm trying to organize myself so I can pass my orals. On rare days when the house is empty of visitors, I feel a rising panic about this work I absolutely must do.

"Man, get over here to Berkeley," he says excitedly. "We've got to walk up and see the scene on campus."

"I can't. I'm outlining the whole history of English literature around the front bedroom wall in different colored markers. I've got to start learning all this shit or I'm dead. I've got to pass orals before Christmas break. If I flunk, I'm out. Then the draft board can have their way with me—and the way they're feeling now about old draft-deferred grad students, it'll be the front lines in Vietnam for sure."

"Hey, come on, man. This is *real* history. It's happening right now. Listen, they tried to throw some activist folks off the tables at Sather Gate. The cops came to make arrests, and now I hear there's a cop car trapped in the middle of a huge demonstration."

"Right on campus?"

"Yeah, right in front of the Union."

I drive to Lon's place south of campus, and we walk up to see. Going in a back entrance to the Student Union, we get up to the second floor and look out a window. Thousands of students have mobbed the area between the Union and Sproul Hall. The squad car is stranded in a sea of young people. From the top of the car, someone harangues the crowd.

"Lon," I say, "this is unbelievable. It's not just the heads, long-hairs, and off-campus radicals. It's the squares, too. It's the whole campus. It's everyone."

"It's just the beginning," Lon says gleefully. "Remember what the Bible says? 'The fathers have set the sons' teeth on edge.' The whole country's got to change now. There's political power in Berkeley, and acid's touching off a wildfire of spiritual power. It's all coming together right here in front of our eyes. It's the beginning of the end for the Establishment."

An itchy stinging on the bottom of my foot pulls me back to the Crag. The sun is high overhead, hot, beating down on my shoulders. It must be close to eleven. Afternoon breezes arriving from the west cool me, licking down my collar, up under my shirttails, and up the cuffs of my jeans.

"It's funny," I think, "that despite everything, we were so filled with hope. We never doubted that the new day was dawning, that the corporations, the military, and the politicians would transform, that poverty, racism, and war in Vietnam would be over, that America would blossom.

"We had a taste of freedom. But not a clue about discipline. What naïveté!

"Look at Striker and me. We couldn't handle it. Just believing in black and white together wasn't enough. With no discipline, our freedom blew up in our faces.

"And right then the Reverend Suzuki came into our lives. He lived a discipline, simple and unshakable. He radiated the freedom of a being filled with joy.

"We hated the disciplines of America, the churches, colleges, military, business world—all so flawed, so compromised, crippled by materialism, tortured out of shape in Vietnam. Suzuki we came to love. Of course, part of that was romance—the mysterious Orient."

Another voice intones, "Oh, shut up. Get off your soapbox. You've got your hands full just doing zazen."

I rock slowly back and forth, smile at myself, and chuckle. I rotate my head and neck slowly clockwise, then counterclockwise, luxuriously stretching out hosts of small muscles that have begun to stiffen and ache. I straighten my legs and take off my socks, carefully peeling the left sock off over the scrape. A few curling fibers of wool stick in the hardening blood. I pluck tentatively at one, then restrain my fingers. I leave my socks off now, to help the scab dry out.

I notice hunger pangs. It would be nice to stop and eat. "Speaking of discipline, don't take a break yet. You've hardly begun to sit."

I rearrange my down vest to get more padding, put my socks on top, and get comfortable. I slowly sit down and cross my legs in the half lotus position. I pull my broad-brimmed hat down tight on my head, tilting the brim against the westerly breezes. And once again I sit, I meditate.

5

Return

It's a month later, seven o'clock on a November evening in San Francisco, the beginning of the winter of 1964. This morning Lou and I dropped acid near the top of Mount Tamalpais. By afternoon we were sitting on rocks overlooking the sea. Now we leave the damp fog of Bush Street and enter the Sokoji Temple. As we walk through a large front room, I see an altar on the far wall with a Buddha statue surrounded by an ocean of cut flowers.

We enter a small inner room and join a group of about fifteen men and women sitting on folding chairs in a half circle. They face a single, empty folding chair. We're mostly young, wearing everything from business suits to torn jeans to psychedelic costumes.

A tiny Japanese man in his late fifties enters and quietly takes the empty chair. His feet don't even touch the floor. His head is shaved and he wears a simple brown robe. He carries a heavy, worn book. He puts his hands together and bows to us. A few in the audience bow back.

"Good evening," he says in heavily accented English. "Thank you very much for coming to listen to my talk. I am very surprised that

Americans are so interested in zen practice." He breaks into a smile, his face wrinkling. "My English is not so good. It may be pretty hard for you to understand. But I will try."

He opens the book, and I see that it's filled with rows of oriental characters. The Buddha statue, the flowers, the strange little man, this curious book—I feel transported to some distant time and place, far from the city that begins outside the door on the foggy street.

Reverend Suzuki attempts a word-by-word, phrase-by-phrase translation of his text into broken, confusing English. I'm puzzled at first. I can't follow what he says. But as the talk goes on, images jump alive in my mind. There is firewood that turns to ash and never turns back again. There are fish swimming that never reach the end of the water, and birds flying that never reach the end of the sky. There are tiny drops of dew that reflect and hold the vast sky and the moon.

Toward the end of the evening, Reverend Suzuki returns again to a passage about enlightenment, struggling to turn it into English.

"So, Dogen says here about an enlightenment that leaves no trace of itself, nothing in the bottom of the cup, no—how do you say it?—no *dregs*. When we practice, we can forget ourself. We can forget the small self. We don't feel our *dregs*. We can maybe begin to feel some big self, something very big. It is really there. We are like the firewood, maybe. Yes, firewood is firewood. But it is already ash, too. Can you understand?

"Some of you worry about this enlightenment. You want to touch it. You want to hold it in your hand. But you are already enlightenment. When this is true, then there is no enlightenment. This enlightenment leaves no traces. But Dogen Zen Master says, this tracelessness goes endlessly, it shines forever through the universe."

Struggling with the word *tracelessness*, Reverend Suzuki pauses, looks up smiling, and says, "Ah, that is very, very beautiful, don't you think?"

"Yes," I think, deeply moved. "Oh, yes, it is."

Something I can't name is welling up in me. It's in the devotion of this small, simple man for an ancient poetry he loves. It's in images from nature that touch the everyday and the eternal—fish and water, birds and sky—and endless sunlight shedding beauty, sweeping forever through an infinite universe.

It was this I felt at the end of my walk with Celeste up into the Berkeley hills that evening last spring. It was this I saw in the golden sun falling down into the bay, in the gently glowing windows of the houses, in the grasses, shrubs, and flowers beckoning from the yards.

"Yes, I'll be here," I say to myself. "I'll hear him talk again. Lon was right."

At the end of the evening, a woman in a flowing white dress serves tea. We all sit silently on our folding chairs, cradling little white porcelain Japanese teacups, which she, one by one, dutifully fills.

Reverend Suzuki accepts our silence for a long while, then asks, with a wry smile, "Did you understand something from my talk? Maybe a little bit? Maybe my talk is not so bad?"

A young man with long, disheveled hair, tattered jeans, and a filthy plaid shirt slowly raises the hand that holds his teacup higher and higher. His hand is clenched, the knuckles white. Surprised, we all watch curiously. Then suddenly he smashes it into the faded hardwood floor. It explodes into shards that fly in all directions, skittering under our chairs into corners of the room. Everyone freezes.

The young man looks at Reverend Suzuki, an expectant half smile on his face.

Without a word, in a single smooth movement, Reverend Suzuki stands and walks out of the room.

We're all still frozen, waiting for him to return, for someone to tell us what happens next. But nothing happens. The lecture is over. We file sheepishly out into the evening fog of Bush Street.

It's an early morning, late in November. Lon and I have driven over the fog-shrouded Bay Bridge from Berkeley to sit zazen with Suzuki Roshi. We sit with several others on the balcony at Sokoji Temple on round black cushions. In the distance, out in the cold bay, great ships sound their foghorns. Quietly, softly, in bare feet, betrayed only by the rustle of robes and the squeak of the floor, Reverend Suzuki passes behind us as he makes his rounds in the middle of a forty-minute period of zazen.

Suddenly, with a whoosh of robes, he settles down behind me in the dim hall. With light, quick hands, he adjusts the position of my shoulders, aligns my neck and head. There's a pause, as if he surveys his work. Then gently he lifts my elbows a tiny bit away from my sides. My hands are in the Buddha's mudra, one palm atop the other, thumb tips touching. But I've been clutching my upper arms against my body. I feel gratitude—and like soft clay being worked by a potter.

It's mid-December, a wet, cold Berkeley afternoon. Fog and low clouds race in from the bay, pushed by blustery winds. I'm walking slowly past Ludwig's Fountain in the square between Sproul Hall and the Student Union, where only a few weeks ago four thousand students rallied against the university administration's strictures on political expression. A few days later, at another rally, some eight hundred people occupied Sproul Hall. To our horror, hundreds were arrested by the Berkeley police and hauled away in police vans. We know now what the power structure is capable of—pure billyclub law. How distant they are from a generation truly dedicated to peace and justice.

But now, after a student strike and widespread faculty support for student demands, President Clark Kerr has offered concessions. Students have returned to classes. An uneasy peace prevails.

As I pass the fountain, I see Ludwig himself, a handsome, alert brown dog, the campus mascot after which the fountain is nicknamed. He sits at the feet of a pretty coed, who leans over him, scratching his ears.

I've just come from passing my M.A. orals. I'm shaken, ashamed, and sick at heart.

"What a miserable, disgusting performance," a voice whispers in my ears. "How could you do so badly? So this really is the best you can do? A second-rater washed out of the Ph.D. program, going home with the M.A. as a booby prize.

"Well, what did you expect?" I think to myself. "How could even four weeks of crash cramming be enough? At least you've got the front bedroom redecorated." I smile wryly, remembering the bold colors with which I'd outlined the major dates, figures, movements, and influences in English and American literature around the walls of the room in which Lon and I gave Striker his first acid trip.

"And what will Barney think?" Barney is the chairman of the American Studies program at the University of Minnesota. A dear family friend, he had steadily encouraged me to hang in with my studies—and had gotten me admitted to Berkeley in the first place. Just last summer, he and his wife, Lucy, had helped me find the mining claim near their summer ranch in the Bitterroots.

"And old Herling. He actually came through for me. He was trying to save my ass." The other two examiners were profs I'd never had. They took sneering delight in showing how abysmally ignorant I was in their centuries. It wasn't hard.

After the hour-and-a-half grilling was over, I waited in the hall, heart pounding, astonished and humiliated. Then Herling called me in.

"Well, Mr. Storlie, I can congratulate you on passing this oral examination. You have now completed the master's degree in English here at Berkeley. But I must say, too, that neither my colleagues here," Herling ducks his head nervously toward each, "nor I, for that matter, feel able to recommend you for our doctoral program at this time.

"You may, of course, prepare further and sit again for this exam. A stronger performance *could* change our minds." He glances expectantly at his colleagues, but neither offers encouragement. One stares out the window and twiddles his fingers. The other, slumped in his chair, faintly smiles.

"Thank you, Professor Herling," I say. "I'll consider retaking the exam. I'm not sure what I should do."

"Of course, Mr. Storlie. This will require some thought on your part. Let us know what you decide. You'll have to reschedule for some time spring semester, at the latest. Good luck, then."

I glance again at the other two. They don't look at me. "Fat chance of passing a second exam," I think. "They just want to be done with me. And why not? Can I blame them?"

Herling opens the door for me and steps outside. He shakes my hand somberly. His eyes seem sad. Then he quickly steps back inside.

"Why did you hate him so?" I wonder. "Couldn't you have gotten to know him better? What is he thinking? What are any of them thinking? The campus just exploded. Surely they've seen it coming.

"I know they know I've been anything but the usual graduate student for the last two years. Yet no one's ever talked to me, asked what's going on with me, asked whether things are okay. No one's discussed my plans here since the year I arrived—and even then, not much.

"Well, they know that you're a goddamned freak. Why should they mess with another burned-out hippie grad student? Am I worth their time? You're just a piece of 'damaged goods,' just what the chairman of the English Department at Minnesota called Jim Wright when he was fired a few years ago. Yeah, you're damaged goods. Jim drank too hard, of course. But at least he's a poet. What are you?"

As I walk down Telegraph toward my car, the scene that a short year ago signaled liberation from the dull, dead, dryness of academia and middle-class American life suddenly looks tawdry and cheap. There is the usual knot of hip young people dressed in a riot of colors in front of the Café Mediterranean, some sitting on the sidewalk, some standing. An ancient VW microbus, painted in wild, psychedelic swirls, leans crazily at the curb.

As I pass them, I suddenly notice the dirt-encrusted feet of a young woman standing on the sidewalk. She wears huge gold earrings and Gypsy robes covered with red, blue, and green patches. And I notice the gritty tracks of tears down the dusty face of a toddler who stands next to her, clutching up with both desperate hands and arms, saying over and over, "Up, up, up."

With an exaggerated, wide smile, she talks loudly and intensely to two male companions with shoulder-length hair, glancing down occasionally to intone, "Later, Sibyl, later, baby. You've already been bothering Mommy enough."

"What's gone wrong?" I think.

I head on down Telegraph past them toward the car, mind returning uneasily to my own dilemmas. "I've got to go for the Ph.D. or the draft board will have me. And it's hopeless here. Maybe Barney would get me back into American studies at Minnesota. He recommended me for Berkeley, and now I've let him down, too."

And as I open the door to the station wagon, I'm wondering, "What should I tell Celeste?"

It's early evening, six weeks later, in January. Lon and Striker pick me up at the airport. I've just flown back from spending Christmas at my parents' home in Minneapolis. I didn't bring Celeste. Angry and disappointed, she spent her Christmas alone at 556.

While in Minneapolis, I asked Barney if he'd help me get into the American Studies Ph.D. program at Minnesota. He agreed. I'm a student again.

Striker is no longer living at 556. He's found a girl and a place of his own. As we head up the freeway toward the city, he asks, "How's Celeste doing?"

"I don't really know," I say. "I haven't talked to her since I left before Christmas."

Lon glances over at me but says nothing. Striker whistles and laughs. "Whooee. You got some *big* trouble coming. She spends Christmas alone, and now she doesn't even know you're back! Why didn't you call her, man?"

"Oh, geez," I say, rubbing knuckles into my forehead, "I don't know what the hell I'm doing. Except I know I've got to go back to Minneapolis for the Ph.D. to stay out of fucking Vietnam. And I know the Berkeley scene is over for me."

"Hey, man, that's okay, take her with you," says Striker. "She'll go. Just play my man Otis, that cut I put you on to when you two had that little fight last fall. Put on 'Try a Little Tenderness.' She'll dig what it's about."

I'm silent.

"Yeah, man, you don't want to," says Striker finally, sadly. "I dig, I wouldn't either. There's nothing in it for a guy to get tied down that bad. I'm just glad *I* don't have to go in there and tell her. She's a nice chick. I mean, she's not just one of these dumb broads hanging out on Telegraph. But that's life."

"What about Reverend Suzuki?" asks Lon. "And acid? Are you still going to do it once a week, like Leary and Alpert? You saw what an incredible place they were in at their talk at the Crystal Ballroom. We can get there, too. Man, we'll burn our karma. I know you've gotta do what you've gotta do, Erik, but this is the chance—the chance for the big one."

"Oh, yeah, absolutely. I know that's where it's at. But I've got to keep on track with the degree, or it's the front lines. You know that. Farmer and I will have to do it back in Minneapolis. We've agreed to do it every week. And this time there'll be no screwing around with diddly little side trips, meth and smack and shit like that. That stuff is nowhere. It'll be one long, pure path to liberation."

"Man, oh, man," says Striker. "That's all just a little bit too far out for me. But I guess you guys know what you're doing. And the Reverend is cool. Lon took me over to hear him a few weeks ago. But sometimes I worry about you guys. That's powerful shit."

"Listen," I say. "For sure, you guys have to come out to the Bitterroots right away in the spring. I'll be there as soon as the quarter is over at Minnesota in June. Farmer says he'll make it out too. We'll get ourselves on track at the mining claim. The cabin is amazing. And you won't believe the incredible wilderness out there. It's perfect."

We cross the Bay Bridge in silence, lights in the East Bay winking on, the bay itself a dark pool. Lon pulls up at 556. A single light burns in the living room window. I wrestle an army surplus duffle bag out of the back seat, then lean in and say, "Well, thanks for the lift. I'll call you guys tomorrow. I've got a month before I have to leave. We can drop acid a bunch of times. And Striker, you really got to see the mountains, too. I mean it."

"Oh, yeah, sure, man," he says. "No question. It'll happen. Just watch your step inside there, now. I'm glad it's you, not me." Striker gives a low chuckle.

I shut the door. The car drives down the dark street back toward the bay, and I slowly climb the front stairs. I let myself in the front door and find Celeste sitting on the couch in a long, red terry cloth robe. The lone floor lamp illuminates her, the rest of the room retreating into shadow. She glances up, then returns her eyes to her lap. I see that she's quietly, determinedly knitting a piece of blue material.

"Hi," I say tentatively, "how's it going?"

"Thanks for asking," she says. "I didn't know when you were coming back. I didn't even know *whether* you would."

"I *told* you I would," I say. "Barney let me into the Ph.D. program at Minnesota."

She glances up again, her dark face clouded, bitter. Saying nothing, she returns her attention firmly to her knitting. The needles click angrily together in the chilly, dark room, and sighing, I drop the duffle in the entry, move across the room, and sit down gingerly in the chair opposite the couch.

I think of the warmth and excitement that filled this room only weeks ago. Now it's cold, drained of life. Between us is Miscorski's girl's walnut coffee table. Regretfully, I notice nicks, scratches, and white water rings marring the lustrous brown grain. I know they weren't there when I borrowed it in the fall.

"Listen, Celeste," I begin hesitantly, "I don't want to hurt anybody . . ."

"I'm not 'anybody,'" she says evenly. "I thought I was your *woman.*"

"I know, I know," I say, "but everything's got to change. It *is* changed. I've got to go back to Minneapolis and go for the degree, or I'm drafted. I can only stay here a month or so, until spring quarter begins at Minnesota."

"And you don't want me to come along," she says with quiet final-ity, not looking up. Her brown fingers work dexterously with the blue yarn. The needles click. Her nails glint under the lamp.

"Well, you know it's not that exactly, it's . . ."

"*It* is that I'm a *negro*, isn't it, Erik?" she says flatly. She looks up slowly, then full into my face. "You don't want to bring me home to your parents, to your hometown. Of course, you were willing to write *me* in Kansas City and invite me out here, have me live with you. That was fine. But that was all."

"Well," I say, "we're *both* away from home. Would you move in with me if we were back in Kansas City?"

"Yes," she says simply, looking back to the knitting, her flying fin-gers. "And it's because I love you. But you were just looking for a replacement chick, a replacement for Lisa. She couldn't take your fucked-up scene anymore, so she moves out of her own place to get rid of you, and you write an old high school girlfriend from Unitarian church camp. We were such *liberal* Unitarian youth. And she's dumb enough to come.

"Perfect for you. Groovy. Because now Erik can dude around Telegraph Avenue and show off his negro mistress, his *negress*." Her final *ss*'s hiss, and I shiver. "And now it's not convenient. Now, it's over."

"Oh, God, Celeste, can't you see? It's not that you're black, it's not that at all. It's just that I just don't know, I don't know where all this is going, or whether . . ."

Suddenly she buries her face in her knitting and tears come, tears that won't stop. Shaking, her shoulders rise and fall with her sobs, and I want to help, do something, but I'm paralyzed. I can't think. I can't touch her. Then I just want to be somewhere else, far away.

I listen for long minutes, and finally I can't stand it. "Celeste," I say firmly, "it's not that you're black. Be sensible. It's *not* that.

Celeste's sobs subside. She continues to sit with her face buried in her knitting. But she's listening.

"It's that I don't want to have such a big commitment. I *can't* have such a big commitment. Maybe I should want it. Maybe I should be ready. Maybe I don't feel enough love for you. I mean, I really like you, I like you a lot, you know that. What *is* love exactly, anyway? Do you really know what *you* mean when you say you love someone? You know, we'll still mean a lot to each other. Things like this happen, you know."

Slowly, she stands. She observes me quietly for a few minutes, then turns and walks out of the room. I hear the bedroom door softly, firmly close with a click.

Restless, dissatisfied, feeling misunderstood and sorry for myself, I roam about the living room. Miserable, I sit down on the couch and rest my head against the cushions.

Suddenly Celeste is standing in the entry to the living room, still in her robe. She looks at me and says quietly, "You know what, Erik? You're a bastard. You're a goddamned selfish bastard. I'm glad I don't have to live with what you are!" She turns and walks slowly back to the bedroom. Again, I hear the door close with a click.

It's summer now, late June 1965. I've driven the old Studebaker wagon from Minneapolis and am staying a few days with Barney and Lucy at their ranch in the foothills of the Flute Reed Mountains. I'm getting up the nerve to move alone out to the old derelict cabin that lies some miles away in the wilderness. In a week or so, Lon and Farmer will arrive.

Last summer, a year ago, when I visited the ranch on my way back to Minneapolis from Berkeley, Barney told me about the cabin. He'd seen it abandoned on one of his Jeep trips up Flute Reed Creek. After checking at the county seat, he learned it was to be auctioned that fall for back taxes. As no one had done the annual assessment work, the mining claims on which it sat had apparently lapsed years ago.

I continued on to Minneapolis that summer, but in the fall Barney went to the auction and bid on the cabin for sixty-five dollars, then sent me the papers to sign. I was a miner!

Now, this summer, my first job is to stake two twenty-acre mining claims around the cabin. Gleefully, Barney loads a gold pan, a pick, and two shovels into his car and drives me and Alice and Harry, his two oldest kids, out to the claim.

"But where should I dig?" I say worriedly. "The Forest Service booklet says we're supposed to have a discovery hole with valuable mineral showing."

"You and the kids just dig a hole somewhere likely," he counsels. "You can take care of the details later." The kids and I look for some place that ought to have gold under it. We pick a dry wash a few hundred yards off in the woods and excavate the requisite one hundred cubic feet of dirt. We've now gone through the motions required by the 1872 mining law.

Barney has stayed behind to admire the cabin and the privy. They caught his eye in the first place because of their sweeping views of the Flute Reed peaks, ten miles across the basin.

We load our pick, shovels, and gold pan back in the Jeep. As we drive back to the ranch, I fret that soon the Forest Service will send an inspector demanding to see the valuable mineral in my discovery hole. "We'll deal with that if and when it comes," says Barney. "The Forest Service has bigger problems than you. Already this summer some crazy old coots bulldozed the hell out of the streambed up in Jack's Gulch looking for gold. Naturally, they didn't bother to apply for permits. They muddied the Bitterroot River for thirty miles downstream. The fishermen and the Sierra Club types are hopping mad. It'll take years for the Forest Service to get around to you."

A few days later, I'm ready to move out to the cabin. I load up the station wagon, and Barney follows behind me in his Jeep, delighted to see me settled in my new estate.

We wander through the broken-down log building. The doors and windows are gone. It has no foundation. The floorboards are rotted out in some places, in others buckled and broken from the settling of the massive log walls into the soft ground. Mouse turds pepper every horizontal surface. Steady afternoon breezes, sweeping off the mountains, rattle and slap layers of torn plastic sheets that hunters have tacked over the empty, gaping window frames.

"Jeez," I think, "do I really want to stay out here alone?" I check out an old log bedstead upstairs. Daylight seeps through the sloping roof boards above. Barney helps me push the bed to a spot where the roof still holds its roofing paper. Later I can throw out my sleeping bag and pad. Downstairs in the back kitchen shed, we examine the broken-down cookstove, the top heaped with mouse turds, the white enamel sides stained and streaked. Finally we walk to the front room and admire the huge stone fireplace. At least I can cook and stay warm.

We hear a car pulling up the long gravel drive to the cabin. We walk out the front door to wait. It's a fifteen-year-old Buick station wagon. It stops and a small, wiry man of about sixty jumps out. Patches of his short, rumpled white hair stand up straight, and his thin red cheeks sprout a week's worth of bristling white whiskers. He wears dirty slacks and a crumpled, sweat-stained dress shirt.

Angrily he demands, "Are you Earik Storkey?"

"Yes," I say, taken aback, unsure what the trouble is.

"I'm Roscoe Ray. I've got the hard rock claims all up and down the mountain there." He waves his hand to indicate the hills behind the cabin. "These here are my claims, too, as if you didn't know. You jumped 'em. Now, I want you and your perfesser friend to clear right out of here. Fast!"

"Now, wait a minute," I say. "I've bought this cabin and I've staked the claims. If they *were* your claims, it's not my problem you didn't pay your taxes or do assessment work."

Roscoe's face turns scarlet. "You're a goddamn liar!" he fumes. "The work is done. It's been done every year and it's filed. And I've got witnesses. Go ask the county clerk, if it'll make you happy. But meantime, I just want to see you two getting yourselves into those vehicles and getting the hell off my claims. Right now. And take this crazy goddamned cabin, too, if you think you own it. Maybe it'll fit in the back of your goddamn station wagon. Otherwise, I guess you can just leave it there where it's been sitting for the last thirty years."

I glance over at Barney, who observes Roscoe quietly, noncommittally. I glance back at Roscoe. He's about five foot seven, like Barney and me. This doesn't look like it could shape up into a fistfight.

"I'm not going anywhere, Mr. Ray," I say. "There's no recent assessment work done anywhere on this place. I've checked that out pretty carefully. And I've staked the claims and done discovery work. As for the cabin, you know it went at auction last fall. I bought it. I'm staying. I'm sorry if this is a surprise to you, but . . ."

Suddenly there's a black six-shooter in Roscoe's right hand. I glimpse lead peeking out from the four exposed chambers.

"I ain't talking to you two sons of bitches anymore," he shouts, dancing from one foot to the other. The gun barrel jerks menacingly. "Do you know what we do with claim jumpers around here?"

I'm in shock. But I hear Barney speak slowly, gently, in a tone of hurt surprise, "Now, Mr. Ray. Just what in the hell do you think you're going to do with that thing? Let's all be reasonable, here. Why don't you just put it away? Something could happen that we'll all regret."

Roscoe comes to rest squarely on both feet. The gun still points at us, but it's steady now, dropped to his waist.

Barney goes on. "I don't think my young friend Erik here meant any harm to you. In fact, I know he didn't. And I'm sure he wants to do the right thing by you. There's going to be some kind of a deal you two can strike here. But before we get into anything like that, I'm guessing he could scare up a few drinks of good whiskey out of that load of gear he's got in the back of that wagon. Then we can all sit down here with a drink and begin to work this thing out so it's good for everyone."

Suddenly sheepish, Roscoe drops his arms to his sides. He turns and throws the gun through the open window onto the front seat of the Buick.

"Well," he says, "I suppose that's about right. Maybe I'm a little overagitated. No harm in just sitting down here and talking everything over."

Shakily, I head for the car and start digging through my gear for the bottle and three tin Sierra Club cups.

It's a few weeks later. Lon and Farmer arrive at the cabin. Lon's beard is now full and wild. His dark hair drops to his shoulders. Farmer's blond mustache droops at the ends. Now and again he thoughtfully strokes a sparse goatee several inches long. I sport a scruffy Abe Lincoln beard. In this mountain valley of cattlemen, lumberjacks, and miners, we're clearly on a mining claim under false pretenses, a scandal to the locals.

It's not gold we're after this summer, but the meaning of life. We will practice the precipitous psychedelic yoga and achieve Perfect Enlightenment. Leary, Alpert, and Metzner announced the plan at Harvard. Guided by their example and the ancient Tibetan wisdom in their manual, we'll take LSD once each week. We'll concentrate this experience by sitting meditation. Here in the mountains, free from city corruptions, we prepare for our imminent enlightenments.

In the back of his little Hillman Husky station wagon, Lon has brought three *zafus*—round black meditation cushions—and a *tatami*, a rice straw mat a few inches thick and about three feet by seven. We place the tatami mat against the north wall in the front room opposite the big windows. It helps bridge some of the rotted floorboards.

Here we will do zazen. Here we will eat meals formally seated on our cushions, even washing our traditional Japanese *oryoki* bowls individually at our seats with hot water, as is done in Japanese monasteries. Our diet will be simple and strict, mostly rice and beans. We have a twenty-five-pound sack of each, bought at a distant grain elevator to conserve money.

But I'm uneasy. Zen meal practice is going too far. Doing things Reverend Suzuki's way at Sokoji Temple was one thing. But this feels like doing it Lon's way.

Farmer, however, is cheerful about the experiment. "Yeah, that's cool. I like sitting on zafus for meals. We don't have to come up with any more chairs. And you know, washing our bowls at our seats saves trouble. We don't have to do dishes except for the pots."

Inwardly I fume. I'm trying to keep up some appearances in the nearby mountain village, where I've come to know a few of the locals. And I don't want to embarrass Barney and Lucy. I know that the locals think the mining claim just a lark. But I sure don't want to look to everyone like a drug casualty on some cult trip.

I'm outvoted, however. "We'll see how this all works on acid," I think to myself grimly.

The day before our first trip, we discuss details at length. My approach is basic. "Well, let's drop after breakfast, do zazen, and hang out in the cabin until we've come down enough to hike a little bit, maybe up to the mine. Later we could head to the hot spring."

"Yeah, that'd be cool," says Lon. "But listen." He takes a serious, conspiratorial tone. "Let's really push this thing as far as we can tomorrow. You know how hard it is to stay one-pointed The last day it's like rolling a needle down a taut thread. We've got to keep perfect balance. Why don't we fast for the rest of the day? Then tomorrow we can get up at five and do zazen. At five-forty we can read the section in Leary's book about holding on to the Clear Light. At six let's drop and keep on sitting—and then just do as much sitting as we can for the rest of the day.

"We've got to break out of karmic game playing. I know I'm into ego games all the time. We can break free into the Clear Light. That's where it's at. If anybody gets into a bad place, we'll read sections from the book."

"Yeah, but what's the point of fasting that long?" I ask.

"Well, you know, it'll clean out your system and the stuff'll hit harder."

"Hey," I say, "it's not like it isn't hitting pretty hard anyway."

"Hey, come on you guys," urges Lon. "You don't know what can happen. Unless we *really* push the limits, we'll never get there. You guys know the incredible groove you can get into when you're not trapped in ego games."

Farmer casts his vote. "Yeah, it's okay with me. I'll do it. Why not try? It's worth it."

"Well, okay, man," I say slowly. "But let's forget this five in the morning stuff. It'll still be near freezing."

"Right on man, good point," says Lon. "Let's get up when we get up and then do it."

We roll out the next morning about eight, hungry and shaky at the thought of what we're about to do. Yesterday our disagreements absorbed some of the dread we know we all feel but don't discuss. Lon gives us each two large capsules filled with a lumpy white powder.

"How much is this?" I ask.

"Well, can't say exactly," Lon smiles. "It's from a good source, and he says take one for a little trip and two if you're serious."

"We're damn serious," I laugh, nervous as hell.

We wash the big caps down with icy water from the spring. I shiver at the lumpy feel of the cap going down, a slight nausea rising to meet it.

We clear our sleeping bags out of the front room and line up the black cushions on the tatami mat. We bow toward our cushions and then away, sit down, and spin around to face the wall, just like at Sokoji Temple.

I settle into sitting in the chill, empty room, my stomach growling with hunger, then filled with butterflies.

Minutes pass. Nothing happens. Have we been ripped off? My stomach is queasy now. Then I shut my eyes and see streamers swirling behind my eyelids, intricate patterns dancing in vivid colors. I open my eyes to orient myself and find the straight yellow-brown lodgepole logs two feet in front of me beginning to ripple along the edges, as if I'm gazing down through a current of clear, rushing water.

Yeah. The stuff works. And it comes on fast. Lon's right about the fasting. Sitting on my zafu, legs crossed, thumb tips touching, I'm solid, grounded, a mountain giant watching the descent of glaciers over eons of time.

I shut my eyes again to enjoy the intricate dance of colors unreeling behind my eyelids, fiery gasses incandescing in the embers of a fire.

A doubt intrudes. Where's the Clear Light? Leary says it should come first, the first Bardo, the first dimension after the ego dies. I'm seeing colors and patterns. Is my karma so bad that I flip immediately into hallucinatory visual forms? On either side of me, Lon and Farmer breathe deeply, erratically.

Suddenly signals arrive from my intestines. Urgent signals. I've got to shit.

Panic strikes through me. My God! Now *I've* got to break the spell. Lon will think I'm just trying to fuck up his trip. He knows I didn't want to do it his way. He'll be angry. I don't want anger right now.

But my guts are on fire. A huge mass of heavy, hot, dark mud moves slowly, glacially, undeniably down through caverns in my lower being. I feel a child's panic. Something's going to happen—I've got to do something—quick!

Breaking the deep morning silence, I grab for the straw mat with my fingertips, spin around on the cushion like a phonograph record, and leap to my feet in a crescendo of morning light. I bolt through the back door in my socks and run a hundred feet to the privy.

Fumbling with buttons, dancing from leg to leg, clamping buttocks tight, I stoop, kneel down, and gingerly apply bare skin to the chill, rough, unfinished boards of the old privy hole. The dark, warm stuff floods from my body through wriggling tubes and pipes that cry out in sheer pleasure—a visceral, stupendous relief.

Jeans around my ankles sweeping dirt and cobwebs off the floor, hands resting idly at my sides, I'm five years old. My body does what bodies have done for millions of years. I lightly stroke the rough-sawn lodgepole pine boards with my fingertips. I watch a spider make repairs to her web, spun over a gap between two logs that lets the morning light shaft through, then gaze wonderingly out the open privy door toward the Flute Reed Mountains.

Sudden panic. The other guys! They're going through this, too. They've got minds, too. What are *they* thinking? About me running out the back door? Of course, Farmer doesn't care. But I can feel Lon thinking dark, ugly thoughts: "That asshole Storlie. Always trying to control the trip. Just had to fuck it up." Or maybe he's thinking, "The poor son of a bitch. He's freaked. Just couldn't handle it!"

I wipe, carefully get up, painstakingly pull up my jeans, button buttons, and start slowly around the cabin for the front door, walking cautiously between the woody sagebrush plants, eyes on the uneven ground. Tiny pine twigs and needles stick to my wool-socked feet.

At the front door, I grip the wooden handle and hesitate, looking up. Ten miles away through a blue-brilliant atmosphere, snowcapped peaks explode into the sky. Muscular cliffs and bare rocky slopes softened by green valleys writhe and twist and transform into flowing colored patterns, re-form into themselves, then dissolve again.

My hand rests on the door handle, but I can't move. My eyes sweep down from the peaks to a red, rusted-out thirty-gallon trash barrel sitting by the Studebaker. Erupting on those surfaces are a million shades of red, of brown, blood flowing, blood drying into dusty, fine-sandy rust, ready to powder off at the touch of a finger.

Still gripping the door handle, somehow, by a tiny, sensitive adjustment of something in each eye, I see the trash barrel go out of focus, and I'm looking back toward the jagged Flute Reed Mountains dancing their ten-thousand-foot peaks into a blue sky. White puffy dragon and whale clouds sail proudly off the tops and over my head.

Another slight adjustment in each eye and I see the empty middle distance—empty yet blue tinged—the empty basin cupped by foothills behind me and mountains ahead of me and meadowlands below. Pure empty air, yet filled with a glistening, pulsing, transparent energy field working its work, a million acres of empty capillary beds of retina and visual cortex registering no color, no thing, registering only itself.

My hand drops from the door handle. I move myself slowly over to a stump upended a few feet from the door and slowly sit down, intricate neurological adjustments piloting a titanic body across the gulf between door and stump. Again and again with that slight, magical adjustment inside each eye, I flick between filigreed red trash barrel, dark exploding peaks, and bluish empty middle distance. The visual elements break into my consciousness like surf into a cove, the energies of eternity, of continents building, mountains rising, tides sucking, the earth in massive orbit circling the sun.

I heave a great sigh, drop my elbows to my knees, my chin into my hands, and smile at the peaks. Again, everything's all right. It's *really* all right!

I notice Lon and Farmer now, carefully coming through the front door, walking with slow steps that feel ahead for the solid ground. I rise to my feet. No words are spoken. We gaze at each other with shocked and frightened eyes—and quickly look away. Together we gaze on the mountains. Then slowly, awkwardly, we drift and wander apart. We can't bear each other. Rivalries and resentments can't inhabit these spaces. Within a few minutes they've each melted into a different part of the woods and I can't remember what direction they've taken.

We don't find each other again until afternoon, and it's evening before we really talk about what happened. We fire up the old wood range back in the lean-to kitchen, start water for tea and dishes, and heat up leftover rice and lentils. Sitting on our zafus in the front room, slowly eating, we quietly talk.

"Man, what an incredible trip," I say. "I can't believe it. Did you see the mountains? You know, I didn't want to stop doing zazen, really. I had to take this horrible shit. I almost didn't make it."

Lon and Farmer laugh nervously. "Yeah, I hung in there for as long as I could," says Farmer, "but the logs started crawling around so had I couldn't look at 'em anymore. I just had to move around."

"Those are mighty caps," says Lon. "I could've sat longer, maybe, but it would've been hard."

"Where'd you go?" I ask.

"Down in the meadow. I just kept wandering and wandering until I was down by the creek, and then I sat for a long time watching it. It's not much bigger than a trickle, but I kind of fell into it with my eyes. Well, and with my ears, too. I'd watch it swirl around little bars of sand and gravel and hear the slurpings and gurglings, over and over again. It was like my whole body flooded with that one little creek."

"I went up behind the cabin onto that high outcrop and lay out in the sun," says Farmer. "The sun got hotter and hotter and I flipped into some nightmare place where I was Prometheus stretched out and chained for the vulture. I could feel the beak ripping out my guts. I wanted to come down and find someone, but I was sure I'd never find the cabin. Things finally cooled out and I walked through the woods and ended up over by the pond. It's full of frogs. I bet I watched them for two hours. It was like I could see a whole little society—there were a king and queen and all their courtiers."

"What *is* this stuff, really?" I ask. "What does it do? How does it do it? Everything else I've ever had is just kid stuff."

"It's something else," says Lon, shaking his head.

Farmer smiles a broad smile. "Hey, they never told us about this at the Unitarian Society."

"That's for sure," I say. "Hey, let me do the dishes. Maybe you can get a fire going in the fireplace. It's getting cold."

We finish eating, and I carry plates and cups back to the kitchen. The sun has set and the old cabin begins to grow dark. I light a kerosene lamp and lift it onto a shelf up behind the warm stove. It stands next to three red coffee cans filled with rice, beans, and brown sugar. I set a dented enamel dishpan on the edge of the stove and fill it half full with water from a bucket on the stove, then add some cold water bucketed up from the spring outside. Stirring in plenty of soap, I drop in cups and plates and spoons.

Warm now, cozy before the stove, I swirl the soapy water idly. I'm a child again, the cups and bowls marvelous craft riding on surf raised by a hand. I reach for my white coffee cup and, holding it before me, observe it for long moments in the gentle pulse of yellow lamplight. I dip it in and out of the soapy water several times, then begin scrubbing the inside with the dish brush.

"What," I ask, "is all *this*, really?"

Here's my cup, shaped from wet clay into a hollow cup galaxy that curves back into itself, then burned by fire into fine-grained ceramic stone. The soap transmutes moving water into a thousand bubbles that reflect rainbow light. Ten-fingered, hairy animal hands calmly, lightly, and deftly manipulate a small galaxy in space.

I gently return the cup to the dishwater. My visual field wells with colored objects. A red bowl, bobbing on the waves, dissolves into capillary beds, networks of interlocking channels through which blood, transparent like water, flows and flows.

"Where does it exist?" I ask, reaching again for my cup. "In the retina? In the visual cortex?" Surely it's out there too in the solid world, now a rainbow of flowing colors whirling themselves into forms—the rough pine bench, the battered wood range, red coffee cans on a shelf, a lamp quietly glowing, log walls yellow in the lamplight. Standing before the dishpan, I hold my cup. The corners of the little kitchen darken to black in the fading light.

It's October 1965—a sunny, crisp autumn afternoon, a Saturday in Minneapolis. I'm back from the Flute Reed Mountains, living in my old basement room in my parents' house, taking courses toward a Ph.D. in American studies, and now teaching full time in a tiny community college that's just opened in a black neighborhood in Minneapolis.

Lon is still in Berkeley. Farmer and I are a church of two. We're absolutely committed to the Leary program. Each week, on Saturday or Sunday morning, we take the sacrament, do zazen, and burn karma.

We feel close to mastery of this yoga. After several hours in zazen, we're calm, sailing confidently on oceans of awareness. Come the afternoon, we climb into Farmer's GTO and tool around town—young buddhas eyeing the girls, buying auto parts at discount, drag racing boisterous teenagers in a hot car that pulls up next to us on Lake Street, doing curbside mechanical work with the hood up and parts strewn all over the boulevard. By evening, we're standing at the old mahogany bar at the Mixer's on Seven Corners, chatting quietly with comrades, secretly amazed as the white foam on our beers goes through endless, gorgeous, cloudlike transformations.

This particular Saturday morning we each rose at six, he at his mother's house a few miles away, me in my basement room, and dropped acid. After several hours of zazen, I drive over to his house. His mother opens the front door and greets me cheerfully. As I step over the top step, I'm aware that the earth beneath it has opened and gapes wide. I say "Hi," noticing the hot flames and fierce magma glowing hundreds of miles beneath my feet. Farmer appears, his face joyful, and we jump in the GTO and take a drive through the city and around the lakes. By afternoon, we're heading to my house to help my parents change storms and screens and wash windows in preparation for the winter.

We work under an old oak tree in the front of the house, which sits on the crest of a hill a block from Cedar Lake. I'm carrying the large, heavy storm panels up from the garage and leaning them on one side of the oak. Farmer washes them with a bristly brush dipped in a bucket of ammonia solution and then squeegees them off. When they're dry, we carry them to my father, who's up on a ladder at the side of the house, removing screens, washing windows, and putting up the newly washed storms as soon as they're dry. My mother is in the kitchen making a late lunch.

The house has some thirty windows, many high and out of reach. After carrying a dozen, I stop and watch Farmer working with the squeegee. He is intently involved. He finishes a pane and reaches out delicately with a scrap of cotton dishtowel to rub out a smudge down in the corner.

"Hey, give me a turn," I say. "That looks fine."

"It is," says Farmer. "El perfecto." He takes a last swipe at the panel and moves it to the clean stack. I move a new window into place and brush it all over with the hot, sudsing ammonia solution—a pungent burst inside my nose—then use a rag to wipe excess water running on the top and sides of the window glass. Firmly placing the squeegee at the top of the pane, I smoothly pull it down and to the bottom.

How wonderful! The ammonia solution runs busily ahead of the squeegee rubber, carrying the buildup of dirt and fog from a year of use and storage. A sheen of solution left by the rubber vaporizes almost instantaneously in shafts of sunlight that penetrate the oak canopy. Light breezes play about the hilltop.

"Well," I think. "It's chores again. At age twenty-four, it's chores. It's wonderful. A long nightmare of drinking and doping is over. Demons were in hot pursuit. What irony. Saved by a drug from drugs. But I'm home again. I've returned."

It's the next day, at the end of a late Sunday breakfast with my parents. We read the papers, lament the latest trick played by the Republicans, chat. The only jarring note has been my new vegetarianism. I refuse the bacon, accept the eggs. My mother is convinced I'll become mal-nourished. As I get up to leave the table, she says, "Erik, your dad and I have to talk to you. We'd like to go in the living room and sit down."

Not too surprised, ready for whatever comes, I carry another cup of coffee into the living room, and we sit. My father, a child of prairie Norwegians, waits quietly. For a moment no one speaks.

Then my mother says, "Erik, I'm frightened. I'm terribly frightened. I saw your eyes yesterday—and Farmer's, too. Your pupils were horribly dilated. I think you were on LSD. Don't you know how powerful and dangerous it is? Your dad and I think we've got to do something. And I'm simply going to insist that you see Doctor Myhre. He's our doctor and he's a good man. He's known you for years."

My father says nothing. Cautiously, he watches.

"Well," I say, "you're right. We did take LSD yesterday, early in the morning, before we got together. And then we each did zazen. But can't you see how different this is? This isn't about escaping some-thing, or getting high and messed up. You saw us. You couldn't really tell we were on anything. This is a yoga. Everything's different now."

"I just don't believe it," says my mother. "I've read about that crazy Leary at Harvard. They threw him out, thank God. And that sidekick of his, too. They simply want to get young people involved with drugs—and with thinking they're some kind of holy men."

Finally, my father speaks, choosing each word. "Remember, Erik, those men are looking for recruits. Young men like you and Farmer."

"I know why you'd think so," I say. "But you're wrong about them. The press is on the attack. The establishment is terrified that LSD wakes people up to the immorality of the war. And to the American rat race. Einstein was the last big step in an age of scientific explora-tion—the *external* world. Now Hoffman's discovery of LSD turns us inward—to an *internal* world—to consciousness itself.

"I know how strange all this seems," I continue. "But it's real. It's a chance, finally, for a real American enlightenment."

"Remember, Erik," my father says, "every generation, for a time, thinks it's found an answer. We're concerned about all this, of course. I'm especially concerned with the anti-intellectualism in what I see of

Professor Leary. And in Buddhism too. The rejection of ideas and rational thought is dangerous—and an old story in this country."

"What exactly happens when you take LSD?" asks my mother.

"Oh, it's hard to explain it, really. But, for example, you see that the world—what's right here in front of us, this living room, these chairs—it's all created by the eyes and brain. You actually *see* the capillary networks in the retina and visual cortex constructing walls, rugs, tables, trees, clouds. Everything is in constant, fluid transformation. It's beautiful—and scary, too.

"And the mind itself stands revealed. It's like a vast, shining ocean, and thoughts are simply waves rolling over the surface. When the waves come to rest, I'm just the ocean. Then I can wash windows. Yesterday was actually a lot of fun!"

"It sounds simply terrible to me," says my mother. "It's your *brain* you're changing—the only one you'll ever have, Erik."

"I know," I say, "I understand. It's hard to say what it is with words. Maybe you and Dad should try it. Maybe you and Barney and Lucy, too. Then you'll *know* what it is."

Shocked, my mother stands. "I wouldn't *dream* of such a thing. And you won't hear the end of this until you've agreed to see the doctor."

My father keeps sitting. He watches quietly, his face relaxed. Do I see the shadow of a smile playing over his lips? Finally, he stands too, for a moment immersed in thought, then looks at me squarely. "Just remember, Erik. You don't have to be anyone's recruit."

Soon Farmer and I are running out of LSD. We have no source in Minneapolis. With my new teaching salary, I decide to send five hundred dollars to San Francisco. This will buy 250 capsules, 250 micrograms each—better than a two years' supply for two of us taking it once a week. I'm no longer into subterranean, beatnik secrets. I decide to be straight, at least with my father.

I approach him one evening as he works at his workbench in the basement. He's preparing to glue and assemble a small cabinet he's building into the wall in my basement study.

"Dad, I've got a question for you."

"Yes," he says, continuing with his work, checking and rechecking the fit of two pieces of wood.

"I'm going to send money to San Francisco to get some more LSD. Farmer and I are going to keep taking it. We're not into sales. This is our own experiment."

"Ah," he says, his voice questioning. "So you're still convinced you're on the right track here? And that your ex-Harvard professors aren't deluded by the very stuff that they're promoting? Ponce de Leon lost much time looking for a fountain of youth."

I hesitate. Finally, I say, "I understand your skepticism. But this thing is genuine. It's huge. It'll change everything. It's Galileo's telescope."

He sets down his work and holds my gaze.

"I don't want to go around hiding," I say. "I want your permission to have some sent to this address. If you say no, I won't do it."

He stands for another long minute, says finally, "Well, I guess that'll be all right," and then turns back to his workbench and the work.

It seems only minutes have gone by, yet hunger pulls me back to the frog. And a mild throbbing in the knees. They've always ached, but now, after years of jogging, aerobics, hiking, and zazen, they teach me my age.

It must be close to noon. The westerlies drop for a moment, the air suddenly still. The sun beats down, hot on my shoulders, and the black rocks surrounding me radiate heat. I look out toward the mountains, then down over sage and timber. I hear the distant roar of a truck engine and the fluctuating whine of a gearbox, as someone bumps and labors up a roadless slope somewhere.

"Bastards," I fret. "They know damn well this area's closed to off-road traffic. They love to grind their way up to the top of any mountain they can manage. Of course, you had your own good times four-wheel driving all through this country twenty-five years ago. Lots of good times. Oh, well."

My knees begin to ache, now. A light sweat breaks over my back.

The bottom of my foot tingles, and I'm anxious to uncoil, stand up, stretch, yawn, and scratch myself all over.

"Don't move yet," I caution. "You're not yet really so uncomfortable. A little hunger and pain will wake you up, wring out these thought forms, clarify the mind."

Over the years, I've learned to evaluate carefully. Is the body just whining? Or does it have a genuine grievance? I'm jury and judge. Zazen should do no damage. Yet pain is inevitable when there is discipline in Dogen's steady, immobile sitting. To move the body or mind for some trivial reason destroys concentration, destroys the zazen itself.

"Well," I think, "we could accept discipline from Suzuki Roshi. We sat hard for him. And we sat hard on LSD. The combination was powerful. But it reached far beyond us. We only dreamed we could master such titanic powers."

Gently, I rock from side to side on my seat on the Crag. This movement eases my cramped knees and allows blood to flow freely back in my legs. Then slowly I sway forward and back, coming carefully to center. Then I sway again from side to side in ever-decreasing arcs, finally entering motionlessness at a balance point of back, shoulders, neck and head. I tuck my chin in slightly and feel the top of my skull supporting the sky.

And I resume my sitting, gently. And gently, I pull the mind back from its many thoughts to rest, for a time, only on itself.

6

Torture and Punishment

IT'S EARLY SPRING, 1966. FARMER AND I HEAR that Tim Leary himself, busted now but defiant, will do a seminar in Chicago on cosmic consciousness. The seminar will focus on nondrug techniques for awakening the mind to enlightenment. We're excited. We decide to take the train down, stay with our old friend Dean, and drop acid for the event. We mail in our registration fees with a letter to Leary that reads in part:

"For almost two years now we've been practicing the weekly psyche-delic yoga that you, Alpert, and Metzner recommend in your great, updated version of *The Tibetan Book of the Dead*. We're eager to meet you in person. We understand why it is impossible for you to provide the molecule, so we will *dilate Mind* before we arrive."

The conference is to begin at nine o'clock on a Saturday morning at a large hotel in downtown Chicago. Farmer and I ride the Zephyr down after work Friday evening, and Dean picks us up at the depot.

Dean's flat is in a grimy three-story brick building in one of the interminable lower-middle-class neighborhoods of suburban Chicago. The side windows look across a few feet of space to more brick walls.

After a few beers with Dean, we turn in. Tomorrow we'll rise at six, only a few hours away.

The next morning we wake to a bleak, overcast sky. We'll drop acid and do zazen early. This will give us several hours to master these energies before Dean gets himself up and drives us downtown.

"Listen, man," I say to Farmer, as we stand blearily in Dean's little kitchen, "I think we should take two caps. It's our chance to meet Leary and for him to see just where we're at now. We might as well go the whole distance."

Farmer's brow wrinkles. "Oh, no, don't you think that's pushing it a bit too far? You know, we've got to get down to the hotel, get into the seminar, deal with whatever goes on there."

"We can do it, man," I say. "Look how well things have been going all winter. We're cool! For almost two years we've been following his program. And there's no one to talk to about it in Minneapolis. And we want to do more than just talk. When'll we have a chance like this again?"

"Listen," Farmer says, "if you want to, go ahead. But I'm fine with just one. Remember, these things are two hundred and fifty mics apiece!"

"Yeah, I know, but I'm ready," I say, eager to show my stuff to the master. "I'll do two and you do one. Then you can pilot us through the hotel lobby," I conclude with a chuckle.

We drop our caps and sit zazen facing the ancient flowered wallpaper in Dean's living room. In half an hour I know I've made a disastrous mistake. I inhabit a body too vast—a cosmos where light years flash across the spaces inside a fingertip. I can't coordinate the motions of this body. I can't stay upright on my cushion. Sighing, trying to cover my confusion, I lie back on Dean's threadbare carpet, chilled, shivering in the gray, early morning light.

Shutting my eyes, I'm helplessly aware of an outpouring of huge, empty energies from every atom of my body, an endless, vacant, exhausting flow that leaves me lost and helpless, stunned, unable to feel fear or pain.

"My God," a muted voice whispers in my head, "is this finally the Clear Light? Is it possible the Buddhas sit in the middle of such vastness?" Infinity upon infinity of fluid energies rush out from my body and mind into oceans of space. But there's no bliss. I simply witness and endure endless, irresistible energies.

For an hour I lie on the carpet, praying for release. I wanted to meet Leary, to show him my accomplishment, yet how foolish, how remote that desire now seems. More time passes, and finally Farmer and Dean, concerned, try to rally me. I look up to see anxious faces bobbing above me.

Farmer says, "Listen, do you think you really want to go? You don't have to. I'll stay here, too. But if you want to go, Dean'll drive us down to the hotel. The seminar starts in about an hour. You have to decide."

I can't reply. I look up at them, helpless, paralyzed.

Then Dean suggests anxiously, "Look, there's no reason for you to go. You can just hang out here."

But this suggestion is terrible. I groan inwardly. This is defeat, failure. After a passionate journey of almost two years, how can I give up this final dream of enlightenment and affirmation by the master? My only hope now for release is to push on.

"No, man, I'll go. But this is the heaviest thing I've ever faced. It's way too much. But we've got to go. Farmer, you just read some sections from the book. That'll help."

Farmer begins quietly reading from The Psychedelic Experience, but I'm beyond hearing words. The clear light energy has changed. Now in the cosmos of my skull an infinity of points once a glowing hot magma— a viscous energy, darkly transparent like honey, burning and relentlessly flowing. Then it erupts all through my body, inexorable, bending joints slowly backward until they snap, twisting arm and leg bones until they splinter. It's agony, but I hang on, try to listen to Farmer's reading of the words, hoping against hope that they will suddenly give their promise of relief, of liberation, of bliss.

But words can't touch these vast empty spaces. "Maybe Leary can help," I think. Groaning, I push up to a sitting position, saying to Farmer, "That's okay, man. Don't read any more. I'm all right. Just give me a few minutes to wash my face and shave. Then we better go."

I go to the bathroom and painstakingly lather my upper lip, cheeks, chin, and neck, then pick up the razor and behold a terrified face in the mirror—the razor suspended, just touching a cheek. I start to stroke the razor down, catching a few stubbly whiskers, then despair.

My hands are so huge, so cold and clumsy, that I fear the icy blade, anticipate the numb slice of a razor cut, imagine red blood welling out to stain the white lather. Cringing, I lift the razor away, set it down, wash off the lather, and return slowly to the living room.

"Let's go, man," I say. "I can make it. I really can."

Worried, reluctant, Farmer and Dean lead the way out into the gray morning and we drive to downtown Chicago. Suddenly we're in the lobby of the Edgewater Hotel, then in a crush of people in an elevator, then I'm following Farmer into a room on one of the upper floors.

Awkwardly trailing Farmer, I maneuver my immense body toward a cushion on oriental carpets spread out in a semicircle on the floor of a small seminar room. Around me are some twenty-five middle-aged folks, mostly professional men curious about Leary. One is a reporter from a Chicago paper. He apparently hopes there's a story here somewhere. I seat myself and try to relax, but the energies pouring thick from every inch of my body are a rising crescendo of pain. Instant after nightmare instant, I make a supreme effort of will not to stand up, scream, run wildly away somewhere, anywhere.

After a few minutes Leary seats himself in the center of the circle and, part Harvard professor, part Irish raconteur, begins an animated exposition of the lessons of psychedelics.

"Now listen," he says, "we're faced with an Establishment that knows its back is to the wall. It's terrified of the psychedelics. It can't handle the alternative consciousness developing all over the country. The secret is out about the meaninglessness of American life as it's presently lived. And about the war—about the collusion of the corporations, the politicians, and the military.

"The psychedelics have catalyzed that rising consciousness. The ruling elite is terrified. They'll stop at nothing to turn the clock back. That's why they've gone after me." He pauses, fixes the audience with a frank stare, then goes on. "If honest seekers can't use the psychedelics, then we'll explore inner space by alternative methods. That's why I'm here. That's why you're here."

My attention wanders in and out. My effort is to stay in my seat. Leary talks about going beyond ego game playing, about the bliss that dawns upon ego death, about access to all this through strobe lights, mandalas, visualizations, yogic concentration.

Then, looking knowingly at Farmer and me, Leary innocently asks who before has experienced a psychedelic drug. "I have, many times," I blurt out, "and I'm on five hundred micrograms of acid right now, and it's too much, way too much. I can't really handle it this time." There's a sharp intake of breath from the audience.

Leary smiles knowingly, wearily. "And how about your partner?" he asks, pointing to Farmer, who sits uncomfortably beside me.

"Yeah, me too," says Farmer, "but I only took half what Erik did."

"Well," Leary says, looking back at me, "try to tell me what's going on with you. What's coming up?"

"Oh, I hardly know what to say," I stammer out. "It's coming on bigger than I've ever experienced before. Every pore of my body gushes pain. And it's like I'm a galaxy looking out at you—and you're another galaxy light years across intergalactic space. I sit here on the carpet and it rises up like surf. I see waves rolling right aross the carpet and breaking on everybody's legs as we sit here. But it's this pain that won't go away. And I'm already three hours into this thing. This time, I know, I took too much."

"Okay," Leary says, "I'm going to take a minute to talk to each of you privately." He beckons to me, and I retreat with him through a door that opens off the back of the seminar room. Leary closes it and sits down comfortably on the carpeted floor of a small room. I sink down heavily to join him. I notice film projectors, some other pieces of equipment, and a few assistants, who had earlier greeted the participants, working to set things up.

"Okay," he says, "now what's happening? Where're you at?"

"Oh, Tim, it's just that I took so much. I can't handle it. It's so huge. There's so much pain. Farmer tried reading to me from your book this morning, but nothing happened."

"But this thing that's happening to you," says Leary, "it's just coming from you, from your own infinite buddha consciousness." He fixes me with alert eyes. "It's really just you. It's your very own hell. And it's your very own way of dying to yourself. I don't think you took too much. You took just what you needed at this time, at this place, to do what you have to do. It's okay."

I'm mute. I have no response to this. After a long minute Leary says firmly, "Let's just go back to the group. I'll talk to your partner. He looks like he's okay. You'll be okay too."

We walk back into the seminar room, curious faces following me like sunflowers. As Leary motions for Farmer to join him in the back room, I edge to the back of the crowd and sit down where I can lean against the wall. I look down at the roiling multicolored carpet and struggle to force my breath to come easily and smoothly.

Soon Farmer and Leary return to the room and take their seats again. Leary is back in the center. He says a few words, the lights are turned off, and he begins to talk. A strobe light ticks on and off in a wild chatter of light while a series of fantastic mandalic images merge into and through each other on a screen behind his head. In the dim light, I see an older white-haired man moving unobtrusively through the circle toward me. I recognize him as part of Leary's team. He is American Indian, his face a mass of genial red wrinkles. He sits down next to me, leans against the wall, puts his arm lightly over my shoulders, and takes my ice-cold hand in his large, warm one. A tiny wash of warmth begins to reach across intergalactic space.

After long minutes, the strobe light and the mandalic images stop. The lights click on. Leary stands and, glancing at the white-haired man, flashes out angrily, "What are you doing? That won't help anything! What he's going through is beyond all that." The man takes his arm from my shoulders and begins to release my hand, but I grip it, cling to it, won't let it go. The warm hand stays in my grasp.

It's Saturday morning, one week later. Farmer's mother is out of town. We can take our scheduled acid trip at his house today. I'm terrified. "What if *that* happens to me again?" I ask myself, as I drive over to his house, cold fear gnawing the pit of my stomach. "But I can't give up now, I just can't give up! I'm not a coward. I won't be beaten. I've put everything I've got into this. I've got to see it through."

Farmer knows I'm worried, but reassures me. "Well, sure, things were bad in Chicago. You really took way too much when we were going to have to be at the hotel with all those people. I knew you should only have taken a single cap. I should probably have just taken a half. Today we'll each just do one. That should be no problem."

"Yeah, sure," I say, trying to feel confident.

We spend a few minutes straightening up his living room and setting out zafus. Then we go through his record collection, pulling out some favorite selections. Finally, we go to the kitchen and wash down our capsules, then return to the living room and take our seats in zazen.

Within thirty minutes I know that, again, it has all gone wrong. My body is a galaxy. I'm adrift, lost, swept through an infinity of capillary beds into endless cellular spaces. A tiny voice shrieks, *I just took half the dose, and it's just as bad. I'm flipping out. I'll never get back, now. I'll be like this forever.*

I slip down off my cushion onto the carpet, lie on my back, and stretch out my arms and legs, trying to relax. Leary's book always said to merge with the fear. Then the bliss of liberation would dawn. But there's only more fear. I curl up in the fetal position and rest my head on my zafu, feeling Farmer's worried glance. "God," I think, "this is messing him up, too."

But I can't hide it anymore. Finally, I groan, "Oh, man, jeez, it's happening all over again. And I only took two hundred and fifty. Something's really wrong. I can't take it, man. You've got to get me to a hospital. I've got to come down."

Farmer, eyes wide and scared, says, "Be cool now, be cool, it'll be all right. Relax. Take it easy. I'll put on some Ravi Shankar. And we'll read some stuff from the book. That'll help. Maybe later we can walk around one of the lakes." He starts the sitar music softly in the background and picks up Leary's book. "What's going on with you? What part should I read?"

"Oh, God, I can't even tell you. But I'm freaked, really freaked. I'm so far out there, I don't think I'll ever get back. Just pick something."

"Okay, okay. Try to focus." Farmer hands me a soft pillow from the couch. "Get this under your head. And breathe real slow and easy. I'll read the 'Instructions for the Wrathful Visions.'

" 'O nobly born Erik, listen carefully:
You were unable to maintain the perfect Clear Light of the First Bardo.
Or the serene peaceful visions of the Second.
You are now entering second Bardo nightmares.

Recognize them.
They are your own thought-forms made visible and audible.
They indicate that you are close to liberation.
Do not fear them.' "

I try to listen, to focus. Yes, nightmares! But Farmer's words recede. I can't hang on to them. I'm plunged into an ocean. I struggle for breath as cliffs of water break over me, crushing me, drowning me.

Farmer keeps reading, glancing up at me hopefully.

"No harm can come to you from these hallucinations.
They are your own thoughts in frightening aspect.
They are old friends. Welcome them. Merge with them. Join them.
Lose yourself in them.
They are yours.
Whatever you see, no matter how strange and terrifying,
Remember above all that it comes from within you.
Hold onto that knowledge.
As soon as you recognize that, you will obtain liberation.
If you do not recognize them,
Torture and punishment will ensue.
But these too are but the radiances of your own intellect."

I start at the words *torture* and *punishment*. Still, there's comfort in their harsh truth. But how *do* I recognize this agony, merge with it, accept that it's mine, see its radiance? Farmer's voice is soothing. But as I reach up my hands to stroke my hair, rub my eyes, I see with horror the hands of an alien. "Whose are they?" I wonder. "How do I make them move? What if they suddenly stop obeying my will?!"

The skin is swollen, quivering, the black hairs starting up like quills.

I struggle up to my knees—Farmer solemnly watching, his pupils darkly dilated—and crawl over to sit in a chair. Across from me is another chair, of ornate dark oak, its yellow upholstery secured by orderly black buttons. It crushes me through my eyes. It transforms and flows, compressed under the terrible weight of eternity, a rock metamorphosing miles deep in the earth.

I shut my eyes to escape it, then helplessly open them and stare again. I watch it flow like a river, moving downstream, moving toward—nothing. In ten thousand years, dispersed, scattered, where will I find its atoms, its energies, the space and time it now drifts in?

And my own body? Stinking, rotten, then nothing but dust. I close my eyes to shut out the horror, and flames rush up from the floor, engulfing the room, eating through flesh, crumbling my bones, licking hot into the cup of my skull.

Late that afternoon at sundown, walking with Farmer around Cedar Lake, I'm jubilant. "Yes," I say to myself, "I die. But these energies are deathless!"

At the north end of the lake, we balance along railroad rails, two lines of iron secreted by the dark earth and stretching toward a sunset. Now off, then back up again, we walk into the huge, drooping red sun settling down into the hills and trees of my neighborhood. My eyes follow the soft rosy glow that travels just ahead of my feet on the polished, rust-pitted rail.

I know that just two blocks away on a hilltop, preparing their supper, hardly dreaming that we're here, my mother and father look out their kitchen windows at the reds and golds fading in the western sky.

We stop on a little bridge over the channel, lean on the railing, and watch the lake darken. Every pore of my body gushes joy.

I say quietly to Farmer, "I don't think I can ever do acid again."

I'm pulled back to the Crag by a left foot that's asleep. Even after all these years, my left hip joint is not as flexible as the right. I rock gently back and forth to start the blood flowing and wiggle my toes.

"He had courage," I think, smiling sadly, shaking my head, suddenly admiring the grit of that young man thirty years ago. "But it finally did beat him. He knew now that Leary and his medicine show had nothing to offer. That the words from the *Tibetan Book of the Dead* had no magic. That only one possibility remained—years of zen discipline slowly unlocking these magnificent, terrifying infinities of body and mind.

"And you didn't, in fact, try LSD again for over ten years. Then, after years of hard sitting, you grew curious. You sought out Gordon Wasson, Richard Schultes, and Albert Hoffman. You had to meet the three serious old men, the mycologist, the botanist, and the chemist, who stayed out of the newspapers and did the responsible work."

Since then, eager for bliss, impatient with the dull, creeping, time-bound mind, how many times have you perched in some eagle's nest, alive with the great mind drug, surrounded by mountains, the valleys winding out in every direction?

How many times have the world and time rolled out like a carpet from under your feet, rolled off your mountain body as streams eternally roll out from hanging snowy cirques and off cliff faces, forever polishing, marbling, enameling the shattered rock into the softness, the smoothness of time itself?

But after each of these ecstasies, lying tired, content by the campfire, I saw the patient, bemused faces of my masters Suzuki and Katagiri, each smiling sadly, each seeming to say, "So it takes this for you to remember the fire that glows in the stomach and heart, awakens each tingling finger and toe, and incandesces the mind. Do you need a mountain and a drug to remember it?"

"Hold it," I say aloud to myself. "Where's your discipline, your concentration? Wake up. Take a look. You're on the Crag."

I open my eyes wide. It's high noon. The rocks, trees, and grasses are bathed in brilliant sunshine. Heat shimmers on the basin floor. My face is shaded by the broad-brimmed hat, but the sun beating down on my shoulders has started the sweat trickling from my armpits.

I stretch out my legs, then lean forward, grip my left foot, and begin to massage the blood back into it. It feels like a warm block of wood. Then it begins to tingle fiercely, and I pull it up to examine the scrape. Licking my thumb, I rub off smears of blood dried around the hardening scab.

I rearrange myself in the lotus position, hands resting in the Buddha's mudra, and start a rhythm of slow breaths. "Too many thoughts," I think, setting my jaw and tensing my diaphragm. I watch my breath move in, move out.

I must sit wide awake, one-pointed—a mountaintop. This nose, prickling with hot windblown dust, these eyes, ears, skin, and tongue are the highest point for miles. My rock-hard skull is, right now, the absolute peak of this mountain.

I follow the inflow and outflow of breath. I count ten breaths, then ten more. Minutes go by.

Suddenly I jerk awake from a doze, bathed in sweat.

"Take a break, Erik," I whisper to myself. Wearily, I shake my head, unwind my legs, pull on my boots, and move down off the Crag.

It's good to stand up, to walk. Hunger gnaws at my stomach and I remember lunch.

"Let's find some shade," I think. Throwing things into the day pack, I amble north along the rugged crest of the mountain, pausing again and again to gaze across steep hills that undulate off toward Bitterroot country. I knead a sprig of sage between my palms and inhale deeply, rubbing it into my cheeks and nose, then circle back and dip down into trees, where the earth holds recent track of elk and piles of moist droppings.

I see a shattered anthill, what had been a careful pile of pine needles heaped around and over a rotting stump. The stump is splintered, the earth torn, pine needles scattered—and not far away there's sticky, fresh bear scat shot through with thousands of half-digested ants.

Down a steep slope I linger by a fallen Douglas fir, an old companion, uprooted by storm winds last winter. It's a giant, the bolt fully five feet across. The branches still hold needles, reddened in death. Roots as big as my waist are shattered and flung upward ten feet above my head, where they clutch flat, angular, torso-size boulders wrenched from the bedrock.

I clamber down into the hole left by the roots and reach above my head to touch thin blocks of rock the size of flagstones. They've been yanked up and suspended by brown, gnarled roots the thickness of my thumb—roots that over decades penetrated cracks in the bedrock and spread out in horizontal umbrellas along the margins between each layer. I trace with my fingers these feathery root systems—delicate fans that crack rock, bringing life to hard places. "Ah, I'll miss you, old man," I murmur, and then lay my cheek on a hanging cluster of root and cool rock shards. At my touch, flakes of granite shower down, rattling against my boots.

I wander back up through timber and, after a time, find shade in a cluster of three Douglas firs, their huge trunks circled on a shoulder of the mountain. They enclose a small room carpeted in years of fallen rusty-red needles. The bolts show scars of lightning strikes from storms blown off the Flute Reeds, the largest trunk scarred clear to the ground. Tracing my fingers over the rent, I feel the two margins of smooth,

103

mounded bark growing in from each side to a close. Dabbling my fingertips in sticky pitch oozing in the crack, I lean forward to press my nose and lips and tongue into the textured bark, inhaling the sharp smell of turpentine.

It's a lovely, shady place, perfect for lunch. Dust blown up from the bare slope below carries smells of grass and the leathery blue-green sage baking in the sun.

I clear a small area, raking aside fallen twigs and branches and dried elk scat with my fingers. I pull off my boots and socks and take a seat on a heap of crackling red needles and tiny brittle twigs. I eat my peanut butter sandwich, linger over the chocolate bar, then finish with the apple, just as my mother taught me to do with brown bag school lunches, because the apple cleans your teeth.

After drinking the rest of my lukewarm water, I lie back, stretch out at full length, and relax.

An occasional cloud builds over the Flute Reeds, floats off and passes overhead, nearly scraping the tops of my trees, which whip occasionally in afternoon breezes.

After a time I think, "I'll do zazen here. It's shady, cool, protected from the wind."

I stand up and stretch, then arrange my down vest and shirt to make a comfortable seat. I sit, again crossing my legs in half lotus and placing the left palm above the right, thumb tips lightly touching. My breath slows, drops into my belly, and smooths out. I drop my eyes down and my gaze rests softly on the reddish carpet of needles and tiny black twigs.

I sit in a fastness of rock and fir, belly full, heart filled with gratitude. For an hour my mind drifts peacefully on the flow of the breath—in and out, in and out. A few black ants, busy in the needles, climb over my hands or up my calves inside the loose cuffs of my jeans, probing, exploring with delicate feet. I ignore the tickling—it's a test of one-pointedness.

Tides of mind stuff ebb and flow, ebb and flow with the breath, surging, pooling in every crevice of my body, flowing out, rolling down hillsides, filling the valley and then rising slowly, effortlessly, to touch the tops of the Flute Reeds.

7

The Flute Reed River Mountains

IT'S THE NEXT SUMMER, 1966. TERRIFIED OF LSD, I avoid Lon and Farmer and seek refuge. I plan to go alone into the mountains, to explore the Flute Reeds. Putting together food for seven days, I pack my backpack and go, fearful, excited. I've got two old Forest Service maps that Barney loaned me. They're sketchy. I know only that these mountains are rugged and little frequented.

On the first day I'm clumsy. The soles of my feet recoil from the jolt of a rocky trail that winds up through dry sage foothills. My skin shrinks from brush that whips and stings my bare legs. Stumbling over a root snaking across the trail, I'm carried forward by the bulky backpack and go down sprawling. I get up panting, grabbing a huge granite boulder to steady myself. The palms of my hands are scraped raw, and I cringe at the rough, granular edges. I make camp early and try to relax.

Hunting for firewood the next morning, I do better. Each foot finds just the right fulcrum on rock and root. I build a fire and set a pot of water on to boil. I see that mice were here in the night. The corners of a chunk of cheese I overlooked in the dark are nibbled away through the tight plastic wrap by fine teeth, leaving many pairs of tiny parallel grooves. I cook oatmeal and raisins, then linger with coffee in the midmorning sun, reorganizing my pack.

Soon I head out on the rough, unmarked trail. All day I move deeper and deeper into remote forest never touched by ax or saw. Here is the original face of the land, the land as the glacier left it, the land absolute. Here are pine and fir and meadow grasses, the deer, antelope, and squirrel that followed the glacier's retreat. All this wells up before my eyes as I slowly march toward the center of the range.

The next afternoon, after a morning hike that brings me up out of the dense timber, I feel I belong again. I leave the trail to follow a nameless creek that winds to the north, higher and higher, up into ghostly white peaks. Under brilliant skies and a blazing sun, I pass two large lower lakes fringed with pine and fir. They're beautiful, but I don't linger. I'm restless, eager to find the fourth lake, the very top of the chain, just a faint, small circle on the old map. Into this, ten thousand years ago, the remnant glacier collapsed—tons of rotten ice and snow.

At the inlet of the third lake, I push through tangles of willows. Then, the creek side steepening and my backpack flopping, I slide on rock faces peppered with loose gravel. Entering a deep declivity, smooth walls rising on either hand, I hop from one exposed boulder to another, sometimes wading, finally crawling on hands and knees up a gurgling watercourse of tiny pools and waterfalls threading down through turf and upended rocks.

Suddenly rock and water end in sky, and I'm standing on the lip of a small lake. It is encircled by peaks, the rugged scattered with low alpine fir that crouch behind rocks, sculpted by the relentness winter winds.

I drop my backpack and throw myself down at full length on the rich grasses. Now, at the end of this third day, my skin welcomes the harsh sun, dry air, and powdery windblown grit. My flesh and bones relax gladly into sharp-edged rocks. Sitting up, I wiggle my buttocks in the lumpy turf, placing the sharp exposed edge of a small rock comfortably between my hams. The creek brims out at my right hand. I pull off boots and wet wool socks and drop in my feet, then snatch them out, groaning with the deep cold ache.

Leaning back against the pack, stroking the cool, wiry green grasses, I look back down on the three lakes below me, each in its basin, the four beaded together by a twisting watercourse that wanders south, now through meadows strewn with giant blocks of stone, now disappearing over the edges of cliffs. The basin, cupping blue sky, was bitten from the circling peaks by glaciers, gnawing, moaning, grinding their icy teeth—century piled on century. In the ten thousand years since their retreat, in fields of rubble and blasted rock, it is these plants and trees before me, just these, that have come to take root.

I sit on thick, emerald turf. It teems with varieties of weeds and grasses, wildflowers and mosses. It creeps in pseudopods of earth, root, and stem as thick as my body, creeps in slow motion a few feet in a century, creeps in great fingers over rock after rock till stopped by snowfield and cliff—a green flesh softening every bitter, glacier-fractured boulder.

The sun lowers, a cool breeze drops off the peaks, and I'm chilled in my sweaty clothes. I rummage in my pack for an old sweater, wool pants, and some dry wool socks. I pull on my boots and pitch the tent, then slowly circle the lake, feeling airy and floating without the pack on my back.

Climbing another steep watercourse, I stand in an immense treeless field of boulders that ends against the great north wall of the cirque. Beneath my boots in the scattered rock and turf, seeps of snowmelt bubble up everywhere, fed by winter snowfields dying against the cliffs five hundred feet above me in the hot, angling afternoon sun. Each spring surrounds itself in grass and mosses, the turf honeycombed with tunnels of unseen small creatures that open out onto the water's edge.

The sun falls toward the peaks at my left hand. Time to make camp. I turn and begin to walk down, honoring the ancient sods and mosses, careful to place my boots only on the rocks, islands in the turf. As I go, the springs now gather into streams, descending toward shelter, the alpine fur reappearing, tangled, gnarled, hugging the ground, hiding behind rocks, resisting yet conforming to all the forces of rock and sun and wind, accepting a life on the edge of this or that house-size chunk of granite—accepting what is and thriving.

With each step down toward more water and warmth, my boots crush increasing, tenacious life, root tendrils following seams in the granite, until suddenly rocks split and meadow and forest are everywhere, home to trout and goat, elk and eagle.

Suddenly I know. I've caught the goddess in the very act of creating the garden! She gathers her strength here, alone, growing more beautiful since the glacier melted ten thousand years ago. She waits. With wonder and a catch in my throat, I fall down on my knees and worship her in the thick emerald turf. Icy water sponges up into the knees of my wool pants as I lean forward and spread my arms wide to gather in the earth, kneading my fingers into the sod. I bury my face in sunwarmed grasses, inhale moist, fecund, mushroom smells, and open my lips, licking my tongue deep into the hairy fiber and grit of the sod.

Tears well up and I'm shaking, sobbing with loss and grief and gratitude. "Oh, I love you, I love you," I murmur into the grass that tickles my lips and tongue, and I hug her close, crushing my face into her belly, crying a small boy's tears.

I can't live without her! I must touch her, stroke her, adore her body, find there the outside of that mind that lies secret, deep. A mind prior to thought—patient, sacred, an ocean of consciousness, its shimmering surface buoying this earth, the plants and animals, the women, the children, the men.

The sun has just swung behind a peak on my right. It's suddenly cold. I move down off the meadow, stepping from boulder to boulder down another steep slope. Above me, angling afternoon sunshine rakes the shattered rock of the mountains into deeply contrasting light and shadow. The bowl of sky inverted over the cirque is a deep brilliant blue. Occasional puffy clouds cap the peaks. Then I'm on rimrock above the lake. I stand for a minute, shivering as cool evening air begins to roll down off the slopes and cliffs above. I see my little blue tent. Good. I'm ready for the sack. I'll eat more cheese and bread and forget about cooking.

Plunging chilled hands in my pockets, I slowly descend the last few hundred yards, following the creek as it widens out and runs, only a few inches deep, over broad bands of glazed, glacier-polished bedrock. At last it drops in a little falls into the lake, glassy now as the wind dies down with evening, gently pulsing, mirroring its cup of rimrock. Standing at the brink of the falls, the cirque darkening, I see a few circles dimpling the surface where rushing white water grows calm as it enters the depths. Trout rising! They're watching for bugs carried down by the stream. Fish for dinner? I'm vegetarian now, mostly, but brought fishing gear as emergency backup. I could cook after all.

At camp, a knot of anticipation in my stomach, I kneel by my pack and assemble a light spinning rod. My fingers, clumsy with cold and trembling with excitement, tie the fine spin-casting line onto a small lure. Several thick-bodied trout lazily cruise a few feet off the rocky shore, making the evening circuit. Beneath the water their bodies are green-yellow. They have flaming red spots at the gills. Goldens.

I stand too abruptly, and seeing me, they spook and dart into deeper waters. I slow down and stalk, heart pumping, moving along the water's edge, waiting for the evening hunger that I know will drive them past wariness. Still they don't return.

I sink down behind a rock and poke up only my head, scanning the water. Now three big ones drift by, cruising just beneath the surface, dabbling the water with their noses. Without standing, moving cautiously, I cast awkwardly from behind the rock.

The lure hits the surface and the biggest goes for it, fiercely outrunning the others. With a jerk I set the hook, then give him line as he rushes out of sight into deep water. I raise the pole, slowly reeling him back, but he runs again. The rod bends double, he breaks water in his fear and rage, and I give back more line, afraid he'll break free.

After a half dozen runs, he tires. Gently, I bring him in close to the shore. At last he rests at my feet in a foot of water, his tail waving, fins pulsing. He jerks his head stubbornly from side to side, struggling against the gnawing hook. He's too tired to run again.

I reach out my hand very slowly from behind, then suddenly get my fingers under a gill and flip him up onto the turf. He's a good fifteen inches, and fat.

I kneel down and admire him, entranced with the golds and reds burning in the fading light. With a pang, an ache deep in my own flesh, I reach with two hands, grip his firm, slippery body belly up, and swing him high over my head, then down sharply to crack the back of his skull on the edge of a fractured boulder lying next to the shore. There's a snapping sound and instantaneously, like a lightning bolt, I feel rows of fibrous muscles up and down his spine ripple under my fingers, a quivering shudder of death. Pulled fresh, living, from the waters, he's a jewel—golden treasure. Now, even as I pull up grasses to cushion his body in my canvas side bag, his vibrant reds, greens, and golds begin fading to a dull silver.

I take two more smaller ones and, hungry, I can't wait. No need to cook anything but fish. I head back to camp and lay them side by side on a flat rock that juts out into the water.

Kneeling, taking up the big one, I sever cartilage under the jaw with a razor-sharp knife, then with a slight sawing motion slit him from anus to gill case, releasing traces of blood and a curve of intestine. With the finger and thumb of my left hand, I grab the loop of his jaw. His sharp teeth drag over my finger, then lightly lacerate the skin as, with my right thumb and fingers, I firmly pull the throat cartilage down and out, shucking gill case and guts. In the fading light the entrails seem to glow, an iridescence peculiar to goldens.

I slit the gut to see what he's eating and find a tangle of insects and stone caddises. I set it aside, and as my left hand returns, about to reach for the next fish, I'm shocked.

The gray-pink heart, just the size of the tip of my forefinger, sticks to the middle of my palm. It's contracting, pulsing—still beating out the rhythm of this life I've just ended. I stare for a long moment, my own heart in my throat, then slowly throw this slight piece of flesh as far out into the lake as I can.

My hands are painfully numb with the icy water. I put them, fishy and slippery, into my pockets for several minutes till they begin to warm up. I kneel down again and with my thumbnail strip out the membrane that holds a line of blood just below the spinal column. I clean the other two, then take up each one for a final, careful rinse.

Back at my pack, I pull leather work gloves on my icy fingers, quickly gather wood, and start a fire in a heap of dry branches in a ring of stones I place by the edge of the lake. Since I packed in only a single aluminum pot, while the fire burns down to coals, I hunt around the camp for green willow sticks.

On a lattice of these laid across the stones, I roast the three goldens. In the heat their eyes turn from clear balls into small, opaque white marbles.

Halfway through cooking, the green sticks burn through and the fish fall into the fire. I jump up to rescue them, scrambling to cut more green sticks and rebuild the lattice.

It's almost dark when the fish are done. I check them with a flash-light. The flesh is salmon pink and running with juices. I brought neither plate nor fork, so I lay them out on a flat rock by the fire, shake out salt and pepper, and eat with my knife and fingers, first popping out their delicate cheek muscles, then eating chunks of flesh off the ribs, finally holding the skeletons like corn on the cob, tail in one hand, head in the other, nibbling off tiny luscious morsels where the ribs meet the spinal column.

Gorging on their fat diamond bodies, chewing grit, ash, and black-ened skin flakes, I don't stop till I've eaten every one—then lean back on the rocks with a sigh, hands and face smeared with their grease.

I sit zazen, cross-legged, for an hour as the fire burns down. The pure, smokeless embers glow in the ashes and, one by one, wink out. It's moonless again tonight. The Milky Way gently pulses over my head. A chill penetrates me—up through my legs and spine from the earth, down into my ears, face, and skull from clear sky.

A thought slowly courses through my mind. "Oh, you beautiful creatures, we all suffer and die. Now your bodies are inside my body. You nourish me, not just with flesh, but with beauty. I rob you. Some-day, in turn, my own flesh will be scattered. To whom will I give nour-ishment? Whose hunt will thieve from me?"

Now the fire is out and I'm shivering. I keep sitting. It's this moment I hunt for. All five senses taste the cirque that surrounds me—deep, still, transparent. Behind me I hear the bubbling rush of the inlet creek, threading down rock and melting into deep waters.

The next morning is clear and cold. Frost whitens my green down bag and lingers on the turf in the shadows behind rocks. I spread the bag out in the sun to dry. After a breakfast of oatmeal, raisins, cocoa, and coffee, I survey the wall of the cirque and decide to head for a cleft between two peaks that might lead down the other side to another chain of lakes. Looking from here, I can't tell whether I can make it. I see several hundred feet of steep slide rock. That I can climb. But it's broken in several places by tongues of snow and dark rock faces. And it winds just out of sight before reaching the saddle. The other side, of course, could be a sheer wall. I'll have to be careful. I'm alone. No mistakes are permitted.

I put together a lunch of cheese, hard unyeasted bread, and chocolate, and pack that, along with water, rain gear, and a jacket, into my day bag.

After walking a half hour up into the back of the cirque, I come onto the slide rock and begin climbing. Here are goat tracks, goat shit, even an occasional tuft of white goat hair on rough, brittle twigs. A good sign. They use this pass.

Soon I'm in steep talus, the sun hot on my back. I break into a sweat and pant in the thin air. I rest for a time, turning around to look back down over the four lakes that step down below me, then begin a rhythm of one breath for each step higher.

Then I'm in a scree slope of fine gravels so steep that even a vibration from my boot starts it showering down all around me. With each step up, my boot slides back, and sometimes I lose ground. I try to place my boots on occasional head-size boulders half-buried in the slope. Dotted along the route, in the lee of rocks, are small green mosses covered with tiny blue flowers. I kneel down to breathe in their delicate honey scent.

Suddenly the scree is pinched off by vertical slabs of broken rock on my left and a tongue of grainy, melting snow streaked with rock dust on my right. Can I go further? I don't want to expose myself to a fall.

After taking a breather, I find I can brace my shoulders and feet between the snowfield and the rock and, with handholds, inch up step by step. Now I see almost to the top of the saddle—another hundred feet of slide rock. Several goat trails cross each other here, and there's a smell I can't clearly distinguish from my armpits.

Head down, I climb slowly and doggedly up the remaining distance, eager to see the other side. As the slope levels off, I look up and stop dead. Thirty feet away, two goats stand just below the top of the saddle. They seem relaxed, easy, eyeing me with curiosity. I stay rooted to the spot. Behind them another line of mysterious white peaks stands up wildly across the horizon.

I breathe slowly, unlock my knees. I'll hold my ground as long as they hold theirs. They shift their weight calmly. Their dark horns sweep up and back to fine points, their coats fluffy with the mountains' perpetual chill. They look at me, then out into the distance, then back at me again. Finally, hooves clattering among rocks, one slowly turns to go down the other side of the pass. The other one follows.

Moving up quickly and quietly, I'm in the notch—fifteen feet of level, gravelly rock that plunges off the other side a thousand feet into a deep blue lake. This is the end of my walk. The lake shimmers in the midday sun, a cluster of slow, lazy spangles winking on and off, a few at a time, at the far end. Great blocks of stone step up on my left and right hands, west and east, impassable, ending in spires fifty feet above me. The notch is strewn with goat track and goat shit. Loose gravel has been stomped into little hollows for bedding places.

Below me, the goats pick their way down along invisible ledges. They seem to walk on air until an occasional rock, clattering, bounding out into space, betrays their contact with earth.

I throw down my day pack, pull off my boots, spread out my soggy wool socks to dry in the sun, and move rocks and sand to create an even place to sit and eat my lunch. Then, cooling down as sweat dries out of my clothes, I pull on a sweater, stretch out at full length, and squiggle and scrunch my back to rearrange several sharp rocks beneath me. My body basks in heat from the sun. A puff of cloud a hundred feet above me scrapes the top of a rock spire that guards the right side of the pass. Fluid, flowing, it forms, half dissolves, then re-forms as warm, moist air moves up and over this great wall and suddenly cools.

I drowse—then come awake on the verge of shivering. The sun lowers. Clouds hang over peaks in the distance and wind gusts through the saddle. I quickly load the day pack, drop a hundred feet, then spot a route up to a high jumbled peak lying to the east.

"Can I get there in an hour?" I ask myself. I don't want to come down in the dark.

"Try it! How soon will you be able to come back here again?"

Circling down and then up to the left, I come onto a ramp of broken rock that has peeled off the walls above in talus ranging in size from an armchair to an automobile—a broken stairway for giants. After three quarters of an hour clambering up and around and over huge blocks, I'm almost there. The talus disappears and I work along narrow ledges, clinging with both hands to cracks in the rock as I maneuver around bulges in the face.

Finally I reach for the very top, find one last toehold, and muscle myself up. Pulling my head above the rock face, I freeze. Twenty feet away on the narrow rimrock is a nanny goat, and between us a tiny kid. The kid eyes me curiously, glances back at its mother, and sensing her agitation, springs back and forth on delicate hooves. The mother darts to her kid, then shoulders by to stand between us.

Suddenly she's sprinting toward me, head down, horns shimmering black in the bright afternoon glare, hooves clattering in the broken rock.

I'm stunned. A twenty-foot drop below me ends in sharp, jumbled rock. I sink down behind the wall and hang, arms extended, fingers crawling into small indentations, one toe tip clinging, heart pumping.

They'll never find my body!

Rocks rattle above me. Then silence.

Minutes drag by, and I slowly pull myself up and peer over the top. They're gone! I worm up over the edge and stand. Fifty feet below me they pick their way through impossibly steep slide rock, the kid going ahead, the nanny, glancing back nervously, following behind.

Shaking, I sink to my knees on the broken rock. She's the goddess too—fierce, protecting, catching me between sharp horns and empty space, ready to trade her own life for her kid's. I watch them for long minutes until they drop out of sight. I shake my head and turn back down toward camp.

Halfway down a long talus slope, I'm suddenly running, sailing, high as a kite, balancing down from rock to rock, mind awake in each foot as it touches, awake in each boulder, sensing, just before contact, its center of gravity, knowing whether to strike it with toe or heel and just where. A torso-size boulder tricks me, stirs suddenly on its own secret balance point beneath my left heel. Thrown off my stride, nearly plunged headlong down the steep, shattered rock, I catch myself— exulting in the split-second dip of my left knee, weight shifting between shoulders with a balancing upswing of my right hand—and run on.

Back at camp just before dark, plopping down on the thick, chilly turf, crossing my arms and legs, I lean back against my backpack. The wind is down and the surface of the lake resolves into a silvered mirror dimpled by widening trout circles. Inside one set of liquid circles, reflected, shimmering, an early star pulses slowly up and down. Dropping my hands into my lap, I stare out into the basin. The immense, still atmosphere becomes darkening transparent tea bounded by rim rock, the cirque a teacup I balance upon my upturned palms.

An indistinct swishing sound behind me pulls my attention back to my three trees on the slope that falls down from the Crag. I tense and open myself out to the forest. Silence. A stab of panic tenses my body.

Slowly, I swivel my head and shoulders to the right and survey the woods behind me. Nothing at all. Then I turn the other way and scan. Again nothing. I settle back—but now twigs crackle, branches whip in the underbrush, and I hear ripping, rending sounds.

It's bear.

Beginning to whistle a tune, I pull on my socks and boots, then turn and tromp off slowly and noisily into the woods behind me. I make my way through the trees and begin a descent into the drainage behind the Crag.

Suddenly there's a loud crashing. I glimpse two brown-black spots, one large, one small, moving away out of sight into a dense thicket of little lodgepole pine a few hundred feet ahead of me. Must be a mother and cub. I walk cautiously up to the point where they disappeared and find another ant stump rent and scattered.

Outraged ants swarm over the duff, rescuing white pods of larvae and carrying pine needles like staves, beginning the huge work of rebuilding. I kick idly at the shards of rotten stump and chunks of sod, scattering ant larvae and ants. Then, feeling ashamed, I step back out of their way. My intervention may have saved them—for now. But it's late in the season. Even if the mother bear fails to return, they have little time to get ready for the months of deep snow and subzero temperatures.

I scan the woods. Nothing. I'm surprised the mother didn't catch my scent blowing over the crest of the hill. Maybe she's a garbage bear, tolerant of humans. I remember the mother and three cubs I found rummaging through my cabin at sundown one evening. I chased them out, screaming and firing a shotgun into the air. At first light the next morning, they climbed back in a window, awakening me with the thud of falling canned goods and crashing dishes.

I turn and stroll back up to my three trees. I pull off my boots and socks, finding the blood on the bottom of my foot hardening nicely—a flexible, brown carapace for my scrape.

I cross my legs and get comfortable, whispering to myself, "Now, let's try a little harder to wake up on this mountain, okay? Remember Dogen's advice!"

I scrunch my eyes shut and hear his words in my mind: "Think of not thinking!"

"And how do I think of not thinking?" I ask myself ruefully.

His answer shouts through my head: "Beyond thinking!" Beneath my eyelids I see a round Japanese face smiling broadly.

"Beyond thinking indeed!" I think, snorting aloud, then sighing. "Ah, if only once more I could ask Suzuki and Katagiri what those words mean. They'd laugh or shout or say nothing—and I'd return to the meditation hall, ready for this balancing act again."

I place my palms in my lap in the buddha's mudra and cast my gaze down softly to the red-brown duff. I watch each breath—inflow and outflow, inflow and outflow, following it down, feeling it fill and expand my lower belly.

But thoughts—now fretful, anxious—darken my mind. The voice in my head whispers, "What if one of the kids is hurt back in Minneapolis? Or sick? You're so damned irresponsible! Oh, I miss them. Remember when they were tiny? At story time, lying on the big bed, they'd wind their arms around your neck, then with little squeaks and grunts fall into sleep. Now they're so tall. It's really time to head back to Minneapolis."

Gently, I pull the mind back to the three trees, back to the breath, back to itself.

But now it's money. "You're running out! You idiot. You thought you could afford a leave from teaching this year. You'll never get through December."

Then I'm back in my ditch. A concerned voice plans, considers, debates. "You've got to daylight the line somewhere. Otherwise it'll freeze up in winter. But that'll take ten more feet of hard digging. Maybe turn the line straight up and install a drain cock at the bottom."

Then it's women. My mind licks into those delicious margins of fine silky hair that run back along each side of the vaginal lips. "God, how luscious!" I think. "How long will it be?" Smelling the juices, I get hard—then laugh aloud at these thoughts in this lost, lonely place.

I uncross my legs and straighten them in front of me, stretch my arms out wide, then high over my head, wriggling my fingers, and finally lie back at full length in the duff, kneading a knotted kink under my shoulder blade against an exposed knob of root.

Finally, I sit again, making minute adjustments to my posture. I watch thoughts closely, trying not to concentrate so hard that, in the end, I lose concentration.

This balancing pours abrasives into my nervous system. My whole body becomes irritated, hot, edgy. I ache. Molten lead flows heavy into my arms and legs, burning dully at the core of each bone. A thick, cold steel bowl, inverted beneath the dome of my skull, clamps down on soft brain tissues.

A voice implores, "Oh, God, let's get out of here, get off this mountain, head down to the cabin. Pour some whisky, build a fire, fry some potatoes, throw on a steak."

Pain in my left knee pierces my consciousness. With fresh determination, I pull myself back, relaxing rigid muscle systems down my back and neck.

"Wake up!" I whisper, and give my cheeks a few light, stinging slaps with my hands. One foot is asleep. The knot below my left shoulder blade signals that, again, my head slumps slightly forward.

I breathe deeply and sway slowly back and forth, centering my back and neck, allowing fresh blood to flow into my feet. The pain in my left knee is an ally now, cutting through thoughts.

"So this," I think, "is my zazen after thirty years—a mind buried in thought, a mole blind in its tunnel. Yes, it's that. And it's also sharp clarity of awareness—I'm here, mind observing all things, mind observing mind, 'snow in a silver bowl.' "

A whiny voice grumbles, "Oh, God, just let this job be done. Why aren't you enlightened by now, once and for all? Do you really have to think all these thoughts over and over again? Isn't it ever going to get any better?

"Remember now," says a whisper, "remember the old stories of the Buddha. He went to meditation three times a day to quiet his mind after talking to students. Thoughts are inevitable.

"Remember Dogen. 'All the universe is one bright pearl.' The scrape is the pearl, the blood is the pearl, the scab is the pearl, the pain in your knee is the pearl, the ants are tiny black scrambling pearls, the bear is a brown mother pearl.

"And each thought is a pearl—a pearl of great price."

I sigh deeply, sway slowly from side to side to center myself, then drop my gaze down to the duff.

8

Master Shunryu
Suzuki

IT'S AUGUST, LATER IN THE SUMMER OF 1966. I drive to San Francisco from the mining claim to visit Lon and to sit zazen with Suzuki Roshi. I stay at Lon's apartment a few blocks from Sokoji Temple. The San Francisco scene is wild. Freaks from all over the country have gathered, are hanging out, grooving, awaiting some "New Age" that's just around the corner. Lon is in the thick of it. A stream of characters flow through his apartment. Weird, costumed men and women—saints, cowboys, beggars, whores, madonnas, amazons—all spout bizarre theories and describe ecstatic transcendences. They're excited, naïve, delighted to be on the edge of this breaking wave.

But my focus now is zen alone. Lon and I go mornings and evenings to sit zazen at Sokoji. I know I can't handle another psychedelic trip, so I decline opportunities as unobtrusively as possible. I'm not eager to tell anyone about my freak-outs.

After a few days, Lon suggests that I participate the next Sunday in an intensive afternoon of sitting meditation with Suzuki Roshi. "This is the trip," he says. "We've got to learn it. Like that record of the monks chanting at Eiheiji we listened to last night. Man, it's obvious that they're *there*! They've *made* it! Imagine moving through life in the monastery with total acid consciousness."

Eagerly, I ask to join the group. I'm accepted and told to get meditation instruction from Katagiri Sensei, a Japanese priest who has arrived recently with his family to help out at the temple. On the Saturday night before the sitting, he meets a few students in a hall at Sokoji, where he's placed a row of round, black cushions. He's much younger than Suzuki Roshi and speaks very broken English. He doesn't smile, and the corners of his mouth seem to be turned firmly down. After making patient attempts to correct our postures, apparently unimpressed with the results, he finally dismisses us, saying, "It takes some time. It's okay. Just try hard."

"Seems pretty strict," I think, as we all file out.

Meditation begins the next afternoon at one. There are about twelve of us, both men and women. Suzuki Roshi brings us to a small room. Spaced around the wall are the round black cushions, each placed on a rectangular black mat large enough to cushion our knees and legs as we sit.

After instructing us on taking our seats, Suzuki Roshi bows toward his cushion, then back toward us. Two experienced students return his bow. He sits down and bows again. Now we all manage to bow in return, and he begins.

"My talk today will be about what we call the Heart Sutra. Maybe you have chanted it with me at service. We call it the Heart Sutra because it is the heart of a very big sutra. I think it is pretty difficult, maybe pretty confusing for you. It is pretty hard even for zen priests." The Roshi smiles and chuckles at this.

I'm intrigued. I've been puzzled by this teaching when we've chanted it in English.

"This is a very important teaching," Suzuki continues. "So I will try to explain something to you. This sutra says that form is emptiness and also emptiness is form. This is true. This is hard to understand, but it is actually so. The sutra tells us something else, too. It tells us that form is also form. And emptiness is also emptiness. Do you understand?"

No one responds. I'm puzzled. I do remember the words *form* and *emptiness* from services, but have no sense of what their meaning and relationship might be.

Suzuki Roshi tries again. "You understand, of course, the word *form*. Everything has a form. A tree has a form. A bird has a form. Human beings have a form. But these forms really are emptiness. Of course, form *is* form. A tree *is* a tree. A human being *is* a human being. That is true. But it is emptiness, too. Can you understand that? Everything is emptiness, too. And emptiness is also form. Emptiness cannot be emptiness unless it is form. But it is really emptiness, too."

The talk goes on, and Suzuki Roshi struggles, patiently and cheerfully, to explain this thing that seems so plain to him. He phrases and rephrases the lines from the sutra until, finally, I'm lost in the words *form* and *emptiness*, and they lose even the meanings I know so well— like the word *cat*, in the child's game, after it's repeated a hundred times. Then my mind's wandering. I listen to a truck grinding up the steep street outside. I watch a pretty girl with close-cropped dark hair dressed in severe zen black across the room. With an annoyed glance, she catches me staring, and I drop my eyes down to the mat.

Now I'm drawn back to Suzuki Roshi's talk. I hear him saying, "This teaching tells us about buddha nature. This is very important. We always want to think that Buddhism is ahead of us, so we are working to catch it. But Buddhism is right here. When we sit down here on our round cushion, this is Buddhism. When we pick up our teacup and drink tea, this is Buddhism. When we get up and go to our meal, this is Buddhism.

"So the sutra says, 'No attainment. There is nothing to attain.' Because you have already attained this buddha nature. But that doesn't mean we should stop our practice. This buddha nature makes it possible for us to practice. It is really so. Everything is this buddha. The word *buddha* is buddha. The letter *b* in *buddha* is buddha. The letter *u* in *buddha* is buddha. The letter *d* in *buddha* is buddha. All things are *buddha*. You are all buddha. Do you understand?" Suzuki Roshi chuckles softly. "So to know this, we sit together. This is our practice."

He stops talking. He sits easily on his cushion, his whole being light and sparkling.

"But to know we are buddha," he goes on, "does not make us so important. We are not so special. Everything is buddha. It is really a relief for us not to be the most important thing in the world, don't you think?" Then he bursts into a peal of laughter. We all look up expectantly, and after clearing his throat, he says, "When I was a boy in Japan, I helped an English lady with cleaning. In her hallway there was a little statue of the Buddha. When I would enter her house, I always bowed to the Buddha. It was very important to me. My master bowed so much to the Buddha that he made a callus right on his forehead. Can you imagine that? So I always ask you to make nine bows at the service. This is to bow to the Buddha, not just outside you to a statue, but inside you too. Now, that lady saw me bowing to the Buddha and she got very angry. She scolded me."

Again Suzuki Roshi overflows with chuckles that shake his small shoulders. "She scolded me for bowing to that Buddha statue. Of course, she is a good Christian lady. For her that statue is just a decoration. Maybe she thinks that I believe the statue is really alive. She is very concerned to correct me. Of course, it is just a Buddha statue. But it is good to bow to it. We just bow to the buddha that is in all things."

He pauses, looking around the room, then asks, "Are there any questions?" A few students make hesitant, feeble attempts to question him. Finally, laughing, he says, "It's okay. We can sit now."

We sit for several forty-minute periods. After the first period, Suzuki Roshi doesn't sit with us, but after ringing a little bell leaves the room, his robes rustling, the old hardwood floor squeaking under his tread. I imagine he retreats to a little office he has. I imagine him sitting at a desk and taking care of correspondence to Japan, or conferring with an elderly man in the Japanese congregation who seems often to visit him. After each forty-minute period of zazen, he returns to lead us in kinhin—walking meditation.

Toward the end of the afternoon, he rings the bell to begin what I assume is the last period of zazen. Soon we can stand up, stretch, and go home to supper. I've never sat this many periods of zazen at one time. My knees, neck, and back are stiff and painful.

As we near what must be the end of the period, I can tell from the rustling of clothing and creaks and squeaks from the floor that others are as uncomfortable as I. Sitters all around me, quietly, stealthily, they hope unobtrusively, are shifting position to minimize the pain. I know we must be nearing the end of the forty minutes. "These folks are just weak," I think. "I'll tough it out. I won't move."

Long minutes go by, but no Suzuki Roshi appears. The old building is silent except for rising afternoon traffic din out on Bush Street—and a quiet crescendo of rustling and floor squeaks from students who can no longer bear their silent agony.

Then it dawns on me. "He's testing our practice. He wants us to sit hard. Well, I'll show him hard sitting. I'm certainly not going to move. I can handle another few minutes. This is real zen."

But more and more minutes slip painfully by, and suddenly it's way beyond a few minutes more. It's endless. "We've got to have been sitting over an hour!" I say to myself. Still, there's no sign of the Roshi. All around me in the room are the sounds of sitters shifting their bodies, sighing, and even a few quiet groans as knees are unlocked and straightened.

Horrified, I think, "It's not a test at all! He's forgotten we're here. Why doesn't someone go get him? Or do something?" I can't, myself, of course, because I'm a newcomer. And if it really is a test, and I interfered, I'd be a complete idiot.

Finally, in agony, composure gone, I join the weaklings. I surreptitiously allow my right foot and ankle to slowly, slowly slip off my crossed left leg—and point my toe down toward the floor so it only falls a few inches and barely makes any thump on the mat. My right knee shrieks at the release of tension, pulsing wildly with the beat of my heart.

Suddenly the bell is ringing. With all the quiet commotion in the meditation room, Suzuki Roshi has crept in to ring it. There's blowing of breath, sighs, and we all turn on our cushions toward the middle of the room and come creakily to our feet.

Suzuki Roshi says, "Thank you for your hard effort. That is all we need to do today." And he's gone.

Stiffly, I walk out of Sokoji and back to Lon's apartment. For a block down Bush Street, my knees burn at each step. At supper with Lon at a Japanese restaurant nearby, I tell him what happened, then ask, "So, what do you think? Did he just forget us? Or was he putting us through the wringer?"

"Hey, man, your guess is as good as mine." Lon laughs, picking at his fried vegetables with a pair of shiny black chopsticks he brings with him so he won't have to use the cheap disposable kind. "Everyone says he *is* very absent-minded, and he likes to joke about it. But you never can tell. He's an old fox. I think it's a teaching."

Then I ask Lon about the lecture on form and emptiness. "This is important, man," Lon says. "Can't you dig this? Haven't you heard the parable of the golden lion?"

I shake my head.

"Well, if you think about it, it's really like that. The gold can be formed into a lion—or anything—or nothing. But's it's still gold, isn't it? So if I point to the lion and ask you, 'Is that gold?,' what do you say?"

"Oh, I suppose I'd say yes."

"Right on," says Lon. "And if I point to the lion and say, 'Is that a lion?,' what do you say?"

"I'd say, 'It's a lion.'"

"And if I point and say, 'What is this, a lion or gold?,' what do you say?"

"I'd say, 'It's both.'"

"So," concludes Lon, "gold is gold, and gold is also the lion, and lion is lion, but the lion is also gold. It's like the Clear Light of the Void in the *Book of the Dead*. On acid, it's what rises up from everywhere in everything you feel, everything you see and touch. It's that flowing energy. You dig?"

"Humph," I say, annoyed that I didn't myself make these logical connections. Why did the words seem so meaningless? "Well, then emptiness isn't really just *nothing*. Just like the Clear Light of the Void isn't just *nothing*. It's the Clear Light."

"I don't know about that," Lon says, returning to his rice and vegetables. "Ask Suzuki Roshi. You'll get a chance if you go with me down to Tassajara next week. A lot of people are working down there. And Suzuki Roshi's going in a few days. They're going to do the first Tassajara *sesshin* at the end of the summer. It'll be heavy. They'll sit a series of forty-minute periods from rising till bedtime. If we work down there for a week or so, we can join. Tassajara is an incredible place. You'll dig it."

"Great," I say. "I'm ready. I just hope Suzuki Roshi won't let zazen go longer than forty minutes."

"Oh, he won't," Lon says. "But it'll be strict. The real thing. A mountain practice led by a real zen master. But he says we shouldn't go overboard, either. We can't just sit sesshins all the time. When I asked him how often I should do one, he said, 'Oh, maybe it's enough to climb the mountain once a year.' "

It's the next summer, 1967. I've driven again from the mining claim in the Bitterroots to visit Lon and practice with Suzuki Roshi. My doctoral course work and teaching in Minnesota continue. And Farmer and I have developed a regular practice of zen at our respective houses, two periods in the morning before breakfast and one period at night before bed.

Lon's moved to a new apartment now, just across the street from Sokoji Temple. His building and several others up and down the street, all old and somewhat rundown, now house numbers of young people who have come to practice with Suzuki Roshi. The Katagiris live at the end of the block.

I find my way to his door, knock, and am surprised by a new Lon. His head is shaved, his full beard gone, and he wears ordinary jeans and a work shirt. There's no trace of a psychedelic costume. I'm uneasy. Head shaving by American zen students has always struck me as pretentious.

After greetings and small talk, Lon serves green tea. We sit on zafus on the hardwood floor in a dining room empty of furniture. He pours in silence. After a few sips, I ask, "How are things going? Looks like your scene has cooled down here a bit."

"Yeah, that's for sure. Things happened this year. I guess I was over-due. Long overdue."

"Ah," I say, raising my eyebrows. And then ask, "What happened?"

"Well," says Lon, "You know how, during the fund-raising for Tassajara, some of us made pretty good contributions, even though, like they say in the newspapers, we had no visible means of support?"

"Yeah, I dig," I say. "I know hundred-dollar bills appeared with surprising frequency in the collection plates. Strange coming from a congregation of poor hippies."

"Well, old Suzuki didn't like it. He figured out where the money was coming from. He's in real hot water with the Japanese congregation, anyway. They're mad as hell about all these hippies swarming around him. They call it 'hippie Sokoji' now. But Suzuki always seems to be able to calm them down. You know what he's like. He's incredibly calm and collected—and happy. How long can you be upset with a guy like that?

"Anyway, all of a sudden we get this hard-ass lecture from Katagiri Sensei about how it's not real zen practice to sell drugs and give money to the Zen Center. He said it violates the precepts. It's got to stop. 'It's only delusion,' he said.

"Boy, you should have seen him when he gave that lecture. Was he uncomfortable! I'm sure Suzuki Roshi just told him he had to do it. Might as well let the first officer handle it."

"So that's going to change your life a bit," I say, smiling, sipping my green tea.

"Yeah, it will, but it's okay. It's time. And it's time for me to make a final commitment to Suzuki Roshi and to the practice here. This is it. I'm in it for the long haul. For real. There's no turning back."

A few days after my arrival, Lon tells me excitedly that Bishop Sumi, Suzuki Roshi's superior in the Soto zen sect, has arrived from Los Angeles to visit Sokoji Temple. Everyone says he's a remarkable man, a great zen master. He's to give a lecture in the evening.

After supper, we join a throng of American zen students at Sokoji. We sit on zafus beneath a low stage on which Suzuki Roshi and the bishop are seated. After introductions, Bishop Sumi begins to speak. To my surprise, he says nothing about zen practice itself. He talks about the Japanese living in America. Then I'm amazed. He seems, in fact, to be scolding Suzuki Roshi.

"We have so many Japanese boys who are in trouble in California," he says. "Many are in trouble in Los Angeles. Many are in trouble in San Francisco, too. It is very hard to think that we are too busy to help them. Some of those young men even will go to the jail. This is a very terrible thing for the boys and their families.

"The Soto Sect has a very important job to help these boys and families who are in trouble in some way in this country. We are not really here to help the Americans. Of course, we like to help in any way that we can. But we must take care of the Japanese people who are in trouble."

I look over at Suzuki Roshi. I'm astonished. Is he nervous, ill at ease? Embarrassment clouds his face. I've never seen him like this before. Though seated cross-legged on his zafu, listening quietly to the bishop, he seems almost to fidget.

Bishop Sumi continues. "I don't really come here to criticize your effort at Sokoji Temple. I know, it is important for Americans to have an opportunity to learn zazen. I know Suzuki Roshi is very sincere. I know you are all very sincere. I accept how sincere you are, and I appreciate this very much. But we cannot forget our young people in trouble. They are begging for our help. So we cannot forget this."

Bishop Sumi stops talking. I hope to hear some rejoinder from Suzuki Roshi, but he simply thanks the bishop for coming and the evening is over.

As Lon and I walk across the street to his place, I ask, "What's going on? Sumi doesn't seem interested in zen at all. It was like hearing some Christian minister talk about the social duty of the church. And I've never seen Suzuki Roshi look uncomfortable like that. It was unbelievable."

"Well," says Lon, "the Japanese congregation is very upset. They really don't like us American weirdos hanging around. Suzuki Roshi always says zen is dead in Japan, anyway. He says he's glad to be here where people are actually interested in real practice. I know he's considering leaving Sokoji. We've got Tassajara now. The next step will be to find a new place in the city. I think it's going to happen."

It's another August in the late sixties. I drive, as usual, from the mining claim to visit Lon in San Francisco and do another sesshin with Suzuki

Roshi. There's now interest in zen in Minneapolis. Once a week Farmer and I join a small group that sits together with Beverly White, a middle-aged woman who for years has been a student of Buddhism. We sit at 5:30 in the morning in her living room in St. Paul.

Earlier in the year, I wrote Lon to see if Suzuki Roshi would encourage us to have a two-day sesshin, even without a master. Lon wrote back, "Roshi says it's okay, so long as you're sincere."

Lon's head is still shaved. He now dresses in dark, solid colors, simple shirts and loose pants sewn by women in the zen community. Zen and the San Francisco Zen Center are his life. He has become macrobiotic, austere, soft-spoken. I see in him at times a medieval monastic dedicated to God and the mortification of the flesh. I have doubts about these trappings of zen, but I too want enlightenment. Lon is the only friend I have who takes this all with the same deadly seriousness I do.

Suzuki Roshi, I discover, is down at Tassajara Mountain Center with some thirty students. Lon says we can join him and sit the last sesshin of the summer. I'm excited. A few years ago, Lon and I sat the first sesshin at Tassajara. I remember the hot spring, the creek, the simple stone-and-wood buildings, the hot, dry California mountains.

Within a few days, we drive down the coast to Monterey, inland to Carmel Valley, then over some thirty miles of rough mountain roads into the heart of the steep Santa Lucia range. Rounding a final bend, we stop the car and look down into the valley. Beneath us, Tassajara Creek winds through a scattering of old buildings. How wonderful to return to this wilderness outpost dedicated to zen.

The sesshin doesn't start for a week, so we're assigned to work crews. Each day we work on rebuilding buildings, repairing a spring-fed water system, hauling soil from the hillsides to create garden beds by the creek, and taking care of the cooking and other routine needs of the community. These days of work are punctuated with two forty-minute periods of zazen before breakfast and single periods before lunch, dinner, and bedtime.

Though I visit the California zen community every summer, I feel, as I often do, left out, on the edge of things. I know many of the old students and officers, but no one acknowledges my presence or talks to me, except to collect a fee and assign a cabin.

After a few days, I suggest to an older student whom I admire that we eat a sandwich together at lunch during a free day, but he declines. His free time, he says, has become "too social." Of course, he's quite social with other regulars.

I feel better when Lon, after the last sitting one evening, stops me outside the meditation hall. He pays me a high compliment. "Erik," he says, "you're sitting beautifully, as solid as anyone in the *zendo*."

As the days go by, I watch Suzuki Roshi work on a rock garden he's begun outside his little cabin. Bubbling, enthusiastic, he seems energized by this hard physical labor under the open sky. This is not the berobed, retiring man I first met in Sokoji Temple, moving with measured tread through its quiet, dim confines, silently bowing to each sitter as he or she leaves the zendo to step into the evening fog on Bush Street. At Tassajara he's everywhere, brilliant and sunny, a reflection of the hot California summer itself.

The sesshin begins—seven days that mark the end of the summer. I worry. I've sat for four or five days at a time before, but never for a full week. Still, I'm eager to test my practice.

The sesshin is hard. We sit from five in the morning till nine at night, each period of zazen followed by ten minutes of slow walking meditation. We're off our cushions only during a daily two-hour work period after lunch and during meals, mercifully taken at tables outside in the shade of great trees. As we sit in silence waiting to be served, warm breezes carry the smells of delicious vegetarian foods.

By the last sittings before lunch and bedtime, I'm in agony—knees burning, my back a complicated knot of pain. Stubborn, I refuse to change position. In the snap of the fingers, in the blink of an eye, enlightenment will pass me by.

Roshi lectures morning and evening. Many of the students are new to zen, and he talks often about the pain. On the second evening of the sesshin, he says, "I know you are practicing very hard. Now after two days many of you are feeling some pain. But if it is possible for you, don't move. Just sit. Don't move your body. Don't move your mind. Sometimes it is very hard, but that is our way. Try to experience the pain as just pain. It is pain, but that is part of our human life. It is actually okay. I can feel the pain too. When I was a young man and had to sit many sesshins, sometimes I imagined my whole body was being swallowed by a great snake. It was so hard.

"Zazen is hard for you, too, of course. It is true. But remember too that zazen is also soft and gentle. Please try to sit with a soft mind like bread dough—you know how it sticks together, and then with fire becomes something wonderful to eat."

By the end of this second day, the pain in my knees has built to a crescendo, intense waves of fierce, dark energy rising up through my body. But Roshi's acknowledgment somehow removes fear, and the waves flow peacefully into the bubble of consciousness that fills my body, a turbulent stream disappearing into deep, calm waters. For a time I mark only purity in the intense dark waves.

Then I'm listening again, aware of Suzuki Roshi's voice going on. "Of course, it sometimes seems too hard, but our practice can help your life very much. The Buddha's zazen is a huge umbrella. In India, you know, it's very hot. You need an umbrella to help keep off the sun." Suzuki Roshi opens an imaginary umbrella, holding its handle with his left hand and extending his right hand high above his head. "Please remember, you can come underneath it here and sit with me. There's plenty of room. It gets bigger and bigger the more people who come inside. You may not believe this, but it is actually so."

During the sesshin, Roshi continues work on his rock garden. Someone tells me that as a young monk his work was stonemasonry. I see him selecting stones from the creek. His helpers carry them to shore, then later move them a few hundred feet up to the garden at the front of his cabin. Occasionally I see him standing there during breaks, observing his stones. Sometimes he comes to a decision and swiftly moves one to its place.

On the fourth day of the sesshin, after lunch, I'm chosen at the work meeting to help Suzuki Roshi and Alan, one of his regular students. This is a privilege. I've never worked with Roshi before. Excited and nervous and eager to work, I arrive early at the rock garden. A few minutes later, Alan arrives. He's tall and muscular, deeply tanned, his head shaved. We stand together, silent, sweating in the hot afternoon sun, waiting for Roshi to come out of his cabin.

To my surprise, Alan begins whispering intently to me about serving Roshi tea earlier in the sesshin. "Listen, man, he was in there during zazen preparing his lecture. I bring in the plate with tea, a cookie, and an apple. Then after the lecture, I go get the dishes. The apple was eaten down to a core so thin it hardly existed. It was almost a piece of string. You could see every seed."

Alan puts his hand on my shoulder and stares closely into my face. He whispers fiercely, "See, man, that's what a Roshi is. He's someone who takes time to do absolutely fucking everything absolutely fucking completely. When he eats an apple, he eats it! He *really* eats it!"

I nod nervously, eager Alan to stop talking, hoping that Roshi doesn't come out of his cabin and catch us whispering. We're supposed to maintain a strict silence, though I see the regular students, and occasionally Roshi himself, break the rule. And I wonder at this tiny old man who looks like a picture from an oriental travel book. What goes on in his mind as he sits in a little screened summer cabin deep in American wilderness, surrounded by hippies, quietly eating an apple down to the thinnest wisp of a core?

In a few minutes Roshi steps out of his cabin. He wears loose work clothes, legs bare from the knees down, a kind of karate outfit. On his bare feet are *zoris*—simple rubber beach clogs. He carries a mason's hammer and rock chisel. I stand stiffly at attention, not sure how to greet him. He bows matter-of-factly to each of us. We return the bows, and he leads us quickly down to the creek side, where he takes off his zoris and clambers into the rushing water.

Standing crotch deep, he beckons us. Alan and I pull off our work boots and follow him in. He begins working a huge light-colored stone lying a few inches below the surface of the rushing water in the middle of the creek.

My diffidence evaporates. How wonderful to be off my cushion, outside in the hot sun and cold creek. The past two days I've spent work periods in a dim corner of the primitive kitchen, washing and chopping endless vegetables, scraping stubborn blackened crusts out of the bottoms of huge rice pots, adding new hot spots to a back already a mass of pain. But now, at last, I can straighten up, stretch out, throw my arms straight back to each side and stare up at the blue sky— burning knee joints flexing, back muscles unknotting, my whole body an antenna for sunlight and breezes.

Roshi hammers steadily on the chisel, its edge placed somewhere on the stone hidden beneath the foaming water. Alan and I stand happily in the creek next to him and look on. Students move up and down the path, busy on various errands. Everyone's expression is easy, serene in the hot sunshine. It's bliss simply to be off our tormenting cushions, moving our bodies, free for a time from pain and the intense effort of concentration.

After a few long, delicious minutes, Roshi pauses in his hammering and turns to Alan. "Please, Alan, you hit the stone. It is too big for us now, but when it splits we can carry each piece up to the garden. Please, strike it right here." He points to a slight cleft, a margin in the light-colored stone, dimly visible a few inches under the rushing, bubbling water.

Alan, bare-backed, bends to the task. Then Roshi turns to me. "What is your name? I'm sorry. I forget so often."

"Erik," I say. "I'm Lon's friend from Minneapolis."

"Oh, yes, I remember. Thank you for coming again to Zen Center. Please carry those stones up to my cabin." He points to a number of smaller stones waiting at the edge of the stream.

I pull on my boots and carry stones for about twenty minutes, then take a breather by the side of the creek and watch Roshi and Alan still working the stone in the middle of the stream. Alan is tiring and slowing down. Roshi says, "It's pretty hard. Let Erik hammer the stone for a while." Then, looking up at me, "Erik, please, you can try too."

I pull off my boots again and enter the cool, rushing water. Roshi hands me the hammer and chisel. Alan stands beside him, tired, solemn.

"Here, you try the stone too. Right here." He points to the cleft, faintly visible beneath the foaming water. I feel it with my fingers—a slight indentation snaking its way around the top of the rock. Positioning my bare feet on the slippery round stones of the stream bottom, I grip the chisel firmly in my fist and begin striking with the hammer over and over again, each blow splashing water up onto my chest and face.

My head and back are hot in the afternoon sun, my legs and hips icy in the rushing creek. I strike the chisel over and over, gripping my toes on the round rocks, struggling to balance, to position the chisel for a solid, accurate blow on that faint margin beneath the rushing water.

Long minutes go by. My blows are slowing down, and I hear Roshi saying above the rush of the creek, "Here, please, I will try again. It is very hard work, don't you think?"

As we watch, Roshi works the stone again. Then Alan takes another turn. Then I go again.

It's cool in the creek. Intense sunlight heats my back and neck and dances on the waters surging around the stone. As my hand and arm return from each stroke, I see sparks of watery sunlight reflected up from flecks of mica in the submerged rock.

For half an hour, we alternate at the hammer and chisel, all three standing close, the icy water from the hammering splashing first on the hammerer, then on the two who wait. The sound of steel on steel pulses over the surging creek, ringing out into the little mountain valley.

Alan and I sense the end of the work period coming. We work furiously, pressing against fatigue, flailing at times and losing our balance on the slippery rocks, pressed downstream by the icy water. We want to succeed, to accomplish this task for the Roshi. He watches quietly.

Finally, in what I know will be one of my last turns—frustrated, aches reawakened all over my back—I straighten up for a second and glance at Alan, who raises his eyebrows quizzically.

Roshi, waiting to take his turn at the stone, smiles at us, his face wrinkling with delight. "Of course, I know you cannot believe the stone can split. But I know it can. We must keep hammering that place. It will split. Sometime it will split." Then with a rising, inquiring, teasing intonation: "Maybe you are not so sure? But I know.

Someday you will know it, too. All we have to do is just keep striking the stone."

A young woman dressed in black zendo clothes, her face freshly washed and her moist brown hair pulled back in a bun, hurries over to the creek side. She says anxiously, "Roshi, work period is already over. You will miss tea."

"Oh, I'm very sorry. I always make a mistake." He bows to the messenger, then to us. We return his bows, and he turns to walk swiftly back to his cabin to change, balancing on bare feet over the smooth rocks in the streambed.

As Alan and I pick up our work boots on our barefooted way to our cabins, I see, side by side on a large stone next to the rushing water, Roshi's zoris. He walked right by them. About to pick them up, I glance at Alan hurrying toward his cabin, hesitate, then leave them and rush back to clean up and get to the first period of zazen before the bell.

Back in place on my round black cushion in the zendo, I think about the stone. Will it really ever split? If one of the young American work leaders had kept me there hammering in the middle of the creek for two hours—for nothing—I'd be furious. But hammering with Roshi, I was happy. He wasn't hurried or impatient with the stone—or with us. It was Alan and I who got anxious at the end of the work period when the stone wouldn't split.

Still, I don't want to hammer stones that never split. But Roshi's a stonemason. He knows what he's doing. His rock garden grows steadily more beautiful up there by the cabin.

One fine day the stone will split and we'll triumphantly carry the opened halves, heavy fruit, back up to the garden. Beaming, Roshi will say, "Of course, you would not believe that the stone could split." The halves will lie there in his garden and he, for one day or many, will observe them, patient, until he knows right where they go. Then, like a hawk, he'll swoop, and each opened half will find its place.

That evening after supper, during the short break before zazen, I see him in the rock garden with three of his old familiar students—three big shaven-pated men—wrestling with another huge stone. They strain to start it moving. Roshi throws the whole weight of his small body against the stone. Finally, with grinding sounds from small bits of gravel beneath, it slowly slides toward a shallow pit he's dug for it. After it settles into the hole, he directs his crew to rock it back and forth so he can observe it in slightly different positions. Finally it's bedded just right.

Afterward, as we all survey the placement, one of the students teases him. "Roshi, why do you want to work so hard? You know, this is our break."

"Oh, I think this is really a problem for me," he says, very quietly, in deference to the rule of silence. Suddenly, he's deadly serious. "Sometimes I think that I enjoy working too much. I am really so attached to work. Thank you." He bows to the three men, who bow in return, and turns to walk into his cabin.

I walk down to the creek to retrieve Roshi's zoris. I carry them back to his cabin and set them down carefully, neatly, side by side, just outside the screen door. If only he'd chance to the door, see me, and speak. There's nothing I want more than to talk to him. But I don't dream of knocking.

Hesitating there, I peek through the screen and see an apple on a plate, a new green and red apple waiting to be eaten down to filigree. When will I eat my apples without haste, completely, with a mind filled with red ripeness and summer? There's no sound in the cabin.

Filled with longing, I walk quietly back down the path and turn right toward the zendo.

The sesshin continues, day after hot summer day, evening after cool mountain evening, zazen after zazen, instant after instant. My back is molten with pain, knees on fire, my mind now faint, overwhelmed with pain and endless thoughts, now fierce and stubbornly determined.

One night toward the end of that week, the last period of the day, I abandon myself to the pain. I mark it rising up. Each instant I endure without moving is a blow struck on the mind stone, on a faint margin barely visible under the rushing waters of thought and time.

Two intense rivers of sensation rise up from my knees. I feel a sudden cleavage, a fracturing. Tense muscles relax along my legs and shoulders and arms. "Oh, please," I beg, a voice sounding in my mind, "let this mind stone split! Let some gorgeous seed spill free!"

Thoughts stop. Swiftly, as water wets cotton, my mind rises up from the little zendo hidden in the dark creek bottom, wicks up the mountain walls to their steep rims, and overarching, engulfs stars in a spangled sky.

The last bell rings, signaling that zazen is over. It's time for bed. We all wearily bow and file out past the yellow glimmer of the kerosene lamps to the stony paths outside.

Later that week, on the last night of the sesshin, Roshi begins the evening lecture by saying simply, "Tonight I have nothing on my mind. Nothing at all. If you want, you can ask me some questions."

There's a pause. Then someone says, "Roshi, what's it like for you to speak English? Is it very hard?"

"Yes, sometimes it is very hard. But if I am calm, then I just see the English words float up from the depths of my mind. They're like fish. I catch them and say them. That is very easy."

After a few more questions, I grow bold and ask, "Roshi, how hard should my effort be in zazen? When I try very hard, I get exhausted, and then I lose my concentration."

"Yes, that is true. So please don't try so hard. But still, you must make effort, too. Without some effort, you will become like that smoky lamp over there." Roshi smiles broadly and turns to point to a kerosene lamp, its chimney blackened with smoke, standing behind the dais. Or does he point to the cook, who sits next to it, exhausted from kitchen duties, his head bobbling back and forth as he struggles to stay awake?

A woman says, "Roshi, yesterday I saw one of the cats eating a little bird it had caught. I wanted to save the bird, but it was already almost dead. It really upsets me that nature is so cruel. I don't know what to think about it."

"Yes, that is hard, it makes us feel very bad. But maybe you could imagine that little bird saying to you, 'Please, please, don't look at me, don't look at me, I am a bodhisattva working out my way, don't look at me!'

"Of course, you will still actually feel some pain. But remember, birth is birth, death is death, and actually birth is already death and death is already birth. We ourselves will experience like that little bird someday. All we can do is find our compassion.

"But that does not mean we can change things. We must accept. The bird dies today. The cat lives. Tomorrow the cat may die. Tomorrow I may die. This is the Buddha's world."

Then someone asks, "Roshi, what about reincarnation? Do our souls really go to another body?"

Slowly, Roshi says "I know I will probably be scolded for saying so, but I can't really tell you. I have no experience of reincarnation. I can't really say anything."

A young woman asks, "Roshi, I get really angry when I see rich people driving expensive cars and wasting so much money when there are so many poor people. Shouldn't we try hard to change those things? Sometimes I think that sitting is just an escape."

Roshi picks up his glasses from the mat and waves them at us. "Well, you think these are mine, of course. Everybody would say, 'Those are his.' Sometimes I ask myself, 'Where are my glasses?' But, you know, that's really ridiculous. That's just a way we talk. Nothing is mine at all." He chuckles delightedly. "Still, I always think, here are my glasses. Well, it is true, you are all very kind to me. You will let me use these glasses for a while. I know you won't take them away from me. You will let me use them because my old eyes are very weak.

"So, it is a big problem for people who own many things that they don't need. But we are here. We don't need so many things. We can practice the Buddha's zazen. It is free. When you were born, you received a mind and body. It is wonderful. We don't have to pay anybody. We can just practice our zazen. And our zazen can help us be calm.

"It is very hard to really help anybody if your mind is not calm. You may think you are helping, but are you sure? This doesn't mean that we shouldn't help people. Of course we should. But it is important to do it with deep calm." He picks up his roshi's stick and smoothly traces a horizontal line back and forth in the air. "Someday, if you continue your practice, your mind can become very even, very level."

Someone asks, "How can Buddhism really flourish in America if we don't have more authentic teachers? Do you think we could get more priests to come from Japan?"

Roshi looks serious. "That sounds like a pretty good idea, but it might not really be so good. There are many things you can't learn from a Japanese teacher. Someday you will have Caucasian masters. It won't be too long. That may be better for you, even if you don't think so right now."

The student whose life was "too social" asks, "Roshi, what about the differences between Soto and Rinzai zen? I understand that in Japan the two orders are hostile to each other. I know we're doing Soto practice, but why is it better?"

Roshi looks pensive. "Well, that is a problem in Japan. For many years when I saw a Rinzai priest, I didn't say anything, but I had a kind of bad feeling. But now it's okay. Now Soto and Rinzai—I think they are two eyes of a dragon."

Then I ask, "Roshi, in Minneapolis we don't have a zen center and it's hard for me to practice regularly. Do you think I should keep a strict schedule of zazen at home every day?"

He knits his brows and, to my surprise, says, "That question is very dangerous for you. My answer can catch you in a trap. Just remember, zazen is very important."

The late summer darkness falls over the valley as we sit in this last lecture. The room is almost dark. Several kerosene lamps cast their soft, yellow light, and the corners of the zendo fill with deep, black shadow.

A million crickets have begun to sound outside the zendo, a giant maraca shaking with rattlesnake hiss. Across the creek, a second maraca joins just off the beat. The whole valley trembles in ecstatic Latin rhythm, and a thousand little shivers bubble up my spine and burst beneath my skull.

Emptiness—an emptiness filled with the fire of being. Moving, rhythmic, transforming endlessly, zazen after zazen, meal after meal, work period after work period, sleep after sleep, day after day, year after year, hammer blow after hammer blow.

Beneath the crickets shaking the valley, drowning the wind, I hear the creek—not just the little riffle near the zendo, but simultaneously riffles and rapids along its whole length. Rippling, gurgling, sucking, sometimes rumbling as a rock is upset and rolls downstream, it flows from the mountains toward me and then past the monastery and away.

Finally, Roshi adds his voice to the crickets and the creek. "This is the last night of the sesshin. Now you will go free. Many of you will go back to the city. You will see all sorts of wonderful things. Please try to contact them gently."

The Roshi, his lined face illuminated, speaks softly, quietly now. I'm transported back thousands of years. This could be India, China. I feel the deep gratitude of a young man hearing an old man's words—an old man who wants nothing, who wants only for the young man to blossom.

"You cannot escape the things in this world. They are just our world. But contact them gently. Do not become so attached. Remember, they are not really real. They are just pictures in your mind. I know that's not so easy to understand. But it is actually so.

"Try not to get too excited. Most of you are young. You want to run and jump and stretch your arms and legs wide, as wide as they can go. That is pretty natural. That's okay. But just contact things gently. Thank you for sitting this sesshin with me. Thank you very much."

The bell rings, signaling the end of zazen. We all bow, rise, and face the center of the zendo. We wait for Roshi to fluff his cushion and arrange his robes. He seems absorbed, his gestures slow and deliberate. Finally he bows, turns around, and bows gently as the bell sounds once more. We return his bow and the sesshin is over.

The next day there is time to relax, wash clothes, swim, and hike. In the afternoon, I go to the old cement plunge fed from the hot spring. Stripping off sweaty clothing, I walk in and am surprised by a naked Roshi about to climb in at the far end of the pool. Standing without robes or stick or attendants, he is suddenly tiny and frail, his yellow-brown skin smooth, childlike.

He looks at me shyly, one hand lightly shielding his genitals from view. He climbs into the pool, and, embarrassed, I follow, not knowing what I can possibly say to this being whom I admire more than anyone I've ever met before.

We spend long minutes standing in the pool together, looking past each other, relaxing in steaming hot water up to our waists.

Finally Roshi says with a smile, bringing his hands up a little above the surface, palms up, dripping, cupping a little water in each hand, "It is pure. It is very pure."

"Oh, yes, it is," I say, feeling the magnificent, empty clarity of the hot, steaming water that flows endlessly from the foot of the mountain. My heart is full. I want to talk, but I can't think of one thing more to say.

We stand quietly together for what seems a very long time. Then he bows, and I return his bow. He turns to go, and I stand waist deep in hot, pure water, head filled with a million questions.

It's August, the next summer, at the end of another long sesshin held at the new Page Street Center in San Francisco. I think I've broken through. For the last several days my body has relaxed into the lotus position hour after hour, heart pumping emptiness, mind pulsing upward into consciousness, then flowing back on itself, a sparkling spring-fed pool. I don't drag myself to the forty-minute periods of zazen. I welcome them—breath flowing, thoughts drifting downstream, bubbles flowing with the current, then quietly bursting.

On the last day I see Suzuki Roshi for *dokusan*, a private interview with the teacher. Entering his study, I bow three times to the floor before him. Seated, he slowly returns each bow. I feel his deep relaxation.

I sit down facing him on a zafu placed only a few feet away, taking what I hope is my most perfect sitting form. He watches calmly, observantly, waits for me to speak—but again, tongue-tied, I have no words.

Though comfortably settled on his zafu, he suddenly stands with a quick, smooth motion and makes fine adjustments in the height of my left shoulder, the position of my hands. He returns to his zafu and sits, rearranging his robes, which make silky, whispering sounds as he moves them into place.

After another silence, he says, finally, with a smile, "You are very calm."

"Only now, at the end of the sesshin," I blurt out, heedless of the irony.

"Lon is from Minneapolis, too, I know. It is very far. How do you travel here?"

"I drive my Jeep. It takes me five days. Would you come visit us sometime? We'd like you to lead a sesshin. Do you remember that Lon asked you whether we should do one together last year, even though we had no teacher?"

"Oh, yes," he says with a nod. "I remember. It is possible I could come sometime. But how do you feel when you are calm?"

"Well, even at the end of a sesshin, my head is filled with many thoughts. They get quieter, though. But I always worry about whether Japanese zen practice is right for Americans. I know zazen is exactly what I need to do, but the Japanese ceremonies and traditions bother me."

"Yes," he replies, looking at me intently, raising his eyebrows. "Japanese zen has many ceremonies, it's true. Don't worry too much about ceremonies. Ceremonies are maybe not so important."

"I guess it bothers me too much," I say. "It seems like the dark robes and ceremonies and everyone speaking softly make zen look like a cult especially for people back in Minneapolis." I pause, but Roshi says nothing, observing me with alert eyes. Confused, I stumble ahead, "You know, I think Americans and Japanese are completely different, like fire and water."

Suddenly he looks me full in the face and breaks out laughing. He laughs long, leaning so far forward on his cushion that his forehead almost touches the floor. I begin to laugh, too.

After a minute he recovers and says, "Oh, yes, Japanese people are very quiet, usually. You know, we just go on like a peaceful river. And the Americans get very excited. I see that. But all we can do is practice the Buddha's zazen together. Zen in America is like a little baby. We have to take care of it. We don't know exactly how it will grow up. A baby cries, the mother gives it some milk."

He smiles. "But you practice hard. I see that. I have practiced so many years, I know when people's practice is lazy or hard. But don't try too hard or you will become exhausted. And don't be too lazy. Just sit. Someday you will know how big the Buddha's world is that we are sitting in. Your zazen will give you some power to do that. But I don't like to say 'power.' That is not right. I think a better way to say is 'possibility.' The important thing about zazen is not that it gives you power. It gives you possibility."

It's a few years later, the fall of 1971. I'm thirty and on my third year of a leave from teaching to finish my Ph.D. Farmer and I have continued our zen practice with the small group in Minneapolis. I want, somehow, to fuse an academic career with mastery of zen. Now I've arranged to study zen with Suzuki Roshi for a full year. I'll live at the Zen Center building on Page Street, follow the daily practice, and use the library at Berkeley for research. I arrive in September to find him dying.

Yvonne, one of his old students, tells me they tried to ask me not to come, but couldn't reach me. I'd been in the mountains all summer. I'm glad they couldn't find me.

That evening Reb, one of the building officers, takes me aside. We sit on zafus in his room. After a silence, he says sadly, "He's dying. We're going to lose him. Of course, there could be a miracle. Why not? But there's jaundice now. Even that is beautiful. He's turning to gold, a golden Buddha. He says to us, 'The cancer is my friend.'"

I'm given a little dormitory room on the cold north side of the building. It's fall, and the sun never reaches here. To save money, and to encourage hard practice, the building is kept cold. On clear days, as I sit at my window to study after breakfast, the room fills with a thin, filtered winter light reflected from sunlit buildings on the hills off to the north.

Suzuki Roshi is now too weak to lecture. He stays in his rooms in the building, attended by his wife and a few close students. But he struggles to be part of the community. He takes short walks in the building. If it's warm, he'll come downstairs and sit on a bench in the little open-air courtyard.

One evening he comes into the meal hall during dinner and stands chatting with some students at the table opposite mine. Turning to walk out, he loses his balance and almost falls. The top of his shaven head traces three small circles in the air as he steadies himself, tightly gripping his short staff to his chest.

"Why," I wonder, "why did I spend the last two years in Minneapolis doing doctoral work? Why did I wait so long to come? At least I'm here now. Does he know what he has done for me? How can I tell him?"

One afternoon, walking down the hall past the Suzukis' rooms on the second floor, I pass him just as he is about to enter his door. Since I arrived weeks ago, we've not spoken. He's been so ill, I've felt it wrong to intrude. He fixes me with his eyes and stands expectant, his hand, tiny and frail, gripping the knob. I stop walking and stand, too, holding his gaze. Does he know I came from Minneapolis this fall to spend the year with him? Has anyone told him?

Again, despite the imminence of his death, I'm tongue-tied. His face is thin, eyes sad and solemn, yet suddenly they regain the old twinkle and he smiles.

My heart is breaking. I can't speak. The smile speaks everything to me. I hear it like words: "O strange American, I know you. You have sat hard for many years, and you have always come back to me to sit. I am dying, it is true, but that is all right. Don't worry. Just remember what I told you. Zazen is very important."

We hold each other's gaze for a very long time, his eyes suddenly alive with humor, mine moist with tears. Finally I raise my hands, palms together, and make a slow bow, all the time keeping my eyes on his eyes. He also puts palms together and bows slowly, keeping his eyes on mine.

I turn away and, walking down the hall, hear him open and close his door very gently. We have said our farewell.

Suddenly I'm back, nestled among my trees, tears tracing gritty lines down through the dust on my cheeks. Where have the years gone? I'm fifty-four, not thirty. The freckled skin on my Scots-Norwegian face has collapsed from the mountain sun, from decades of summers enfolded in these pine-and-fir-forested hills dropping down from the

Crag. Now Roshi is dead. Even Alan is dead, who was young like me on that hot summer day in the cool of Tassajara Creek.

Still, I sit. As Roshi told me, I sit. I sit here on the mountain in wind and sun—now struggling and cursing, plagued with regrets—now suddenly ecstatic, every finger and toe tingling with joy—now gliding to rest, words all gone, the mind stuff an ocean dabbling a bright sand shore. "Yes, yes," I think, "one bright pearl is its name."

Day after day, year after year, I strike the mind stone. I hammer—some days weak, some days strong—hammer blow after hammer blow. Should the stone never split, I hammer still, hammering with the joy of that day in the rushing creek. Hammering with tall, tanned, broad-backed Alan. Hammering with Roshi, who stands at our sides bare-legged, diminutive, his sunlit mind teasing. "Oh, Roshi," I whisper. "I'll hammer forever."

I stretch out my legs to ease the ache in my knees and bend double, dropping my forehead to touch my knees. I sit back, pull up the neck of my T-shirt, and slowly wipe the tears from my eyes and cheeks, a gesture I always smiled at in my young son. I smell a puff of warm air, fragrant with sweat, rising up from my armpits and chest. The cotton comes away streaked with the fine yellow-brown dust of the basin. I stand up, stretch, and slowly walk to the edge of the trees.

A chill afternoon breeze wafts ten miles from Flute Reed snowfields. I shiver. The mountains are bluish as the sun drops to the west, throwing the east- and north-facing slopes into shadow. "Ah," I think. "Let's head back up to the Crag for a final sit."

I gather my things back into the day pack, shoulder it, then caress with my fingertips the dark, rough treads of bark on each of my three trees.

With palms pressed together, I bow to each of the four directions. "Thank you," I whisper at each bow, then shout "Ho!" as loud and long as I can. There's no echo. The shouts are carried off by sharp gusts of wind.

I slowly walk out of the shade of the forest floor, along the open hillsides, through sage and angling sunlight, back up toward the Crag.

I stand for a moment at its base, gazing out into the crystalline atmosphere, then clamber up the jumbled outcrop to my three leveled black rocks. I open the pack, take out my red vest, and fold it again into a cushion. I sit down, cross my legs, pull my hat down hard against the afternoon breezes, and sway from side to side, forward and back, centering myself.

Flapping overhead, a solitary raven catches my eye. He coasts down to sit on the top of a dead fir and squawks fitfully. His fussing annoys me and I turn to observe him. His black feathers are ragged. He pointedly ignores me, staring down into the trees.

Then Suzuki Roshi's words drift back to me. Shutting my eyes, I see again his small body, buoyant, graceful, as he sat at ease on his cushion at twilight that evening in the zendo at Tassajara, the creek rippling, the crickets sounding. Opening my eyes, I whisper musingly to myself, "Nothing on my mind. I have nothing on my mind."

Now the late summer grasshoppers busy themselves, flying with clack-clack-clacking through the sage, their days numbered by imminent frost. Sitting among these rough black rocks still holding the noon heat, I'm almost hot again. Then a cloud floats by to the west, casting its shadow, and I shiver, cooled by gusts blown off the mountain fortresses before me. A thousand feet below, the basin floor shimmers. My hands lie relaxed, palms up, on my knees.

9

A Year at the Zen Center

AFTER SUZUKI ROSHI'S DEATH IN DECEMBER, I stay on living at the Page Street Zen Center till the next summer. I'm older than most of the residents—a refugee from the Berkeley sixties, but now a college teacher and doctoral candidate. I throw myself into zen practice, sitting daily zazen and the monthly sesshins, and driving each day to Berkeley to do dissertation research in the library.

Ever since arriving in the fall, I've been tested. Shortly after being assigned my cold north room, I get a roommate. He's lived at Zen Center before. Everyone knows about him but me.

He appears in my room one afternoon—stocky, in his late twenties, hair dark and close-cropped, wearing jeans and a flannel shirt. He drops several old army duffle bags and a cardboard box and introduces himself.

"Hey, man, good to have you on the scene. I'm Ron. Wow, you sure got this place neat. Uh huh! Another anal-retentive hard-practice type! My own practice is to be messy. But that's cool. That'll be part of your practice now, too."

"My practice?" I say. "I don't think so. By the way, I'm Erik." I stand up off the mattress-on-the-floor bed that serves as furniture and offer my hand. "Just leave me half of the room. We'll get along fine."

By evening the entire small room is filled with Ron's clothes, books, shoes, papers, religious paraphernalia, and miscellaneous clutter. Every surface, including my bed and desk, is covered. Ron, it turns out, has just begun a career selling futons, traditional Japanese sleeping mats that are now gaining popularity.

"Hey, man, look what you're sleeping on," he comments, as I start to climb into bed. "It was worn out years before the Zen Center got this dump. Just cheap dormitory crap to begin with! Four inches thick on this cold concrete floor? You'll kill yourself. In a few months you won't be able to practice your zazen. Now, I've got a deal for you. This is a spiritual investment! Get a king size, double-thick futon. Since you're a zen student, I'll let it go for wholesale—a little thing I do for members of our zen community. That's less than what you'd have to pay for a queen at my store. I'll personally deliver it."

"No, no, Ron, I'm doing fine. All I ask is that you get your stuff organized tomorrow morning. You can probably skip the work period since you've just moved in."

The next day is a Saturday. After morning lecture I skip work period myself to have coffee and cinnamon rolls at a zen hangout near Market Street. It's not considered good form to skip work period, especially to go drink coffee and eat sugary sweet rolls, but I always find Alan, the poet Philip Whalen, and other less-than-pure zen students. Afterward, walking back up the block to the Zen Center, I cross to a little Chinese grocery and buy a pint of half and half. I glance up and down the street, then stand on the corner and gulp it down, hoping no zen student walks by. The vegetarian diet has left me with an immense craving for fat. I head up to my room to check on Ron. Entering, I see new stuff scattered about on top of the old stuff—and a young female resident under the covers with Ron. "Hi," I say noncommittally.

They watch me intently. Ron says, "Well, hello. I hope you're cool with my having visitors. I'm sure your thing isn't celibacy. I mean, that's really not what zen is all about. You dig?" He turns to the young woman, who lies peacefully on her back, arms behind her head, now staring up at the ceiling. "It's not *your* practice either, is it, darling?"

"Nooo, not really," she says, smiling, gazing coyly at the ceiling.

This is too much. I sit down on my bed and angrily push aside a pile of Ron's clothes. "Look," I say, "I don't really care what you two do as long as you don't do it when I'm here. And I'm gone most of the day. So, for Christ's sake, enjoy yourselves. But I can't handle your shit everywhere. My bed and desk and this side of the room are mine. I mean mine! Keep your goddamn shit on your own side." I trace an imaginary line with my finger between our mattresses and move stuff off it until a six-inch no-man's-land of concrete floor appears. "Dig it?"

"Yeah, I guess we can work that out," says Ron, clearly pleased to have provoked me.

"Cool," I say, and begin tossing stuff onto his side of the room.

Within a week of his moving in, he seems to disappear, although more stuff keeps appearing in the room. The young woman never turns up in bed again, though she gives me lingering smiles when we pass in the halls. I smile back, torn, but I don't fall. I'm here to practice, I tell myself.

Ron honors my line of demarcation, and his side of the room stays in chaos. I bring friends in just to see it. On my side everything's put away, the single bed on the floor made up with a few blankets, a small wooden desk covered with some books and papers. My steamer trunk sits at the foot of the bed. Ron's side is litter on top of litter, right up to the line in the middle, where suddenly the concrete floor reappears, then a small rug I have next to my bed.

I tolerate him for a month. Then suddenly I realize he's not been around for a week.

I return from the library on the Berkeley campus one day, and his things have disappeared—except for a few stacks of futon sales literature.

I'm quickly given a further test. For my work assignment, I'm given trash, garbage, and compost. My station during the daily work periods is the rear basement entrance to the Page Street building. I collect and carry down garbage, sort cans and bottles for recycling, stockpile organic vegetarian garbage, and sweep up the area inside, as well as the sidewalk and street outside. I also maintain the little wooden altar that hangs on a pillar inside the heavy rear double doors. I'm to light incense and bow each day before and after my duties.

Far from the zendo, Buddha hall, and library, this is definitely low-prestige work. Even kitchen duty is preferred to this, for most residents attach spiritual significance to the correct preparation of vegetarian food. But I grew up doing dirty jobs—household chores, home repair, hardware store work, auto repair. I accept the test and get intimate with refuse.

To the surprise and gratitude of the cook, I volunteer to haul organic garbage to Mel's garden at the Berkeley zendo. One morning each week I pull the back seat out of my 1965 Studebaker Lark V8 and load in three or four thirty-gallon plastic garbage cans filled with slimy vegetarian slop. Cruising the Bay Bridge at seventy-five in overdrive, sickly sweet-sour smells wafting to the front seat, I pray I don't have an accident. I pull up to the Berkeley zendo, ring the bell, and Mel and I haul the cans to the backyard and dump them in compost bins. Even in winter, the plants in his yard flourish, and I begin to take personal pride in the fertility of the ground. Once the cans are emptied, Mel and I drink morning coffee and play recorder duets.

My garbage enthusiasm extends to the sacred ceremonies of the rear entry. This isn't the Unitarian Society of my childhood, so I put aside secular doubts and get serious about the altar. I want to honor garbage, trash, waste, and compost. I rummage for a wine bottle in the green glass barrel and, holding it by its neck, reach inside the barrel and smash it against another bottle. In the Zen Center workshop I drill a hole in a block of hardwood and insert the neck upside down in this base. This creates a graceful vase-shaped green glass sculpture about six inches high with pointed shards arcing up into the air. I call it the Buddha of the Realm of Infinite Landfill. This I add to the rear entry wall altar.

For several mornings I light incense, chant, and bow to the Infinite Landfill Buddha. But upon making his rounds one morning, Steve, the work leader, informs me that my altar is unacceptable. "Sure," I think. "It's unacceptable because it's unconventional." But Steve sticks to safety issues.

149

"What if someone's down here and stumbles against it? They could get hurt."

"What?" I say. "This is a low-traffic area. No one comes down here, and anyway, it's placed head-high on that pillar. There's no danger and you know it."

"No, I really don't think I do know that."

Heatedly, in the dim light of the basement, we argue.

"Listen," I say, "for someone to be injured on that thing they'd have to be seven feet tall. It'll never happen!"

But the work leader is adamant. I remove the Infinite Landfill Buddha.

I grow used to petty rules and petty controversy. Early in my stay, I learn that if I refer to "Suzuki," a certain officer will challenge me: "Don't you mean Suzuki *Roshi?*" Then for a full week everyone debates whether residents, to minimize dirt in the building, should have two pairs of zoris—"inside" zoris and "outside" zoris.

Meals are taken formally in the zendo on Saturday mornings using oryoki. The ritual use of these bowls is complicated. Wearily, I come to expect that a certain officious young American will come to me after each meal, offering corrections to my food handling, napkin folding, and sequence of putting bowls and utensils away.

Finally I get snappish. My own technique was taught me a few summers ago at Tassajara by a different but equally insistent young American who is now an important priest. I mention his name and my critic is silenced.

I begin to frequent the "flop" room, a disreputable haven off to the side of the kitchen with old couch cushions thrown about on the bare floor. On a stained counter next to a stove top are cups, tea and coffee pots, and various containers of tea and coffee and sweeteners—even white sugar!

Too much time spent here raises questions about one's purity. Those who laze about the floor chatting and drinking full-strength black coffee are scorned by "hard practicers." One morning, as I'm spooning two spoonfuls of sugar into my coffee, a hard practicer eyes me balefully and warns, "Don't you know that white sugar is worse even than heroin?" I nod, smile, and continue stirring. The hard practicers even lobby for elimination of the room, but fortunately, these efforts are beaten back.

One morning after breakfast I'm sitting with Dainin Katagiri Roshi, Suzuki Roshi's assistant, together against the flop room wall. I'm discussing with him the developing zen group in Minneapolis and our hope that he would move there to teach zen. He has already visited several times. We understand the uncertainty of his situation with Suzuki Roshi's illness, but we want him to come if it's possible.

A young woman, a hard practicer, enters and offers Katagiri a cup of herbal tea. He shakes his head, saying, "Please, could I have a cup of coffee? With cream and sugar, please?" She raises her eyebrows, but brings him the coffee. Later I hear hushed talk in the kitchen about the dangers of toxins to the young Roshi's health.

It's in the flop room that I become acquainted with Hoitsu-san, one of Suzuki's sons, who has come from Japan to see his father during this final illness. He frequents the flop room after breakfast, obviously curious about these young Americans who have absorbed the last twelve years of his father's life.

He's a youngish man, a priest, full of talk and good spirits—a breath of fresh air. His credentials are impeccable—a priest and Suzuki Roshi's son. "So zen need not be unremittingly puritanical and dour," I think.

I'm curious about this window onto Suzuki Roshi's past. I ask Hoitsu-san what effect a lifetime of zen practice had on his father.

"Oh," he says, "he has changed very much in one way. When I was a boy he was strict and got angry very easily. One day I was going to school and playing by a lake along the way. I was playing so much I was going to be late to school. He caught me. He was so angry, he just picked me up and threw me into the lake."

I chuckle. "That certainly doesn't sound like your father to me. I've heard that he gets angry at zen students sometimes, but not like that."

"Well, you see," says Hoitsu-san, "zen practice has helped his anger very much."

I'm surprised to find the arts ignored. When Gary Snyder reads at the Zen Center that year, he leads off by saying he can't think of a better audience for his poetry. Yet the zen students are mostly unresponsive. Except for a few polite questions, they sit stone-faced till the evening is over.

I've brought my violin and discover a woman resident who also plays. On a few occasions we try some duets, but even though we play in the afternoons, she soon tells me she's heard complaints, and we must stop.

I'm puzzled. Many students have stereos and play rock in their rooms. Ancient Chinese and Japanese masters were artists, musicians, and poets. Everyone is proud of Suzuki Roshi's calligraphy.

But still, the heartbeat of the place is the daily meditation, the monthly sesshins, the silence. After the sesshins—up to seven days of intense meditation together—jealousies and rivalries diminish, kinks straighten out, and I'm simply grateful for my opportunity to be here, to sit with these men and women who struggle, however imperfectly, for something great.

For weeks in the late fall, the Zen Center is in a flurry of activity preparing for the ceremonial installation of Dick Baker as abbot. Buddhist dignitaries from Soto headquarters in Japan and from around the world are invited to this event. Everything must be in apple pie order. Along with other ordinary residents of the center, my work is to clean. After insuring that my basement, hallways, back entry, and rear sidewalk are spic and span, I move on to other tasks of vacuuming, mopping, and dusting in the bathrooms and common passageways on the floors above.

The installation is of huge importance. After its completion, Dick Baker will be a zen master. He will be addressed as "Roshi." He will be the spiritual leader of the Buddhist communities at the Page Street center and Tassajara. He will, in theory, have received an imprimatur from the Buddha's own mind, transmitted in unbroken succession from masters to disciples over two millennia.

There's concern among some of his peers that Dick is not equal to this responsibility, that Katagiri Sensei should assume it. Some students talk of leaving the Zen Center to follow other, more interesting teachers, like Trungpa Rinpoche, the remarkable and mercurial Tibetan master.

At a lecture a few days before the installation, Katagiri urges that Dick be fully accepted and supported. He talks of the difficulties of succession, that these difficulties were common in ancient China and Japan, too. He tells an old story of a master who is, at first, rejected by his students. "But he became great," Katagiri concludes, smiling "Dick Baker will also be great, a great priest, a very great priest."

Finally the day arrives. Students and guests crowd the hallways. The ceremony takes place in the Buddha hall. Important guests are seated on zafus inside, a few of the less hardy seated on folding chairs, which earlier this morning I helped place along the back wall. Seated students spill out into the hallway. Finally, at the rear, there's standing room only, and I stand at the back of a crowd, watching a procession that moves slowly down the stairs from the Suzukis' rooms and into the Buddha hall.

Suddenly I have my last glimpse of Suzuki Roshi, a tiny, helpless figure in beautiful, royal robes shining with whites and golds. He's borne up by several of his old, devoted students, who slowly carry him to the Buddha hall. I'm amazed to see him out of his usual brown and black. Today he's clothed for eternity, a frail king on his journey home to vast emptiness.

Now the procession is inside. Still standing at the back, I listen for a long time to the drone of the chanting. Finally, long before the ceremony is complete, I slip up the stairs to my cold north room and, for the first time in years, sitting on the bedclothes, sob like a child.

It's early morning, the first day of the seven-day *rohatsu* sesshin, held just before Christmas. During zazen, Baker Roshi makes a quiet announcement. "This morning Suzuki Roshi died. He stayed with us until the beginning of the first period of zazen. Then he let go."

Dick pauses, then goes on softly, "Yesterday, I asked where we could find him after he was gone. He said nothing, but a tiny brown hand came out of the bedclothes and traced a circle in the air."

We sit for the next seven days knowing that he stretched to reach the beginning of one more sesshin, and touched us, before leaving.

On the last day of the sesshin, I'm assigned during the afternoon work period to help clean and rearrange the Buddha hall. The room has large sunny windows on two sides that look off to the south and the east. The floor is almost entirely covered with rice straw tatami mats. I dust and vacuum while Angie, a young woman priest, rearranges the altar.

First I vacuum the masonry floor, then all the zafus. Toward the end of the two-hour period, I begin on the tatamis—and suddenly the tatamis are Suzuki Roshi's body. Then every surface in the room is his body. I feel the vacuum tickle and massage. With every stroke of the brush, he shivers in delight, a puppy stroked and scratched all over.

Light streams through the big casement windows. The straw mats glow like ripe field corn, their edging cloths black like the spaces between galaxies. I vacuum and vacuum, every roaring stroke vibrating up my arms and legs and spine.

The bell tolls the end of the work period. I put away the machine, hoses, and brushes and return to my cushion. Tomorrow, I know, I must go forward without him.

It's an evening in late January 1972. Professor Edward Conze lectures to about thirty of us at the Zen Center. His subject is the movement of the Buddha's teachings from Sanskrit into the Chinese texts. A man of perhaps seventy, a German, one of the great European writers on Buddhism, he's spending this year as a visiting professor at Berkeley. Many of us attend his lectures regularly.

He's sarcastic about zen, which he considers trivial and upstart. The real Buddhism, he insists, originated and matured in India. Further, as one whose world was destroyed by Hitler and the Axis powers, he's contemptuous of the Japanese. When he sees zen students in his classes, he grumbles about the militarism of "Samurai Buddhism." Nevertheless, despite his gruff, rough treatment of us at times, we see that he's deeply gratified by our serious interest in Buddhism and in his work.

But tonight he's agitated. After seating himself uncomfortably on a large zafu raised with several small mats, he spits out in heavily accented English, "So, it seems that it is necessary, after all, for the Americans to do the graveyard meditations. Like the old monks in India who sat in the boneyards and burning grounds, learning that the body is only rotten meat."

Pausing, Conze glowers at us through the thick lenses of his glasses, shaking his head and grizzled mustache, then accuses "So a young man is handsome. Or a lady is beautiful. Maybe she has, oh, such beautiful breasts." Conze makes a curving flourish in the air with his hands. "But when the surgeon cuts through these beautiful breasts with a scalpel? What is beneath? There are ribs. And he saws through those ribs? There are lungs. And fat. And blood. Disgusting, is it not? Then we know what the body really is."

Taken aback, I glance around the room. Other students, stoic on their cushions, look puzzled, too. But we're used to unconventional lectures and occasional tirades.

"So," Conze continues, glancing at us, "now I have been told that all that the young Americans want to do for each other is just to lick each other's bits." He pauses, then firmly emphasizes his words: "Yes, you just want to *lick each other's bits*." Accusingly, he stares around the room. "And this way," he concludes, "it is not even possible for the woman to be taken care of. She cannot be satisfied."

He stops, uncharacteristically out of words. Then a bold, handsome young woman from the university raises her hand. She regularly attends his lectures on campus and has come over to hear him tonight. He looks up and nods, and she firmly breaks the silence, saying, "Oh, Doctor Conze, that's just not true. A woman can be satisfied that way."

"Oh?" Conze roars, outraged and embarrassed at being contradicted by this particular superior authority. "Oh? So you have found, after all, the one who can do this for you? I see! I see!"

The young woman falls silent and drops her eyes, abashed. Thus saved from himself, Conze rummages through his notes, then shifts ground completely. He softens. Suddenly he's even complimentary.

He expresses pleasure at seeing young people learning the Buddha's teachings and even admits ruefully that the most he can manage in

Buddhist practice is mindfulness, paying careful attention to what comes before consciousness moment after moment. He complains that his old legs don't permit him to sit long in the Buddha's meditation.

But soon he recovers himself and, shifting his large bulk uncomfortably on his oversized zafu, turns on us again, observing that a key virtue in Buddhism is "friendliness"—a virtue he finds singularly absent in zen students. "What good is this so-called 'zazen,' this sitting on the ground all day, if you don't have simple friendliness?" he demands. "If that is not there, you have not even *begun* real Buddhism."

We say nothing, and his irritation subsides into grumbles: "I know all about your little Buddhist groups. You find some rich old ladies to pay the bills so everyone has time to walk around looking very solemn. Then you each hope everyone else is thinking you have achieved enlightenment. Humph! Not very likely, that one.

"So," he goes on, a sly smile creeping over his lips, "for an example, look at your very own officers. Right here in this room we have most perfect examples of the three Buddhist evils. That one there," he says, pointing to his first victim, who sits a few rows back, "is a good example of the *greed* type of personality. It is a very greedy one. That is clear from the body type. Very much work remains to be done there." The greed type chooses not to meet Conze's eyes.

"And right here," says Conze, pointing to a second officer, who sits zazen with perfect form in the front row, "right under my very nose, is the classic *delusion* type. It is an unfortunate karma, but one must after all accept whatever comes to us from our past lives, eh?" The delusion type maintains a stony equanimity.

"And finally," Conze goes on, "right there in the back I see a fine example of the *hate* type. I myself am a hate type, so I sympathize. It is not pleasant to be a hate type. For the hate type, it is very hard to enjoy the foolishness of the world. However, this type is further advanced than the other two types. This type is intelligent enough to begin to understand how things really are. But we are an unpleasant sort." The hate type squirms on his zafu and tries to look amused.

"Now," says Professor Conze, delighted to have insulted American young people, zen, the Zen Center, and the three officers, for whom we know he has, in fact, affection, "let's get back to our subject. But first, someone bring me a chair so I can stretch out my legs. And a lectern. We have much matter to discuss here tonight."

It's an afternoon about a week later. I've arranged to meet Professor Conze in his office. He leans back in his chair and peers at me through his thick glasses. "Well, here I am," he says, not unkindly. "What is on your mind? I know you're one of those zen students."

"Yes," I say. "I'm living this year at the Page Street center. I'm also doing a dissertation comparing zen and American puritan styles of meditation, looking at the way in which each has a yogic discipline that catalyzes a nonordinary state of consciousness. The puritans called it 'assurance of justification.' Buddhists, of course, call it many things—*satori*, *samahdi*, enlightenment, what have you."

Professor Conze grunts, leans back in his chair, then asks, "So why are you so interested in this zen stuff? Everyone in America seems crazy about zen. The real work was done in India centuries ago. You must go back in history to find great minds filled with enlightenment. A mind like that—a truly enlightened mind—hasn't appeared for many centuries."

"Well," I say, "what else is one to do? Where else is one to find masters?"

Conze snorts, "Of course, no one thinks European Buddhism is important. Actually, now it is quite old. There are very good people. Very good. But everyone has to run wild after some Oriental guru. It's absurd. Like this Trungpa."

I'm intrigued. Chögyam Trungpa Rinpoche is causing a huge stir these days. A number of Suzuki Roshi's students have left Dick Baker to join him. Curious to meet him myself one evening after a lecture he gave at the Zen Center, I went up to talk. He stood, sandwiched between two large male disciples close on either side. Stepping forward to address him, I hit a wall of alcohol stench and caught myself before taking an involuntary step backward. Yet despite a high state of intoxication, he gave lucid answers to my questions in flawless English.

And one evening just a few days ago, my old roomate Ron from futon sales reappeared. As we stood talking with a group of people in the hall, he pulled aside one of the young married women and solicited her to come spend the night with the Rinpoche. To my astonishment, she went, leaving her husband to climb disconsolately to their room alone.

"It sounds like you're not very impressed with Trungpa," I say. "But he's gathering many disciples."

"A man without character," says Conze, "an exploiter. He took advantage of the British Buddhist community. We threw him out of England and hoped we'd heard the last of him. Now your country must deal with him."

Changing the subject, I ask, "But Professor Conze, why do you dismiss the zen schools? Don't you think that a true understanding was transmitted from the Buddha through the Patriarchs to Bodhidharma, and through him to the zen schools?"

"Pure fantasy," he snorts. "There never was any historical Bodhidharma. An old wives' tale. Everybody loves, of course, their own mythology. But tell me now. What exactly is on *your* mind?"

"Well," I begin hesitantly, "I want to ask you for your advice. You're a scholar and a teacher. And you're a serious student of Buddhism, as well. For years I've been struggling for some way to pull these two halves of my life together. I don't know that it's even possible. Do you think I can harmonize a commitment to enlightenment with a career of study and teaching? Right now I can't give up the academic work—or maybe it's just that I won't. But it leaves me feeling divided, unable to pursue either wholeheartedly."

Conze observes me intently though his thick glasses. "Yes, I can understand this problem. So you study the American puritans. They had some kind of mysticism, of course. But I think you should think about the big fish. That might be more important."

"What?" I ask, puzzled.

"The big fish," he says again. "The big white ocean fish. What was his name who wrote about it . . . ?" He squints his eyes, trying to remember.

"Oh," I say, "You mean Moby Dick? The white whale? Melville?"

"Yes, yes, of course. Herman Melville. There's something very interesting there, don't you think? A great mystery, the biggest creature on earth, and a quest. But it's not my field. This is all I can think of."

I thank Professor Conze and leave. On my drive back across the bay to the Zen Center, smiling to myself all the way, I think about Emerson and Thoreau and the transcendentalists—and "the big fish."

The Zen Center stands on Page Street at the edge of the Fillmore, San Francico's black ghetto. The residents in the few blocks around are a mix of poor blacks and whites, a few Asians, and a smattering of zen students. Most days, I jog a three-mile circuit through the Fillmore. Pedestrians, upon hearing my running footsteps approaching, anxiously turn to check out who is overtaking them from behind.

Early in the winter, I often slip away on a Friday night to a black blues joint some blocks away. The band is fine, and they bring a tall, leggy singer who dances in the center of a raucous crowd, pulling a short, tight skirt high up on her thighs.

As I'm walking there one Friday night, a gang of six teenage boys herd me into an alley and demand money. Zenned-out, unafraid, I smile and apologize, extending my arms and hands, palms up, in a gesture of embarrassed appeasement.

"Hey, guys, I'm sorry, but I haven't got shit. You know that Zen Center up on Page Street? I live there and none of us have money. But we always try to help the folks. And you can sure have whatever I got."

They grumble, mutter curses, begin to mill about—and then one says, "Ah, fuck 'im," and they scatter on up the darkened street.

My post as rear entry garbage sentry gives me another window on the neighborhood. I come to know an old, near-sighted, and pathetically obese white woman who lives in a deteriorated basement apartment across the steep, narrow street from my doors. How, I wonder, does this helpless old creature survive here? We talk occasionally from sidewalk to sidewalk.

She says she has little money to care for herself and eats whatever food she can laboriously carry home from a tiny and expensive neighborhood grocery nearby. I begin bringing her leftovers from the kitchen. She seems confused about her own history and family—a vague story of different cities, different jobs, a husband who's dead, children who don't visit. She doesn't seem sure what cities they live in.

One evening, setting trash and garbage out for the early morning collection, I see her walking home with two teenaged black boys. Each carries a small grocery bag. As they approach, they eye me uneasily. Clearly, I'm a complication.

As she fumbles for her keys, I shout loudly across the street, "Hey, how's it going? So you got some help tonight?"

Nervous, flustered, she says, "Oh my, I got so turned around today. I don't know how it happened. It's never happened before. But these boys," she nods to each one, "said they'd walk me home. I was so tired I didn't know how I'd carry my bags."

I linger outside my doors, the officious janitor, conspicuous, checking locks, rattling knobs, picking up and crushing a beer can and throwing it inside my back door. I stand stolidly with arms crossed and toss more pleasantries across the narrow street. I chatter, wondering. "Will these guys split or try something?" I'm ready to sprint for the phone.

She tugs on the heavy wooden door to her cave. Encrusted with seventy-five years of paint, the last layer a glop of gray, it creaks open and the bottom scrapes heavily along the sidewalk. It takes her whole weight to move it. She turns and fumbles in her purse, then hands each of the boys a dollar.

Taking their dollars, the boys hesitate at the door, eyeing me again. Breathing heavily, she carries in her small bags of groceries, one at a time. Suddenly the boys turn on their heels and dart swiftly away up the steep street.

By now she's disappeared into her basement rooms. I lock my own doors and follow her in. A stench of dank, fetid bedclothes, uneaten food, and ancient rancid grease hits me full in the face. I gasp, sickened.

Breathing through my mouth, I find her in a little dimly lit kitchen area. "Weren't you afraid?" I say. "You've got to be careful, you could be hurt!"

"Oh, I don't think so," she says, looking up. "Don't you think they were nice boys?" Bent and obese, her face floats below mine in the dim light, matted strings of greasy gray hair flying in all directions—a crazy old sunflower. "You know, I get so tired and there's nothing else to do. I have to go out every day, you know. I've got to get something to eat. I don't think they meant any wickedness." She breaks into a toothless grin.

Returning early one evening, I park my car behind the building and, at the corner, meet a corpse face down in a puddle of blood. His throat is slit. Down the street ten feet is another puddle, red gouts thickening on the hard cement surface. Then I see dark pools continuing on down to the middle of the block. With horror, I realize that spurts from his jugular struck the pavement as he made a last run for his life.

When the police arrive and he's turned over, I recognize him—a slender, handsome young black man with a neat goatee that makes him look Ethiopian. He came often to sit evening zazen.

I follow the trail down the sidewalk to the rear entry of his apartment. Two detectives are photographing glass scattered below a broken second-story window. Large crystalline sheets lie atop one another, smeared with his darkening blood. He was pushed through the window, his throat sliced by a shard that fell edgewise just ahead of him.

It's spring. I join the first practice period led by Baker Roshi. For three months, some fifteen of us will sit intensively morning and evening throughout the week and attend all sesshins. Each morning after breakfast we gather for tea, an informal occasion when Dick answers questions about practice. I like him. But can he help me with the questions I've carried across the continent for the old Japanese master? He's only a few years older than I am. And he's not Japanese.

Nevertheless, at the end of the practice period, during dokusan at five o'clock one morning, I open up and tell what drives me—a doctorate, teaching, writing, wilderness, and ultimately enlightenment. I want to achieve mastery of zen. He listens carefully in the quiet, dim room, the only sounds the occasional whine of a garbage truck making early morning rounds.

"Erik," he says finally, "your house has too many rooms in it."

"I know, I know," I interject. "But it's all one house!"

"You can't live in them all," he shoots back. "When will you shut some doors and turn the key?"

"I don't know," I say.

"Are you going back to Minneapolis at the end of this year?"

"Yeah. If I don't return to teach, I'll lose my job. I've been gone three years. And I've got to finish my thesis."

Chuckling, Dick says, "We'll give you a doctorate here. Not the usual kind, but it'll be genuine."

"I know what you mean," I say, "but I'll have to think about it. My roots are in Minnesota. I love the bay, but zen in Minnesota is real, too."

"Maybe," he says, "if you can find it. We'll miss you. It's been a hard year with Suzuki Roshi's death and all the changes. You're older than most of the students. You've been steady. It's been a big help."

"Why, thank you," I say, pleased to get this acknowledgment.

"Someday you must go to Japan. It's important to see what zazen is like when you're not just sitting in someone's living room."

I nod, an image forming in my mind of a zen practice that is less personal and idiosyncratic—a practice that's a normal part of a culture, like a physics class in America.

"But be careful," Dick continues, "about going back and starting a zen group. As soon as you're the leader, your own practice will stop developing."

Surprised, I nod. I've never considered myself even remotely qualified to lead a zen group—not yet. I'm light years from that vision of the clear light thrust upon me six years ago in Chicago one chill spring morning.

I bow, Dick Baker bows, and I step quietly through and close the door.

I'm brought back to the Crag by intensifying pain in both knees. I rock my body from side to side in increasing arcs, release my right foot from on top of my left, and stretch out my legs. The pain reaches a crescendo, then quickly subsides.

Glancing over, I see the raven has fled from his branch. I didn't notice. I stand gingerly, my legs stiff, carefully balancing on bare feet, enjoying the sun's warmth radiating from the black rocks into the soles of my feet. Then I step idly down fifty feet from rock to rock, testing my balance, finally leaving the rocks to meet sage and hillside.

I stand for long minutes at ease, observing the lengthening shadows thrown by the great Douglas fir that follow the crest of the Crag, then notice, off to my left, beyond trees thirty yards distant, a blur of brown. Bear again? I freeze, and then three cow elk and as many young move cautiously into the clearing—edgy, nervous, gazing toward me with soft faces. The wind coming over the crest of the hill didn't give them my scent. The cows are huge. Reaching only their shoulders, the calves seem to stand on stilts.

Now they catch my movements. For a time all six brown faces are lowered in my direction. I see concern and curiosity. Then the cow nearest me makes her decision and turns to run. The others follow noisily, pummeling the turf, plunging through crackling underbrush and scattering fallen branches.

Happy, I turn and, step by careful step, make my way back up the jumble of the outcrop to stand by the three leveled black rocks. In my absence the raven has returned. Again, he pointedly ignores me as I gather myself into a sitting position. There is slight achiness now in both knees as I pull them loosely into a half-lotus position. I begin watching my breath. It flows easily, in and out, in and out. My body is erect yet easy, every bone and muscle falling naturally into its place. This, I remember, is how Katagiri Roshi used to look toward the end of a seven-day sesshin.

I shut my eyes and awareness is everywhere, an ocean. Thoughts arise and sink into a shimmering surface. Then thoughts cease. I'm an ancient tower, a lighthouse shedding beams of light over a silvery night sea, a mountain marking the slow, massive slip of glaciers down its sides. Everywhere, inside and out, all the world is one bright pearl.

10

Master Dainin Katagiri

IT'S EARLY SUMMER. A WOMAN FRIEND FROM Minneapolis and I drive from the San Franciso Zen Center to Monterey to talk with Dainin Katagiri Roshi. He moved there a few months after Suzuki Roshi installed Dick Baker as the abbot of Zen Center. We want him to move to Minneapolis. And we are ready to ask formally to become his students.

In the last few years, he's visited the growing group of zen students in Minneapolis several times. This last year at Page Street, I've been lobbying him to come to Minneapolis and lead us. During that time, it had seemed possible he would replace Suzuki Roshi. Now, with Dick Baker's appointment, he seems guardedly interested in Minneapolis. In any case, despite years of refusal to compromise my independence, I'm finally ready to declare allegiance to a teacher. There seems no other choice if I'm to achieve mastery of zen.

Katagiri Roshi and I sit on black zafus facing each other in the small back room of his house in Monterey—his zendo that year. After a few minutes of small talk, he waits for questions.

My heart pounds. "What am I doing here? I never made a commitment, even to Suzuki Roshi! Why make one to Katagiri?" Sweat pools in my armpits and drips down my arms. It runs out my short-sleeved shirt and plop, plop, plops on the black mat.

Katagiri watches, then says, "Oh, yes, I once sweat very much when I was a young man and had to go to dokusan with an important zen teacher who visited the temple. It was pretty difficult. But it's okay."

I blurt out, "I'd like to be your student!"

"Accepted!" That's the end of it.

"Now," he says, "I would like to tell you an old story. Please tell me what you think.

"When Tozan Zen Master was still a student, he was asked by his master to show his spiritual power. He stood up and walked out of the room, saying, 'So long!' "

Katagiri pauses. I want to respond, but my mind's a blank.

Before I can say anything, Katagiri adds, "Later, when he was a master, Tozan had a disciple who left the monastery to go to a hut in the forest. For a while this student came back to the monastery for food, but one day he stopped. Tozan sent for him to ask how he got his food. The student said that heavenly beings brought him food. Tozan told him he had a crack in his practice through which the heavenly beings could appear. But the student still stayed alone practicing in his hut, and finally one day he was enlightened. To express deep appreciation of his student's understanding, Tozan went into the forest and burned the hut.

"Now, why do you think Tozan burned the student's hut?"

I say nothing, but I'm thinking, "He's already got my number. He knows I avoid the ceremonial practices at the Zen Center. He knows I disappear into the mountains in the summer." I say slowly, "Well, I guess Tozan wants to stop his student from having a practice all by himself, so he gets rid of the hut."

Roshi says, "Oh, but he burned the hut as the student's reward for becoming enlightened. But it is true that individual practice is not usually our practice."

"Well," I think, "I'm not exactly being told what to do here. In the first story, Tozan expresses his enlightenment by walking away from the master. Remember how careful Suzuki Roshi was when you asked him whether you ought to practice by a strict schedule?" Still, the hint seems clear. My independence is a roadblock. "Well," I ask, "was it wrong for Tozan's student to go into the woods to practice alone?"

"It doesn't make sense to call it wrong. But remember, in our practice it is not important to meet heavenly beings. Our practice is very ordinary."

I nod.

In our first meeting as student and teacher, Katagiri Roshi lays his finger on the rift that will always divide us. I refuse the traditions of Japanese zen—shaven heads, robes, chanting, a Japanese name, ordinations. And I refuse the informal American culture that grows up alongside—loose black shirts and pants, military haircuts, vegetarianism, whispered voices, even an American speech that begins to drop its articles, its the's and a's, in imitation of the Japanese teachers. I'm not into zen, I often grumble to myself, to stir up my family or be noticed on the street. I've done that already.

I ask, "Roshi, sometimes I wonder if Soto zen is clearly focused on enlightenment. I wonder if it isn't like all the other religions—really worried about keeping itself going, getting people to accept its doctrines and call themselves zen students, or Buddhists, or whatever.

"For example, I'm confused by all the concern about the zen lineage and so-called transmission of the Buddha's mind from master to disciple. It seems pretty exaggerated. Do you really think that some magic happened when Baker Roshi was given transmission and installed as abbot, that something actually passed to him that he wouldn't otherwise have? Now, Professor Conze points out that Bodhidharma is a mythical figure, that he didn't really exist. So in reality there was no continuous, direct transmission of the Buddha's mind from India to China to Japan."

Roshi looks taken aback. His eyebrows contract and his lips purse in distaste. With mild indignation, he protests, "Oh, Bodhidharma is very important. He really existed. That is very certain."

As a Westerner raised in the tradition of free inquiry, I'm about to press the issue—but go silent. Does he find the question barbaric? Suddenly I see in him the Christian missionary, sorely pained that his

American Indian convert, puzzled again, asks once more what's wrong with the Great Spirit and why only the Jesus god can save.

We sit without words for a moment. My question drifts in some huge gulf between our cultures. I don't want to offend him. I've just become his student.

Then he looks at me quite seriously and says softly, "The only thing I have to teach is emptiness. Just emptiness. That is all. That is the most important thing. That is really our way."

"So nothing else," I ask, "Is part of this teaching?"

"No," Roshi says. "Emptiness is the whole teaching. Emptiness is complete."

We go on to discuss my dilemmas, my connection to friends and family in Minneapolis, my love for the mountains and wilderness, my teaching and study, my drive for enlightenment—the many rooms Dick Baker warned me against. Sitting quietly, Katagiri listens to all this, then says finally, "Don't worry about zen now. Just finish your studies. That is very important. It is hard to chase two rabbits at the same time."

"No, no," I say, shocked at this suggestion. "I must do zazen, too!"

Roshi says nothing.

Driving back up the coast to San Francisco, I mull over this exchange. Is Roshi pushing me to give up one or the other? I know I must practice zen. I want enlightenment. I want to be a master of meditation, a zen master. But I know also I must finish my studies, or voices will whisper that zen is the latest excuse, another escape from fears of inadequacy, a final failure of nerve.

And soon, I tell myself, the academy will need my zen training— and my Ph.D. It can't forever ignore the existence of consciousness, of pure awareness itself, dismissing it as an inconvenience and embarrassment, as some curious epiphenomenon. Soon, surely, the universities will want professors whose training goes beyond the surface intellect, beyond the thought formations by which mere images of reality are constructed. And I'll have that training—along with the requisite Ph.D.

Then my generation will winnow religion for its fundamental truths. The chaff of zendos and ashrams, of Bibles and sutras, of black and orange robes, of shorn and shaven heads, will be blown to the four corners of the earth, with only hard, sweet kernels remaining to be gathered and ground and baked into exuberant bread.

As I enter the outskirts of San Francisco, I'm firmly resolved. Somehow, I'll fuse this Eastern practice of empty awareness to the rigorous intellectual structures of Western learning. Anything less is failure.

Later that spring I drive back down to Monterey to again urge the cause of zen students in Minneapolis. Sitting in the Katagiris' small living room, I try to persuade him.

"Roshi, it's a perfect time for you to move. Baker Roshi is taking care of the San Francisco Zen Center. Things seem to be going smoothly there—and you will always return to lead sesshins and practice periods. The midwest has many people interested in zen. Don't you think it's time for a teacher to come to the middle of the country? We call Minnesota the heartland."

"Yes," he says, "this may be a good time. But I have to think very carefully. I promised Suzuki Roshi that I would help take care of Zen Center. But I will think about it. I am very interested."

I'm encouraged, but I wonder if his interest is shared by his wife, Tomoe-san, who has brought us tea and now listens quietly to our conversation. Outside, their two little boys play in the warm sunshine.

"Tomoe-san," I say finally, "you have never been to Minneapolis. The winters are cold and full of snow, and the summers are much hotter than San Francisco. Yasuhiko and Ejyo will have to go to different schools and make all new friends. Do you really want to go?"

Tomoe-san looks at me brightly. "It is okay. Wherever *he* is," she says, laughing and pointing at Roshi, "I am okay."

Some weeks later, several women zen students from Minneapolis visit the Katagiris in Monterey, and upon my own return to Minneapolis in the early summer, I learn that finally he and his family have agreed to come.

Later that summer, Katagiri Roshi arrives in Minneapolis to lead a five-day sesshin. He and his family won't be able to settle here until late fall or winter. But we don't want to wait that long for a sesshin with our master. His small group is eager to practice hard.

The day before the sesshin begins, I pick him up from the family with which he's staying. As my parents are gone on vacation, I've offered to have the sesshin at my house. Roshi and I drive over so he can see the house and think about arrangements. After a brief tour of the rooms, I suggest that the large living room be cleared of all furniture, which can be stored in two bedrooms. He can sleep in my room. The rest of us, about eight men and women, will throw sleeping bags out on the floor—women in the living room, men in a basement room.

Then we sit down at the kitchen table to write out a daily schedule on a yellow legal pad I take from my mother's desk. Since I'll be the *doan*, the one who rings bells indicating the different events of the day, I watch carefully. He writes:

4:30	Rise—ring bell
5:00	Zazen
5:40	Kinhin
5:50	Zazen
6:30	Service
6:50	Breakfast
7:20	Break
7:35	Zazen
8:15	Kinhin
8:25	Lecture

At this point, I interrupt his writing. From past experience at sesshins, I know that breakfast never gets done on time and people line up, frustrated, trying to use the bathrooms during the short break afterward.

"Roshi," I suggest, "maybe we can allow more time for the break after breakfast. We'll have eight or nine people here, so we'll need time to use the bathrooms. Then the time for the next zazen might go forward to seven-forty or seven-fifty. That's easier for people to remember, anyway. It's kind of confusing to start things at thirty-five minutes past the hour."

Roshi pauses, looks at me questioningly, then says, "No, I think it is okay. It is not so bad even if people have to hurry a little bit." He turns back to the schedule and completes it. The last entry is

9:10   Bed

But I have several more improving ideas for the sesshin routine. As usual, the afternoon tea break is only twenty minutes long. The house is a block from Cedar Lake, which has lovely wooded pathways. "Roshi, you know it would be very good if people could have more time at the afternoon break. That would permit them to walk down to the lake, which is very beautiful. Probably some of the new students can use more time to stretch their legs, too."

"No, no," he says firmly, the corners of his mouth tightening down. "This is enough break."

I'm desperate to loosen the schedule. I'm afraid if things are too strict, we'll lose some of our present members, let alone attract more. One member has already repeated her therapist's horror at what she must endure during sesshins. The therapist asks how a practice that demands, and seems even to revel in, such self-inflicted pain can be anything but masochism.

Trying a new tack, I mention to Roshi a second member's wish to use work time to do something socially beneficial, some activity worthy in itself as well as helpful in making zen acceptable to the Minneapolis community. "She suggests we use the work period to gather litter along the lakeshore. I've got the plastic bags. It would be a very good and useful activity."

"Zen is really useless," says Roshi, chuckling. "It is not good for anything."

"But this schedule may be too hard for people, at least right now," I protest. "Why do we need such a strict, rigid schedule?"

At this, Roshi straightens up from the table. He says, curtly, "Yes, the schedule is strict. But it is not really so strict." He looks at me intently. "After all, we have vowed to save all sentient beings!"

Then relaxing, he says, "The sesshin is a wonderful opportunity for us. In sesshin, all we have to do is sit together. We can try to sit very hard." He smiles and makes a fierce twisting motion with his hands, as if wringing every last drop of water out of a washcloth. "Every human being has a certain smell, a kind of stinkiness. In sesshin, each person can squeeze out his stinkiness, maybe, even just for a little while."

It's the fall of 1972. The Katagiris arrive and we house them in a lower apartment in an old fourplex near the University of Minnesota. We convert an upstairs unit to a zendo. Next door is a huge old house in which three families that are deeply committed to Katagiri Roshi live communally. Now we must raise money, repair and redecorate, thread through tax proprieties, devise a political structure, and learn how to relate to the Roshi, his family, and each other.

The practice is strict. Roshi rises six days a week to sit two periods of zazen with us at five in the morning. Five nights a week he sits in the evening or gives a lecture or instruction. During the day he works on his lectures, meets with students, and occasionally gives a presentation to a high school or college class or a community group. Every month we have a two-day sesshin, and several times a year we sit for five to seven days.

In that first year, the founding members have meeting after meeting in the dining room of the big house next door to debate and approve the articles of incorporation and bylaws by which the new organization will become a nonprofit religious corporation. We meet evenings and Saturday and Sunday afternoons. We sit on straight-backed chairs around a large table drinking cups of strong black coffee. How shall we govern ourselves? Is the Roshi's word law? Or is this a congregational organization in which democracy rules? Katagiri has no hunger for power—he's deferential and gladly accepts the group's judgments about the new structure.

Most of us prefer a democratic, congregational form, but some argue that Roshi should make absolute decisions. He discourages this idea. One of us argues that the organization should make decisions only by consensus. This idea gains support, but several of us, including Bob Pirsig and his wife, vociferously disagree. Over more cups of coffee the debate rages, with Katagiri looking somewhat nonplussed, perched cross-legged on his straight-backed chair, cradling an empty coffee cup in his lap. Finally, shyly, he asks, "Can someone please explain this word 'consensus'? I don't understand."

Chuckling, I say, "Well, Roshi, it means that everyone on the new board of directors has to agree before we can do anything. And if we don't agree, we have to keep on having a meeting like this until everyone agrees. So things would be like this all the time."

"That's *not* a fair description," says the proponent, with rising irritation. "We're a spiritual community. Roshi, how can we maintain a sincere spirit if we don't fully work out our differences? It's essential that *all* of us be in agreement with steps we take."

"Oh," he says, raising his eyebrows, "Of course it is very important if we can all agree. Let's discuss some more."

Another hour of increasingly testy debate goes by. It's clear that there won't be consensus on the consensus proposal. Finally Roshi says, "Maybe it's not possible for us to go forward if one person can make us stop. I think maybe we shouldn't try this 'consensus.' " A vote is taken and majority rule is adopted for the normal actions of the board of directors. As the newly elected secretary of the soon-to-be incorporated Minnesota Zen Meditation Center, I'm pleased to record the decision.

The next year is wonderful. I marry Jeanne, a lovely young woman who also teaches at the college, and we move into a spacious apartment near the new Zen Center. My doctoral coursework is done. I'm closing in on the dissertation. And for the first time in my life I'm at the center of an organization, not standing outside with my nose pressed against the window. Roshi talks to me about everything—low water pressure in his apartment, health insurance policies, car repair, fund-raising, schools for his boys, buying a Zen Center building. I begin tutoring Roshi and Tomoe-san in English each week in their small apartment. Soon I come an hour early before his lectures to help with the English in his translations and commentaries. I'm proud to have this role. There are a dozen of us who have founded this organization and are involved in its activities almost daily. But somehow I feel I'm Roshi's right-hand man.

We have a picnic that first summer. Nancy Pirsig, a natural social director, organizes it. We'll celebrate our success as a new zen center at one of the city lakes. We bring our children, charcoal grills, and hot dogs (not everyone will eat them). We drink beer, play baseball, and behave as if we were normal Americans. Instead of wearing his usual robes, Katagiri Roshi shows up in a baggy pair of shorts. And he wears a white, round sailor cap—it hides his shaven head. He seems a teenage boy, happy and relieved of the burden of puzzled midwestern stares. We chuckle at his short bow legs, a legacy of some thirty years of cross-legged sitting.

Roshi and Tomoe, Bob and Nancy Pirsig, Jeanne and I, and several others sit together at a large picnic table. We eat brown rice and hot dogs on paper plates and drink beer in paper cups.

"Well, Roshi," asks Nancy, "how does it seem now that you've been in Minnesota for almost a year?"

"Oh," he says, smiling, "it's very nice. I think I'm very lucky to come here."

"But did you enjoy the winter?" someone asks, laughing.

"Oh, winter is pretty good," he says quizzically, raising his eyebrows. "I think that cold temperature is pretty good for us. Especially for Tomoe." He smiles at her.

"Oh," she says, "I get used to it. And the boys like very much to play in snow."

"I think," he says, "it is good to go away from San Francisco. San Francisco is a kind of paradise. It's by the beautiful ocean and the mountains, and it never gets very cold. It's a kind of paradise for spiritual practice, too. Many people are interested in religion. When I first came from Japan, I was very surprised. So maybe it's really too easy. I'm really glad to be here.

"But there is one problem in America. I can never get lazy. There is always some students interested in zen and crazy to sit every morning. Even when I am lazy and don't want to get up, I think, 'Oh, I must go. Someone will be there.' "

We all laugh at this, knowing Roshi never misses morning zazen unless he's sick. We can hardly imagine that he ever just wants to stay in bed.

Bob says wryly, "If it'll help, Roshi, I promise not to come to morning zazen next week."

"No, no, that's okay," Roshi says, shaking his head. "You better come, even if I am lazy."

"Now, tell me again," Nancy commands. "Why did Bodhidharma go to China? And why did Katagiri come to Minnesota?"

Roshi laughs delightedly and says nothing. We laugh, too. This is a standing joke we like to tease him with.

The conversation lags for a moment, and I offer to refill Roshi's paper cup.

"Oh, no, thank you, I'm okay," he says.

"It's a picnic," I say jovially. "Have some more."

"No, no," he says firmly, raising his hand palm upward in the zendo gesture of refusal for an offer of more food or drink. Somewhat chagrined, I nurse my own second beer.

Nancy says, "Roshi, Bob has an idea on the oryoki sets. We've found a potter who will make the bowls, but it sounds like we can't get the setsu sticks any time soon." The group has been eager to use traditional monastic eating bowls in the zendo. But we haven't been able to get the cleaning sticks that go with each set.

"Yes, that is our problem," says Roshi. "I wrote, but they are very slow in Japan."

"Well," says Bob, "we'll take care of that ourselves. I'll bring some power sanders to the Saturday work period, and we'll begin making them. It's simple enough."

"Oh," says Roshi, quite surprised. "So we can really make them ourselves? That would be wonderful."

"Sure," says Bob. "I've got some beautiful rosewood in the keys of a marimba I made as a kid in the fifth grade. It's a wonderful hard wood." He chuckles. "I never played it. It can reincarnate in setsu sticks. I'll cut out the basic blocks. Then in a few days we can shape and sand several dozen. That will complete the sets."

"Ah," says Roshi. "That will be very nice. Thank you very much."

"You're very welcome," says Bob. Then, with a twinkle in his eye, "But, you know, why stop there? Let's make our own chopsticks too. Poplar trees are the perfect wood, and we've got lots of them in Minnesota. And lots of free zen labor. We'll begin the Minnesota Zen Chopstick Company."

"Excellent," I say. "Why buy what we can make ourselves? We can recycle the leftover wood for toothpicks. What do you think, Roshi?"

Not quite sure whether his leg is being pulled, Roshi replies, "Oh, no, it's not really necessary that we make our own chopsticks. I think to make the setsu sticks will be enough."

"But Roshi," I say, "Bob can really do it. You should see the machine shop in his basement. He finds the dharma in his machine tools."

"Oh, yes," says Roshi, laughing, "the dharma is everywhere. But still, I don't think the zen center needs to be the factory for chopsticks. So please, don't let us make any chopsticks. It is enough if Bob can make us just the setsu sticks."

As the afternoon wanes, there's a baseball game, a mix of children and adults. We laugh at Roshi running the bases in his sailor cap and shorts. Then it's evening and everyone goes home. It's early for a Saturday. But the tone of the group is set by morning zazens that begin at five every day except Sunday.

It's lunchtime at one of the first sesshins held at the new zendo. We have our oryoki sets complete—each with utensils, including Bob Pirsig's setsu sticks, and three nesting pottery bowls, wrapped in a white cloth. The noon meal is the big one. We'll have spaghetti noodles for the large first bowl, salad for the second bowl, and some roasted nuts and raisins for the third small bowl. Eight of us sit cross-legged on the floor on our zafus. We form together a U shape around the room facing Roshi, who sits in front of an altar placed in the bay window of the little living room.

We anticipate the lunch prepared in the kitchen at the back of the apartment. We're solemn, grateful to cease zazen, even though we remain on our zafus while we eat. Our napkins are spread carefully on our laps, our bowls and chopsticks and spoons and setsu sticks placed before us with neat precision.

The bathroom, unfortunately, adjoins the living room across a small hall. A young woman struggles to use the toilet quickly and quietly and get back to her seat before lunch. As we sit in stoic silence, sounds reverberate embarrassingly through the silent room. Finally, with downcast eyes, she leaves the bathroom and returns to her seat.

The cook stands ready at the back of the room amid various pots. At the end of the meal chant, Roshi bows to the cook. The cook bows and walks in slowly, majestically, with the pot held at eye level. He halts before Roshi, then bows again. Roshi bows again in return. The cook sinks to his knees and raises up a tongsfull of spaghetti. Roshi bends calmly forward to receive noodles in his laquered priest's bowl. But the cook's hand keeps rising—there's no end to the noodles. Sticking together, the strands form a continuous rope.

The cook struggles for composure. I think, "My God, why didn't the idiot cut them into shorter lengths?" Determined, the cook rises from kneeling up to one foot—but the noodles rise as well. Higher and higher go his hands, but longer and longer grows the cable of noodles. Now the cook's arms are fully upraised and the noodles still descend into the pot. Paralyzed, none of us dares break protocol and run for a knife.

Then I hear muffled snorting. Across the room, Bob Pirsig's head is down, his stooped shoulders shaking with suppressed sobs of laughter, which occasionally explode past a hand pinching his nose and pressing his lips. I scrunch my eyes shut and breath hard into my stomach to keep from cackling myself.

It's the last day of the sesshin. Bob Pirsig and I are in the zendo drinking our coffee during the afternoon break that follows the work period. Most of the other students are in the kitchen. Two wait in line to get into the bathroom.

In an undertone, Bob hisses, "Just look at it!"

"What?" I ask, looking up from my coffee.

"You know," he says, "that thing." He jabs his finger toward the mokyugyo that arrived just days before to the delight, it seems, of all the students but us. It sits next to the doan's seat near the altar. The mokyugyo is a traditional percussion instrument made from wood. It is hollow and beaten with a small padded stick to establish a rhythm for the chants. Ours is the size and shape of a half-deflated soccer ball. A wide slit cut in one end allows the vibrations to come out. It sits, squat, on a little embroidered cushion.

Bob and I had objected to sending to Japan for it. Like me, he is afraid of making zen seem too strange and cultist in our native mid-west. Unlike those who have arrived from around the country, we have family, friends, and colleagues here who are intensely curious—and dubious—about this thing to which we're so deeply committed. It's hard enough to invite others to see us bowing and scraping and then on our haunches mouthing incomprehensible Sino-Japanese syllables. It is insult upon injury now to be seen following the beat of some strange, alien drum.

Taking a drink of coffee, I comment sourly, "Doesn't really have much of a sound, either, after all this trouble and expense to get the damn thing. You'd think it was the holy grail. All it does is make a 'thunk.'"

"I know," Bob grumbles. "It's a goddamned one-note marimba. When will they learn?" He returns to his coffee. "At least I got them to stop making that swill they called 'Tassajara coffee'—two thirds decaf and completely worthless."

"Yeah," I whisper, "for a long time I'd spend the first three days of a sesshin with a splitting headache. I thought it was just my bad karma."

The bell rings to call us back to zazen. We stand slowly and stretch. Then Bob's face breaks into a huge smile.

"You know," he whispers, gesturing at the mokyugyo, which seems to grin back at us, "the damn thing looks just like a pufferfish. On Saturday, I'll bring a tin of sardines. We'll slip it a few."

It's later that summer. I arrive at the Katagiri apartment below the zendo an hour before he's to give his Wednesday evening lecture. My job is to look over his translation of a text he'll discuss tonight.

Roshi and I sit in the small living room on zafus placed on either side of the coffee table. The surface is littered with texts in Japanese and Chinese. At hand are Japanese-Chinese and Japanese-English dictionaries. Tomoe-san quietly brings us each a cup of green tea. Roshi bows to his cup before picking it up and sipping. I follow suit.

He's presenting one by one the commentaries of Wanshi on various zen stories. His talk tonight is about Nansen and the cat. Our heads bowed over the table, I look at Roshi's rough translation. After adopting various suggestions on wording and sentence structure, he has a version:

> The monks of the east and west halls at Nansen's monastery are arguing over a cat. Disgusted, Nansen calls them together. Holding the cat and a sword, he threatens to kill it if they can't say something penetrating. Confused, the monks remain silent. Nansen slices the cat in two.
>
> Later that evening, Nansen's friend Joshu returns to the monastery and Nansen tells what happened. Without a word, Joshu places his sandals on his head and walks out. As he leaves, Nansen says, "If you had been there, the cat would be alive."

This is exciting. I've read this story again and again for years. It's always puzzled me. I ask, "But Roshi, why would there be such an argument between these two groups of monks? Were they arguing over who the cat belonged to? I don't understand why it was so important. Besides, I thought monasteries usually didn't have pets anyway."

"Oh, no," he says, "it was not about who owned the cat. In ancient time in China, whenever monks met each other—and the laymen, too, if they were really serious about Buddhism—wherever they met, on the stairs, in the hallway, they didn't just exchange greetings, saying, 'Good morning,' or 'Good afternoon.' They discussed some aspect of zen. They would discuss seriously with transparent sincerity. So I think this argument was about whether the cat had buddha nature. So, in these times, maybe you can understand how awful and how fierce this argument was."

"Ah," I say, "you know, it sounds like the arguments of the Christians. In Europe, century after century, they had many bloody wars."

"Oooh," says Roshi, his eyebrows upraised, "so you see how dangerous. Maybe you can see why Nansen cuts the cat."

"Yeah," I say, chuckling, "but some of your students are upset by the story. We're supposed to be compassionate. And most of the Americans are vegetarians. What do you think about Nansen killing this innocent cat?"

"Well, that is a big problem," Roshi replies. "Wanshi calls Nansen 'resourceful' and says, 'The resourceful man is beloved by everyone.' I'm not so sure about that word in English. But what if Nansen did nothing but talk to the monks? It is true that the cat dies. That is not so good. That doesn't show so much the buddha's compassion. That is why Joshu goes with his sandals on his head."

"That's never really made sense to me, Roshi," I say. "What's the point of walking out with his sandals on his head? Is Joshu saying he wants to keep his feet and head connected—that he doesn't want to end up like the cat, cut in two? Or is he simply showing that he's free from normal behavior like wearing sandals on your feet? Maybe he's saying that what Nansen did is okay, that they're both zen masters and therefore free from following the precepts."

"No, no, not free from precepts, not bound by precepts. But Nansen is the 'resourceful' man. He acts in the moment, here and now. Maybe right, maybe wrong. Maybe if you have a child, it does something very wrong. You give it big blows, even before you think. I don't think you give big blows to your daughter, to your son, after thinking whether it is good or bad. Whatever you think, you already hit. Certain circumstances require some intimate, immediate response, regardless of whether you like or dislike. A resourceful man is like Nansen, who gives big blows suddenly to sons or daughters with Buddhist compassion in order to wake them.

"The more you love your children, the more you act strongly. There is no space to think of what to do or to think whether it is good or bad. Nansen's behavior is really like this. Nansen gave big blows to his monks with his big hands, his big buddha hands. That way is really beyond criticism whether it is good or bad."

Chuckling, Roshi smiles at me. "Maybe you heard, Erik, that one time in San Francisco my boy lit fires to the screens? The Japanese screens burn very easily. I couldn't imagine such a little boy trying to do something wrong, making a big fire. Maybe the water in his well is one foot deep, but his waves are very big. Even first-grade children create their own troubles."

"So, Roshi, did you hit him?"

He laughs. "No, I didn't hit him. But I was very upset. Tomoe-san was very upset. So we were very strong in anger."

"But Roshi, I'm still confused about Joshu putting his sandals on his head. It still seems to me like he approves of Nansen and he shows it by also doing something unconventional—like a hippie."

"Oh, no, not like the hippies. The hippies in San Francisco did anything they want without thinking and said they were free. Then they come to the Zen Center and think they really know Buddhism. That is a big confusion."

"So why do you think Joshu puts his sandals on his head?"

"'Oh, I think he puts the sandals on his head and says to Nansen, 'Sandals are not something to put on your head. When you use the sandals as they are in the proper way, the sandals will be really alive in the proper way.' That is Joshu's sugggestion. So it also says, 'Why don't you think a little carefully how to use the cat's life—life itself. When you use the cat's life as it is, cat will really be alive.' Then Nansen understands so well Joshu's suggestion. That is why Nansen said, 'If you had been here, the cat might actually have been saved.'"

"Ah," I say, "that's wonderful. I never could make sense out of those sandals. So Joshu lets Nansen know that what he did missed the full possibility of—what?—of shaking up the monks as well as respecting the cat—of affirming life itself in the cat as well as in the monks."

"Yes, maybe so," says Roshi. "But it's still not a criticism of Nansen. Nansen acts. He just acts. He is the resourceful man. But maybe Nansen should think carefully a little more. Maybe he should think more carefully how to use the cat as it is. I think Dogen really knows this."

"Oh," I say, "what does Dogen say?"

"Dogen is very sharp. Nansen cuts the cat in two with one stroke of the sword. But Dogen says Nansen should cut the cat in *one* with one stroke of the sword." Roshi brings his hand down swiftly in a short sword stroke, hissing between his teeth and tongue: "*Ssshhhooo!*"

"It means you should know what is the difference between the cat's life, or Nansen's life, or a monk's life. They are different. They are all the same. Still, a certain situation requires an immediate response."

"Cut the cat in *one*," I say. What does *that* mean?"

"Ah," says Roshi, looking at his watch. "We have only ten minutes before the lecture. Now, do you think when I translate Wanshi's word as 'resourceful,' it is good? What do you feel by that word 're-sourceful'?"

"Oh," I say, "it's perfect for Nansen. It suggests energy, vigor, and being ready for anything that happens."

"Yes, that is right," says Roshi, finishing his tea.

He bows to me, I bow in return, and we rise to go into the zendo for lecture.

Aches in my knee and under my shoulder blade rise up into conscious-ness, bringing me back to the Crag. It's afternoon, the sun falls more than halfway down the sky. I've known these pains—old, familiar friends—for thirty years. They alert me to bad posture and to tensions I carry. And they force me awake.

"Athletes are plagued with pain too," I think. "They get injuries that dog them the rest of their lives. But that's okay. People accept it. No one expects a champion football player to be pain free. He buys a restaurant and gets prescription dope.

"But how do you explain to people about the pain in zazen? They want meditation cheap—an overstuffed chair. They want Enlighten-ment Lite.

"Zazen calls the great bluff of the universe. Thoreau went to Walden to discover if existence is mean—or sublime. Zazen displays each mo-ment freed from the clamor of human action. It's a mind stone. A touchstone. I strike this stone and see how much base metal mixes with pure gold.

"I just sit still. I see what's here. Without Dogen's steady, immobile sitting, this is something that simply can't happen. Just as without years of disciplined motion, a dancer can't move beautifully."

And now, indeed, sitting here on the crag. I see etched in con-sciousness, moment by moment, exactly those things that would move me off my seat. There's sharp stinging in the scrape on the sole of my foot. My bladder has filled and feels dangerously taut. Stubbornly, I remember Suzuki and Katagiri's words: "It's good if you don't move at all."

I sit on for long minutes. The ache under my left shoulder blade is constant, the muscle beginning to knot. The pain in my knees, especially the left, is sharp, agonizing.

A voice whispers, "It's okay to quit. What's the big deal?"

But I think to myself, "No, I won't move!"

Long minutes go by and suddenly it's huge. My bladder seems bursting, the pain in my knees monstrous, and sturdy doubts now shoulder into my mind. "Look at you," they say. "How weak you are! How endless your thoughts! How useless your pain! You'll never come to the light."

Fiercely, now, every muscle knotted, every fiber of my mind stretched to cracking, I think, "No, I will not move!" And I'm emptied of thought. There's only pure, clarified struggle—a surging, relentless flood of mind energy fiercely demanding that I abandon my seat. With a supreme effort of will by which I repulse it, instant by instant, and sit on.

I sit. I sit. Then suddenly tension is gone and I'm light, airy. Every motion of my body and mind is clear, transparent, arising in vast stillness.

I'm a dancer, dancing in motionless motion.

Calm now, relaxed, I unwind my legs, stretch, sigh, and carefully stand up, feeling the dark pain under my shoulder blade and in my knees break and diminish. Attentive to my bladder, I take a dozen slow steps down off the Crag and let fly into a crevice between two black rocks. Then I swing my arms from side to side and finally do a series of standing stretches, bending my spine slowly, carefully, in each direction as far as it will go.

I look for the raven. Shaken by afternoon breezes that buffet the Crag, he clings, determined, to his branch. A gust yanks at my hat, which suddenly flies off my head and sails down fifty feet into the grass.

"Come back, come back," I yell joyfully, then pick up small rocks and test my aim. Out of a dozen tries, only one gets near the mark. I fire again and this time dent the crown.

I step easily with bare feet down through my rocks to pick it up, then head down, absorbed in each step, make my barefooted way back up to my seat on the Crag.

11

Doubt

IT'S A SUNNY, SUBZERO LATE AFTERNOON IN December 1975. Roshi, Bob and Nancy Pirsig, and I are walking through an old Spanish colonial mansion on the east shore of Lake Calhoun. The house is a wreck, most recently used as a halfway house for addicts. The windows leak, the walls are peeling, the ceilings show irregular circles of water damage.

Bob Pirsig's book has become a best-seller. He and Nancy have offered to donate twenty thousand dollars toward the purchase of a building. After endless discussions of options, the group is ready to make a decision.

As the others wander through the empty house, I step out to a sun porch that overlooks the lake and sit on a low radiator beneath the front windows. Subzero air drifts through cracks in the glazing, chilling my knees. The sun sinks in the west across the lake, shimmering over a mile of crusty, wind-sculpted snow, then filling the white, plastered room with glowing pinks and golds. I know we'll buy this building.

It's the spring of 1976. Marion has arranged to have a dance at the old firehouse near Seven Corners. We're raising funds toward the purchase of the house on Lake Calhoun. Having a dance feels like a return to the sixties, the good times of Country Joe and the Fish and the Avalon Ballroom. I sell tickets to skeptical old friends. I want them to understand. I want them to know I've not graduated from drug burnout to a religious cult. I want them to know zen is not about rigidity and puritanism. This, I tell them, will be a very good time.

The band is fine. The firehouse is crowded with zen students, their friends, and folks from the neighborhood who just want to dance on a Saturday night.

Around ten o'clock, an old buddy who teaches with me at the college, another hippie Ph.D. from Seven Corners, appears at my elbow. We've drunk and doped together for years. He points up a stairway and motions for me to come. Puzzled, I follow him. At the top, on a dark balcony overlooking the dance floor, he pulls out a joint and lights up. The flare of his lighter illuminates our faces, and I see dancers on the floor looking up curiously.

I hesitate. This isn't exactly what I'm here for. But it is a Seven Corners dance. Besides, I'm not a zen puritan. I didn't sign on to achieve some cult purity. I hate sanctimonious stuff about the evils of drugs. I wouldn't even be here if it weren't for psychedelics.

It's a moment of truth. Roshi and Tomoe-san have just left the party. With a broad smile and a flourish of his hand, delighted to put me in this bind, my friend graciously reaches me the joint. To appreciative stares from some of the unregenerate zen hippies on the dance floor, I—a member of the board and recording secretary of the Minnesota Zen Meditation Center—toke up.

At the lecture on the following Saturday morning, I'm surprised when Roshi begins discussing drugs. He names no names nor mentions time or place, but he expresses special concern about marijuana.

"I know that some people use the drug marijuana. But that is not part of real practice. That is only self-indulgence. It is delusion. So think carefully about this."

As I learn he will often do, Roshi offers his criticism impersonally, in public, at a lecture.

It's an evening a few weeks later. Tonight Bob Pirsig gives a benefit lecture to raise money for the purchase of the Calhoun house. The members of the Zen Center have been busy for weeks making arrangements and getting out publicity. I've driven all over town offering flyers to local businesses for their bulletin boards and tacking them up on telephone and light poles. The tickets are very expensive, but Bob is a phenomenon now. Advance sales are brisk. And what, we all wonder, will he say to the crowd?

As my wife and I enter the Children's Theatre, a new hall connected to the Minneapolis Institute of Arts, we're delighted. We see city officials, state legislators, even the Mayor and Speaker of the House, and a host of other well-dressed men and women. At last, I think, we'll get some broad interest and support for the Minnesota Zen Meditation Center.

Bob's talk works. He discusses zen and zen meditation in simple, compelling terms, congratulates the Twin Cities for having attracted a genuine meditation master, and begs for community support. Though he talks for over an hour, the audience is intent, absorbed. He concludes by telling the story of Bodhidharma, punctuated with slides of ink drawings—Bodhidharma with various angry scowls, brows beetling over his glaring eyes. "This is what happened to *him*," Bob says, "when he sat and stared at the wall for nine years." The audience chuckles. "We do it for two or five or seven days in a row several times a year. And here is me after five or six days of sitting!" Bob flashes on a picture of Bodhidharma with a huge head that threatens to topple him to the ground. The audience roars.

After the crowd has left, my wife and I congratulate Bob on the talk. Flushed, exhausted, he grips his fists in front of his chest, a few inches apart, as if forcing two things together. "It was a long talk," he says with a fierce chuckle, "but I crossed the wires and gave them full voltage. I think I shorted out their circuits. I think they got it!"

It's 1977. I go to the Katagiris' to work with Roshi on a lecture. They live in an apartment we've made on the second and third floors of the remodeled Calhoun mansion. In the last year, I feel his growing impatience with my tutoring. I know visitors to lectures are at times completely confused by his words. Of course, some students think the problem is that they're not sufficiently advanced. But working closely with him, I know he often can't put Japanese into accurate English. "At least," I growl to myself, "let's get the paradoxes translated clearly—even if they don't have solutions."

Today he's preparing to lecture on Hyakujo and the fox. Tomoe-san shows me into his study, a back bedroom on the second floor.

We bow. I sit down across from him at his big desk on the floor. He shows me working notes in which he's translated the story. With some help in searching for English words and reworking awkward phrases, he puts together a narrative:

> An old man has been attending Hyakujo's lectures. One day he stays behind.
>
> Hyakujo asks, "Who are you?"
>
> The old man replies, "Once in the time when the Kashyapa Buddha preached, I was the abbot here. Then one of my students asked me, 'Is the enlightened man bound by the law of causation?'"

"Now," says Roshi, "I'm not sure how to say the answer of the old man. He says, maybe like this, 'There is no result from the law of causation.'"

"Well," I say, "that doesn't make it very clear. What does he mean that there is no result?"

"He means," says Roshi impatiently, "that he is not controlled by causation. He thinks that maybe he's free from any causation. It's a ridiculous answer, of course. All human beings arise in this world of conditions."

"So," I say, "the old man thought that his enlightenment, or what he thought was his enlightenment, meant that he was really no longer a part of the human world, that he was beyond it, or above it?"

"Yes," says Roshi. "Is it better if I say that the old man says he has no *influence* from the law of causation?"

"Yeah," I say. "I think that works better."

"Okay," says Roshi, blowing out his breath, "I will write down that the old man answers his monk's question, 'There is no influence from the law of causation.' Now I want to think about the rest of the story." Roshi and I again bend over his notes and, with some further rewording and rephrasing, complete the narrative:

The old man tells Hyakujo Zen Master that he has been punished for this foolish answer by being reborn for five hundred rebirths as a fox. And he says to Hyakujo, "Please give me an illuminating remark."

And Hyakujo says, "No obscurity in the law of causation." At these words, the old man is enlightened.

"Okay," says Roshi, looking up from his notebook hopefully, "do you think the students will understand this English?" Then smiling, "Maybe it will not be so easy to understand the story."

Hesitantly, I say, "Well, I am still a little worried about that last answer." I run my finger along the line, reading aloud, "No obscurity in the law of causation." "Can you say some more about that? What does it mean that there's no obscurity in causation? Causation is not necessarily something that is or is not obscure. I'm not clear about that."

Grimly, I think to myself, "Why go through this whole story if the punch line just claims to dissolve obscurity by saying something isn't obscure. There's got to be more to it than that."

With rising irritation, glancing at his watch, Roshi says, "Don't you think the students will get some feeling from these words, some taste of the story? Maybe it will not be so clear. But I think they will get some feeling."

"Sure," I say, "but often they go away confused." I hesitate uneasily, remembering the enthusiastic audience at Pirsig's fund-raiser a year ago. Many of those curious strangers have come to the Zen Center, once or twice, and never returned. "I mean, they get confused not by the difficulty of the koan or of zen, but they get confused because they can't really understand the English. When you just say there's 'no obscurity' in causation, that's what we call begging the question."

"What is exactly 'beg the question'?" Roshi asks, puzzlement on his face.

"Well, I guess that's kind of off the point," I say. "What I mean is, Hyakujo seems just to give an answer like, 'Don't be confused, be clear,' to the old man. What else does the original seem to say?"

Roshi looks back over his text. "Well," he says, "it means something like he is neither caught by causation or free from causation. He is just *in* causation. To say he is caught or he is free is something extra. Maybe it's good to say he is 'one' with causation."

"Ah," I say, brightening. "That sounds fine. That helps me, anyway. You know, I think it's very important that the translations not only be accurate but also be in powerful English. I've seen some of the early translations of the sutras. It's hard to get through them. They're dull. They don't move the reader. The language has to have fire."

"Yes, maybe so," says Roshi briskly. "Now it is time for lecture. Thank you very much for your help." He bows, I bow, and we rise to go.

It's fall. My wife and I have just returned from the mining claim on Flute Reed Creek. I begin to feel guilty about these trips. I encouraged Roshi to come to the midwest. He never takes a vacation. Yet I go away for two months every summer. Is my time in wilderness only self-indulgence? To me it seems deeply spiritual and grounding. Am I obligated to be here at the Zen Center all the time, too? Roshi seems to think so, although he says nothing directly.

After the Saturday schedule of zazen, breakfast, lecture, and work, I walk upstairs to the Katagiris' apartment at the Calhoun house. We chat, standing at the door.

He asks, "How was your vacation out west?" I'm distressed by what seems his pointed emphasis of the word *vacation*.

"Oh, it was good, thank you," I say. "But you know, it's not exactly a vacation. It's a lot of work. The cabin needs lots of repairs, and we spend time carrying backpacks far into the mountains. It seems important to me to know the mountains. I feel something very deep there."

"Oh, yes," he says. "*Vacation* is very good for human beings. I'm glad you had a good time. And how is Jeanne?"

"She's good," I say. "But she's ready to be back in Minneapolis. I wonder when you would like me to come again to work on English?"

"I think," Roshi says slowly, "I don't want to have any more tutoring right now with my English. Thank you very much."

"Oh," I say, surprised and hurt. "Well, that's fine. Just tell me and I'll be happy to help again anytime."

"Yes, I will tell you."

"Thank you," I say.

"Thank you very much," he says, bowing.

I bow and leave.

It's a Saturday afternoon in the early spring of 1978. After the morning schedule of zazen, lecture, work, and lunch, Roshi invites me upstairs for tea. We sit on the couch in the living room and Tomoe brings in cups and a teapot. We chat for a few minutes. Then Tomoe says excit-ɪ ıllʏ, "Ɍ̣ɔɟɭıl ʌʌɭʌ I ɟɦıɪɟɭ ıɑ̃ʌˡıɪ boyıɴɢ ʌ ʌɪɛw ʋuı. Ḷ̌ıłlı, mıɪyɦr ıᴛ ıɪ possible you can help us?"

"Why, of course. That's great," I say. "Do you want another Datsun? Or maybe a Toyota? They're supposed to be very good Japanese cars."

Roshi says with a twinkle, "Oh, we don't want the Japanese car. We want a big car. What do you think about Chevrolet cars?"

I'm surprised. Finally, Americans are worrying about dependence on fossil fuels and the extravagance of Detroit's dinosaurs. And I know how thin is the shoestring on which the Katagiris live. They're frugal in everything, from both habit and necessity.

"Well," I think, "Detroit has done some downsizing. And with two boys, I bet the Katagiris are sick to death of that little car of theirs. What an adventure. To come to America and finally get a big Ameri-ʟʌıı ʟʌı!"

"A Chevrolet might be fine," I say. "What can I do to help?"

"Well," says Roshi, "it was very confusing for us when we went to the place where they sell cars." Roshi's eyes get large. "And they are very expensive. But maybe there are some that are not so expensive."

"Oh, I think so," I say. "I'll do some checking. It's easy for me. You want four doors, of course. It'll be easier with the boys."

"Oh, that would be very good," says Tomoe.

"And how about color?" I ask, smiling.

"Maybe we can get red?" asks Roshi, tentatively.

"Why, I think so. Certainly, if we order one. I'll call around today and let you know what I've found out tonight."

As I leave, I promise myself that I'm going to get them a big, red, four-door American car, and I'm going to get them the lowest price in town.

After endless head knocking with car salesmen, both over the phone and at several car lots, I've worked out a deal with a Chevy dealer on Lake Street.

It's a Friday afternoon. Tomoe, Roshi, my wife, and I sit in the sales office. The four-door red car with desired accessories at the cheapest price in the state of Minnesota has just been delivered. Foster, the new car sales representative, is a middle-aged man whose red face and fat neck seem painfully squeezed by the collar of his sparkling white shirt. He eyes me balefully. On the phone earlier in the day, he assured me that I'd stolen his and the company's profits on this one.

I'm delighted. Tomoe and Jeanne have worked on the Katagiri's budget so the car is affordable. It's done. Sitting at the desk across from Foster, papers spread out between them, Roshi reaches in his sleeve for his checkbook.

Then Foster, handing Roshi a pen across the desk, casually interposes, "Now, Pastor Katagiri, there is one detail. I hate to bring this up, but we've just now had a price increase come through. We weren't expecting this, of course, total surprise to us, but I am going to have to get an additional two hundred and twenty–five dollars on your car. I know you'll understand that we're in the automobile business to serve customers, but we can't *lose* money and stay in business. You'll notice too that this kind of unfortunate situation is covered in our purchase agreement. I'd like to, but there's really nothing I can do at this point."

"Goddamn it," I sputter, coming up to my feet, "why didn't you say so on the phone? This is absolutely ridiculous. I want your manager in here. You haul us all down here and . . ."

Roshi raises his hand and gently waves the pen. "It's okay," he says quietly. Then he adds, with a touch of pride, "We can do that. Don't worry about it, Erik." He opens his checkbook on the desk, saying, "Now, show me how much."

Foster smiles at me.

In less than an hour, the Katagiris drive off in their large, red, four-door American car.

It's early summer, another late Saturday afternoon. Tomoe serves us tea upstairs in the living room. As we sit on the couch, Roshi pulls out a brochure describing a meeting of Buddhist teachers in San Francisco. All the heavies are to be there, mostly Asian men. Dick Baker, of course, is included. "Roshi should be teaching him!" I think.

"Are you going to go?" I ask innocently.

"No, they didn't send me an invitation," he says.

"I see," I say.

"Oh, it's not important," he says. Then after some talk about the various roshis and roshi wannabes, he sighs, "Sometimes I just wish I were swimming in the big ocean."

"Well," I ask, "where is the big ocean?"

"Yes, that is always the question," he replies, softly, sadly.

It's the late seventies. I'm almost forty. My wife is pregnant with our first child. As usual, I do the annual seven-day sesshin scheduled between Christmas and New Year's. About twenty of us are sitting.

It's the sixth day. Snow lies deep outside and now Canadian high pressure has brought bright, clear skies and crackling below-zero temperatures. The zendo is cold, especially at five in the morning. I wear a heavy sweater and long johns under my wool pants.

Now, after fifteen years of practice, I can minimize the pain in my knees and back, but there's always the mind. I was sleepy in the first days of the sesshin. Now, as I wake up, I fight distraction and endless mind wandering. Each day has betrayed my lack of attainment. Fifteen years and no enlightenment. Will this work ever be done?

After a period of zazen in the midafternoon, the doan strikes the little bell. We all rise for ten minutes of kinhin, slow walking meditation. What a relief to straighten the aching knees, change the posture of the back and neck, just to stand up. Winter sunlight slants into the room. Roshi is upstairs holding dokusan.

After seven days of silence, we're seasoned, calm. We flow around the perimeter of the room, hands folded at the solar plexus, eyes dropped at a forty-five-degree angle onto the oak floor ahead. We're aware of each silent person, each body and mind. We don't look at each other, but we know, we can feel, as each passes through the peripheral vision, how she is doing, how he is doing.

Oh, this poor one, this little sad one went down and cried in the basement during afternoon break for the first two days. She seems okay now, though subdued—a bit pale and wan. I don't even know her name yet. I heard it at work meeting but forgot it. My body becomes firm but yielding, welcoming, as she passes through my vision at the center of the room. "Hang in there. Don't give up," I silently telegraph.

And this one is still tired—this one who kept nodding at five in the morning beside me, head sinking down, down, then jerking awake; then down, down, again jerking awake. Once he hit the top of his head on the wall with a thump. Even when Roshi makes an occasional round during zazen with his roshi's stick, sharply striking sleepy sitters twice on each shoulder, within a minute this sleepy one is nodding again. For the first two days it irritated me. And on the morning of the third day during the first period of zazen, Roshi, patience frayed, leapt from his seat screaming, "Wake up now! Wake up! Wake up!" and hammered the back of the poor sleepyhead with his roshi's stick in hard, crackling blows. Now I feel sorry for him. I know his frustration and struggle. He's a beginner. I admire that he sticks with it and will finish.

And this one. She's fiercely determined and tight as a drum. She hissed a correction at me five days ago in the kitchen. I'd failed to bow to the kitchen altar before helping to serve lunch. "Don't bug me with your trip," my eyes shouted back. But now it's okay. "Be strict. Be fierce," I silently encourage.

This one, he's struggling with his divorce. What hell to be here thinking about money and kids and a life falling apart! He came any-way. "Hang in there, old man," shouts my body, as the periphery of my vision caresses his, and we pass each other slowly near the altar.

Then it's my turn for dokusan. I go upstairs, worrying, wondering about my lack of progress, my endless compromises among teaching, wilderness, family, friends, and zen.

With a bow at the door, I enter Roshi's upstairs study, then make three bows to the floor. Roshi, seated on the floor on his cushion, returns them. I sit wearily on the round black cushion that faces him a few feet away, carefully adjusting my posture, continuing in silence for many minutes until he asks, "Do you have some question?"

"Oh, yes," I say. "I'm just not getting anywhere in my practice. I try to come to zazen every day, and I sit all the sesshins, but it seems like nothing's happening. Then at school I'm under pressure all the time. You really can't do a good job when you're teaching as many classes and students as they give us, and the next thing I know I'm angry at students who don't do their work and still want good grades. Then I get home and my wife's pregnant and, of course, she needs time. And we have to do different things to fix up the house before the baby arrives."

"At school," Roshi offers, "when you feel distracted, you can just sit for a few minutes quietly at your desk in your office and let your mind come to rest. That may help you."

"Yeah," I say, "I do that sometimes, and I can try to do it some more. But how can I use the Zen Center to deepen my practice more?"

Roshi frowns, the corners of his mouth draw down, and he says, "That is maybe the question of a Pratyeka Buddha. Maybe you should ask how you can *make use of yourself* at the Zen Center to deepen your practice!"

"Zap!" I think. "That wasn't really such an innocent question. Usually he's not so attentive to the nuances of English."

"Yes, okay," I say, "it's not that I just want to use the Zen Center, but I guess what I can't seem to deal with right now is that my whole life seems like a distraction, like it's constantly blocking me. Sometimes I just want to get rid of it. I wish I could focus completely on zazen. I know I can't do it now, but wouldn't I make faster progress if I just gave up everything and did nothing but zazen?"

Roshi explodes. I've never seen him so angry. Though one hand still rests lightly in his lap on the palm of the other hand, thumb tips lightly touching in the Buddha's mudra, he hisses, "*That* is a very stupid question!"

Stung, I shoot back, "Okay, if that's a stupid question, tell me what is a *smart* question."

Steely now, Roshi looks me in the eyes and says with quiet contempt, "That is *also* a very stupid question."

Stumped, furious, I sit for a few minutes, heart pumping, mouth bitter with adrenaline, determined not to say one single word more. I make my bows, Roshi quietly returns them, and I return to the zendo to sit.

Walking down the carpeted stairs, resentment floods me. So this is what I get for all my efforts and my sincere questions—a slap in the face. A goddamn slap in the face! If I'm not going through all this to get enlightened, what am I doing it for?

Back at my seat, carefully adjusting my posture to keep pain evenly distributed among my spine, ankles, and knees, the words return. *"That is a very stupid question!"*

"Oh, fuck you!" I fume to myself. "So you don't like my quarrels over new ceremonies that drive people away. So you're disgusted that I don't accept even the lay ordination. Damned if I'm going to wear that ridiculous black ceremonial bib around my neck and get a Japanese name.

"Yeah, sure, I should've told eighty-year-old Uncle Albert over bourbon and lutefish on Christmas Eve, 'Oh, Albert, by the way, I'd prefer it if you didn't call me Erik anymore. My Buddhist name is Tofu-kuku.' It was bad enough to put him through a Buddhist wedding ceremony."

Finally the period is over. We all rise slowly, bow, fluff our cushions, and begin walking our slow circle around the room. I notice the muffled voices of Roshi and another student penetrating the thick hardwood floor above. I hear his laughter, then the student's, quieter, subdued, and I smile.

"Erik, wake up," I say to myself. "Your dilemma is repetitive and boring."

Passing the altar, I slow almost to a standstill, my foot creeping forward only a few inches with each step. I want to enjoy the Christmas cactus that Tomoe-san places there every year. My eyes linger on the gorgeous red explosion, blossoms tumbling in arcs off the oak altar top. Christmas sesshin after Christmas sesshin, I savor this cascade of red, this contrast to black mats and round black cushions, to the polished oak floor, to the austere thing we do here. Today, in midstep, drawing near, thinking of Christmas and the Christ child, I resist an impulse to fall down on my knees and worship.

Outside, northwest winds blow over the mile of frozen lake. Subzero gusts rattle the old ill-fitting casement windows and send cold drafts billowing along the floor. Inside, we twenty sitters hear the frustrated grind of a failing car starter motor. Listening, despite our aching knees and backs and necks, we're grateful to be doing nothing and going nowhere. The motor pulses slower and slower. Then silence.

We sit. We sit. We sit. It's now after dinner, the last period of zazen. "Well," speaks a wry voice in my head, "did you take all this trouble to get your own personal zen master living in Minneapolis and then expect him to kiss your ass?"

"No, of course not," I think. "But don't I deserve a little sympathy and support after all the years of hard practice, all the time and money I've donated to zen?"

"Oh, come on," says the voice, "shut up, Storlie. Don't take yourself quite so seriously. Maybe it's time for you to burn down your little hermit's hut. And by the way, to hell with Roshi, too. He's got his own problems."

My left knee, the site of an old cartilage surgery, aches with a fierce burning. Soon pain drives all thought clean out of my head. Maybe I'd better change position, ease up on that place.

"No, to hell with it.

"Remember what Roshi says about sesshin: 'It's like putting a snake in a tube. For a little while, anyway, the snake cannot make a choice—it can only be straight.'

"Remember what he says about sitting: 'Just keep your mind on the mat.' "

So I sit! I sit! I sit! Hammer blows to the chisel, chisel biting the mind stone, again! again! again! Every nerve, every fiber in my body glows with a fierce concentration that devours the pain in my knees. The palms of my hands, the soles of my feet vibrate with fire. My eyes glare at the line where the baseboard meets the floor. My skull fills with painful, concentrated energies begging for release, yet suddenly gleeful, awake, watching themselves.

The bell rings. The day is over.

Slowly, I pull on coat, hat, mittens, and boots and walk out into a star-studded twenty-below night.

At a two-day sesshin later that winter, Roshi asks during dokusan, "How is your life now? Is it okay?"

"Well," I say, "things seem to be going a little better. You know, you always say enlightenment is like an eel. You grab it, and suddenly it's gone through your fist. I'm getting a little better at doing all the things I have to do without feeling so frustrated, just doing each thing with full attention. And I've tried to take time at work sometimes to calm my mind. But I still get very angry at students."

"But sometimes you have to get angry at students. That is pretty natural, part of being a teacher, don't you think?"

"Well, yeah, up to a point, if it doesn't go too far."

"Anger is part of our human life. When it's like the thunderstorms here in Minnesota, it's okay. They just come and are very noisy and exciting. Then they are gone and the sky is blue again. Anger is just anger. But it's pretty natural when you are caught by it."

"Yeah, it's hard not to be caught. But I'll keep trying. What I've been noticing now, though, is that my zazen really works when I'm absolutely involved in all the other parts of my life, without hesitation, completely, not trying to escape them. Then, in some way, all of those parts—dealing with students, getting the house ready for the baby, even keeping the car going when it's below zero—helps my zazen. Or really, I guess it's more like it's part of my zazen."

"Ah, yes," Katagiri says excitedly, vigorously nodding, "that is exactly right! You know, you can't just pick up one side of the piece of paper. But human beings always want to do that. I do too."

We sit together for long minutes, peaceful together, silent in his study.

Finally I say, "You know, Roshi, I don't know if I'll ever be ordained, even as a lay Buddhist. Somehow it doesn't fit for me. It wouldn't be right for my family and friends. And the people I teach with would never understand. Everyone would just think I'm crazy. How can that help anyone—or help them to learn zazen?"

Smiling, he says, "It's okay. Don't worry about it. Just have the good spirit of a zen student. Just sit." He bows, I bow, and I leave.

Roshi calls and asks me to join him at the "Smorgasbord of Religious Cultures," a gathering hosted by a new age church near the University of Minnesota. He'll give a presentation on zen there. He's often reluctant to participate in such things, but we hope this will help advertise our existence in Minneapolis.

After the presentation, at the end of the afternoon, one of the organizers, an enthusiastic middle-aged woman, urges us to attend a final session led by a mystical dancing rabbi. Shy and not very ecumenical, Roshi politely declines.

"Oh, please, Katagiri Roshi," says the woman. "We'll be so sorry if you don't enjoy this experience with us."

Pressed, reluctant, Roshi agrees.

We walk downstairs into a large basement room and join about thirty people sitting in a circle on the floor.

The rabbi—giggly, clad in a black robe—talks about "transcendence with and through body," then stands in the middle of the group and begins to move in graceful circles, hands stroking the air.

"Easier," I think, "than getting up at four-thirty in the morning and sitting zazen all day until you collapse into bed."

There's a tugging at my sleeve. I turn. It's Roshi. He inclines his head toward a side door near us, whispering, "We can go now."

What? In front of these seekers, sitting rapt on the church basement floor, we should insult the mystical rabbi? He looks to be, after all, a nice middle-aged gentleman.

I hesitate, but Roshi holds my gaze, insistently nodding toward the side door. We get to our feet. The faces of the workshop participants follow us as we head for the door.

Ducking quickly through it, we find ourselves in total darkness. Damn! Then our eyes become accustomed to a dim light creeping in underneath the door, and we each explore an end of a long basement hall, feeling with our hands for a light switch or another door. Long minutes pass. No luck. Then finally, to my relief, at the top of a stairs, I find an exit door.

It's locked.

The escape is foiled. We've no choice but to go back. I open the door, Roshi goes through, and I follow him back into the workshop. We try to walk quickly and unobtrusively through the room, but the rabbi halts a sacred movement in midstep and, along with the entire assembly, observes us quietly, his eyebrows raised.

As I drive Roshi back to the Zen Center, he says nothing about the incident, nor do I. We drive in silence. I'm mildly amused. I understand Roshi's impatience with what he considers frivolousness. On the other hand, we were guests.

That Saturday, at the end of his regular lecture, he describes the religions smorgasbord and all the different things he saw. Finally he tells about the mystical dancing rabbi.

"Ah, but the Katagiri is very ignorant," he concludes, laughing ruefully. He raises one hand high above his head and with the other measures down to the floor. "The Katagiri ignorance is very deep, like this, as deep as the ocean. Can you imagine what I did? I walked out! I just walked out!"

He motions sweepingly with one black berobed arm, index finger jabbing toward the side of the room. He makes the noise small boys make when they fly toy airplanes. "*Sssshoooo!* I just walked out. I didn't want to stay. I am always pigheaded, you see. Even after so many years of practice, I am always so pigheaded. So maybe next time I can do better. I will try to stay."

It's the fall of 1979. I teach full time. I am now the father of an infant girl. Desperately I try to juggle these demands while maintaining full involvement in Zen Center activities. Roshi has announced that he will lead a three-month practice period that begins in a few weeks. I want to sign up for it. But it would take me out of the house mornings at 4:45, as well as two evenings a week and much of the day Saturday. Further, I'd have to sit a two-day sesshin each month and the seven-day rohatsu sesshin before Christmas.

I call one morning before my classes to arrange to talk with him. He's free, so I walk over to the Zen Center to ask for some kind of flexible schedule.

I enter the back door, leave my shoes in the basement on a shoe rack, and walk upstairs to the Katagiris' apartment. I knock, he opens the door and we bow to each other, and he leads me down the hall to his study. We sit down on zafus, he on his side of his long, low desk, I on the other side.

As we chat about some details of the financing of the country land purchase, Tomoe-san brings us cups of tea. She asks about the new baby, and I thank the two of them especially for making lovely patches to go in the baby quilt that Zen Center members had put together before the birth.

After she leaves, I launch into my question. "Roshi, I want very much to do the practice period, but with my teaching and the new baby, I don't see how I can do it. I really shouldn't be out of the house so much."

Roshi nods and looks at me expectantly.

I go on, "I wonder if you would make me a schedule for a practice period that I can do myself. I could talk with you regularly, maybe once a week. I know family life must be part of my practice now. But I want to practice zazen hard."

Uncomprehending, Roshi says, "It's okay if you can't do the practice period. There is no problem. You can just pay attention to your teaching and to your family. For some time into the future, you will have to be pretty busy."

"I know, Roshi," I say, "but I don't want to lose the thread of my practice. It seems like my life just gets busier and busier, and I can't really focus clearly on zazen at all. So my idea is that you could write up a schedule that I could keep strictly, but maybe not so many evenings away from the house. I could do all the morning zazens. And the lectures. And several sesshins. Then we could talk at certain times. That could help me to keep a strong practice."

The corners of Roshi's lips turn firmly down. "So it is your idea that you should have your own *special* practice period?" His emphatic enunciation of the word conveys impatience and contempt.

"No, no," I say, "I don't really want a *special* practice period. But if you're not willing to do this, it's okay." I'm embarrassed, sorry now that I came to him with my struggle. I didn't think that I was asking to be special. But I wanted him to help me practice as hard as I can.

A voice in my head grumbles, "He sure has plenty of time for the budding new priests!"

"It is not necessary," he says, "to do practice period at this time. Maybe some time in the future you can do it."

"Yes," I say. "I'll see. Maybe I can arrange to handle this practice period, after all. Most of the time I'd be gone will be in the early morning when the baby's asleep."

"You should think carefully," says Roshi. "Do you have any other question?"

"No," I say. "Thank you very much."

We bow and I leave.

Back in the basement, sitting on the stairs, pulling on my shoes, I'm upset, filled with angry questions. "Does he really think that the only reason I'm doing this is just to be special? I really do want to practice hard. Is he going to be my teacher or not? And I have to work. How does he expect me to pay bills? And my damned generous Zen Center pledges? I'm a father now, too. How does he expect families to raise kids?"

At home, that evening, I discuss the practice period with my wife. She agrees reluctantly that I can do it. The next morning, after zazen, I sign up.

It's the last of a series of rancorous meetings debating plans for the country land. The Zen Center has recently purchased a tract of beautiful undeveloped pasture and woodland in the hills of southeastern Minnesota. We're preparing to seek funds for buildings.

Roshi and several newer members of the group want these buildings designed after Eiheiji, Dogen's temple in Japan. There will be separate large halls, a Buddha hall for chanting and services and a zendo for zazen. In the zendo, there will be cupboards for personal belongings at each sitting place so students can sleep together. The goal is to recreate Dogen's original thirteenth-century practices.

I'm convinced none of this will work. In a final appeal, I argue, "This is Minnesota. We should build something that fits our land. We have no traditional Japanese materials or carpenters. And the winters are very cold. A Japanese-style temple will be impossible to heat.

"Besides, we can't afford to build two buildings just so the chanting and bowing can go on in a separate space from zazen. We'll be lucky to get one building built. And we will need dorms. Are a mixed group of men and women really going to sleep and dress together in the zendo?"

Others answer me, explaining that this is the real Buddhism, that we must go forward with confidence, that miracles happen when one's karma is pure.

"Don't expect that kind of miracle in Minnesota," I say angrily. "No one in this state is going to donate big money for such a thing. There just isn't much different in Japanese culture. Can't we be realistic and settle for some kind of three-season camp arrangement? That's how most church groups do it."

As so often happens to me now in Zen Center meetings, I feel outflanked. When I point out that our escalation of ceremonialism drives away potential students, effectively reducing our support for a city expansion or country buildings, I know other students dismiss me as an egotist and troublemaker. I, too, want expansion and country land. But I know I'll be one of those who feels duty bound to cope with budget shortfalls.

Worst of all, I've lost Roshi's support. Does he now just feel I'm in the way?

Finally, Roshi resolves the matter. The meetings have gone on too long. Reluctant, saddened by the lack of harmony among his students, he speaks quietly. "This is Dogen's way, this is our way. We should try to do it."

I'm bitter. Does he confuse black clothes and shorn heads with commitment? Does he misread passive-aggressive behavior as egolessness? He seems now to listen only to students who have arrived in the last few years. Students eager to don robes, shave heads, and play priest and priestess. Students who lack the practical work skills that enabled us to tear apart and rebuild the Calhoun house. Students who could never have raised the money to buy country land in the first place. "How," I wonder, "can he be so naïve?"

It's a Saturday afternoon that spring. I'm anxious to get home to my wife and infant daughter. My day at the Zen Center began with zazen at five in the morning, then breakfast, attendance at lecture and tea, and finally a work period before lunch. For me, the work has stretched into the afternoon because of a plugged basement toilet.

Halfway down the stairs, on the way to the toilet, I argue with a board member who wants someone to install a vented exhaust fan above the altar. She and some others feel they're getting allergic reactions to the constant burning of incense during meditation.

"Listen," I say, "do you have any idea what's involved with getting into the chimney cavity and bringing in power for a fan? Let's just cut down on the amount of incense we burn. After all, this isn't a huge, drafty Japanese temple. It's a house."

"No," she replies firmly, "we've talked to Roshi about that. He feels it's very important to follow Dogen's practice in every way."

Of course, Roshi may have said something like this. But I know how often his words are taken out of context to justify whatever someone wants.

"Look," I say, fuming, "two weeks ago someone took the storms off the basement windows for ventilation. Now we can't even seem to get the screens back up for the summer. Meanwhile, the place is filling up with mice, but no one wants to use poison or traps. This vent just isn't a very high priority for me, not right now, anyway."

With a look of pained but patient forbearance, the board member turns and continues up the stairs.

"On her way home!" I grumble to myself. "Oh, well, at least her little kids'll get a chance to see her. She'd never disappoint Roshi by not showing up at five Saturday morning, so no doubt she was in bed before they were last night—and gone before they got up."

Now it's almost three. The toilet's working again, but I'm in the alley, where squirrels have scattered orange peels, melon rinds, apple cores, and miscellaneous vegetarian slop across the grass and pavement. The mess has to be rebagged or the city won't collect it.

What about my own weekend chores? What about the baby? Disgusted, cursing squirrels and the careless zen students who threw plastic bags of this stuff unprotected in the alley, I see three brand new priestlets—two women, one man—in full black regalia tripping in clogs down the back alley on their way to a special priest meeting with Roshi.

These are recent converts. They arrived only a few years ago. Where were they when I gave thousands of hours and dollars to bring Roshi to Minnesota? Now they'll give lectures and lead seminars. I'll do chores. After fifteen years of fierce practice, after giving everything to this group, am I relegated to dirty work?

I'm suddenly reminded of Philip Whalen's poetry reading at the Loft last winter, a fund-raiser for the Zen Center. Afterward, he wanted to see Seven Corners, the Minneapolis equivalent of Greenwich Village and North Beach. He wanted to drink at the Mixers, a place I helped make into a legend. I should have been the tour guide for Philip, but Natalie and her friends spirited him off without saying a word to me. I was left behind to fold and stack the folding chairs.

"These prisses should be up to *their* nuts and cunts in veggie garbage," I grit through my teeth, watching the black backs and shaven heads disappear into the building.

I know they're going up to be served tea and cookies while discussing the sacred details of "priest practice." And my place in this place? They call me when cars don't start, when toilets plug, when insurance forms are neglected, when progress reports are due in Japan, when money runs out.

Oh, I know what they say. "Well, it's really a shame, but Erik has so much ego. He can't accept even the lay ordination. He just can't accept Dogen's way."

Now, with each orange peel dotted with spent herbal tea leaves, with each slippery melon rind skittering along the concrete, eluding my fingers, a voice rages, "Ego? Damn right I've got ego. And so do you all, you silly, whispering, passive-aggressive twits. You just hide it. You go to the zendo, cross your legs, and hide. You're sitting in a building that Pirsig's ego bought and that a half dozen strong male egos rebuilt with their own hands. Without us you wouldn't even be here.

"Or maybe you think I've got a problem with dirty work? I can handle stinking garbage. I can plunge shit-smeared tampon-plugged toilets for the rest of my life. But why should I?

"You priests want to learn the correct sequence of bows when offering incense at the altar? Come here, come close, my black-berobed pretties. Let me demonstrate the Buddha's way of picking up rotten tomato slices smeared on alley concrete. Let me show you the correct sequence of plunges when breaking up a huge black turd in a toilet badly plumbed by volunteer help."

Suddenly, hands full of apple cores, I come to a halt before a pile of coffee grounds. "Cool it, Erik," I think, upset now by my pounding heart and roiling stomach. "Let the garbage lie. Maybe it's time to quit being a good zen student. Go home, tend to the wife and baby, wash your own windows, fix your own slow toilet, and paint the baby's room.

"Of course your ego is huge. But does being a flunky help? Did you spend fifteen years of time and money, put an academic career on hold, and take a hundred high-dose acid trips to become one of those tired, middle-aged men hanging around the church basement—the reliable, regular volunteer, the sincere guy who'll always sweep up after the crowd, the deacons, and the preacher have all gone on home?

"You go home. To hell with the garbage. Go home. This is all making you sick."

I straighten up and toss the apple cores back on the cobblestone path, then sighing, pick them up again and finish the job. As I head for home, cutting through the Zen Center yard, a piece of advice Roshi gave me years ago echoes in my mind: "Don't stick your head too far into the cave of the church or you'll smell a very bad smell. It's true, even in the Soto zen sect."

I come back to the Crag filled with sadness. The day wanes, I'm tired, and even the jumbled black rocks seem draped in mourning. I uncurl my stiff legs, stretch them straight out, and lean over to embrace a shoulder-high boulder that sits on my right hand. I rest my head on the hard, jagged top, hugging it with my arms. My fingertips knead into the warm, rough surfaces. Looking up, I see that the raven, reproachful, continues to ignore me.

"How could you have been so self-absorbed?" I ask myself. "And naïve?" I shake my head. "Yes, you really did believe, even at thirty-eight, that zen would not have the frailties of other human institutions.

"You thought a religious organization could shuck its religious paraphernalia and hierarchy just for you. You thought that the Japanese Soto zen sect could take Dogen's advice and cast off its own body and mind.

"Maybe you read too many zen stories. Some monk in ancient China wanders from monastery to monastery for ten years, and then some famous master slaps him on the cheek, or breaks his eating bowl, or screams, 'Not one, not two,' and then 'at that moment the monk was truly awakened.' Did you really think that that was how it would be?"

Suddenly, I remember the Christian high school group, curious about Buddhism, that came to hear Roshi's Saturday lecture in his first year in Minneapolis. We gave them refreshments afterward, everyone sitting around a large table. One of the girls, her fresh face bright and wondering, asked Roshi, "Are you enlightened?"

"Yes," he said simply, with a smile, cradling his coffee cup, and went on to other questions. A few of us looked at each other in surprise at this quiet affirmation. We never asked him that question.

Then once again I remember that Saturday afternoon cleaning the alley. Sorrowfully, I whisper to myself, "Whatever the right or the wrong of it, after that, something was over for me." I stopped coming to zazen regularly. I stopped sitting sesshins. And even when I did come to Saturday lecture, even when I saw Tomoe subtly nudge Roshi in my direction during tea time and we exchanged a few words, even when I knew he was as incapable of reaching out as I, I didn't care anymore. I had thought we were special to each other. Of course, he had warned me against "using" the Zen Center. He had warned me against wanting a "special" practice. But I did want his love. I could no longer believe he really cared about me. Was his interest in my practice only proportional to mine in the priesthood? Now I felt used.

I rub my cheek into the rough, grainy surface of the warm black rock, comforted by its harsh reality. I sigh and sit up again, wriggling my toes. I pull up my left foot and examine the scab. It's a hard, tiny turtle shell now, dark brown, testimony to the quiet efficiency of the body.

"Why did you stay away for so long?" I ask myself. "Why did you stay so bitter? Couldn't you just be his friend?"

I look up from my mournful black rocks, from the mournful black raven, searching the sky and distant mountains for comfort in their beauty.

12

A Death

IT'S SEPTEMBER 1987. I'M SITTING THE FIRST sesshin I've sat in years—seven days on the country land in the hilly oak and maple forest of southeastern Minnesota. The thirteenth-century temple isn't here, never got funded, never got built. Now I wish I'd worked for it, at least as a patient, doubting friend.

Roshi is approaching sixty. I'm forty-six, divorced, busy with my kids and a new woman friend, no longer active at the Zen Center, doubting myself again, doubting the million decisions that have led to this place in just this way. Sadly, I think, "This should be my second home."

During the week, I sense Roshi's pain that the plans crumbled, his disappointment that all we have is this rough three-season camp—just what I'd argued for from the beginning. A sadness, at times, pervades his walk. His health, never strong, seems to be failing.

I'm grateful to be here, grateful to sit with him again—taking meals, hearing lectures, clearing weeds that choke the plantings of nut trees, sitting, sitting, sitting, hammer strokes on the chisel, chisel biting the mind stone, again and again and again. Who would have believed twenty years ago that such a place as this would blossom in Minnesota?

It's the fourth day of the sesshin. Some twenty of us sit in the little, rough-sawn oak zendo on the side of a hill that sweeps up into forest. We're bundled up in sweaters and sweat clothes. It's been chilly and damp all week, with frequent autumn clouds and showers. At the afternoon lecture, Roshi talks, among other things, about the difficulties and confusions that Americans experience when they become Soto zen Buddhists.

"Of course, it is very hard," he says. "I know that. The customs of a Japanese monastery seem pretty unusual in this much in world. Maybe sometimes they in in ridiculous. But it is our practice. We can just try it. All we can do is plant a seed. Maybe it can grow.

"I always ask you this question. How does the tiny pumpkin seed grow into the gigantic pumpkin fruit?" Roshi indicates something tiny between his thumb and forefinger. And then something huge, spreading his arms round and wide, embracing the air.

"Maybe this Zen Center is a little seed. Someday it can grow into a big pumpkin fruit. We cannot know for sure.

"I remember how I felt, a funny-looking Japanese person who came to the United States. Everything was very strange. It was hard to understand this new world. It was very hard just to live. I knew I was not really an American. It is pretty natural then if this Japanese person decides he doesn't want to stay in America. He doesn't want to be a citizen of the United States.

"That's okay, of course. But then, what if this Japanese person says, 'I think I would really like to be a big part of America. I would even like to be the president of the United States.' Someone will say to him, 'Well, after all, it is necessary for you to become an American citizen first.'

"Then this person feels some disappointment. Of course, it is really ridiculous. He must be a citizen first. But we are human beings. We always want like that sometimes."

Roshi chuckles. "How can you be the president of the United States without joining this country?" he asks again, musingly.

Sitting on my cushion, I smile to myself. "Yes. I'm the one who refused to join the Soto zen sect, yet threw everything into becoming a zen master. Remember how angry you were when he said once in a lecture that the zen priests were the 'professionals,' as if your practice was something less?"

But today I'm touched that Roshi talks to me again in this way, chiding me indirectly, in lecture. I feel like a young man, long away from home, who returns and now welcomes a fond father's rebuke. "Yes, he's right. It really is ridiculous. And yet, on the other hand, it isn't entirely! Can enlightenment really be about joining something?" I shift uneasily on my round, black cushion.

"Well, Erik, here you are, thinking things through, as usual. Roshi always said that it's not important to be smart, that that's not the real zen. I suppose you've just outsmarted yourself once again."

On the afternoon of the last day of the sesshin, I have dokusan in his little cabin. It's snug and pretty, the only building that nears completion.

"Roshi," I say, "this country center is very beautiful. It seems unfinished to you, I know, but think how amazing it is that we're all here sitting together, almost thirty people in the middle of bluffs and woods. We're warm and dry, we're eating good food. We even get hot showers."

"Yes, it's true, it's beautiful here. But I would like to do more." And he talks about the numbers of students he wants to come here, the possibility of winterizing for a year-round practice.

"It'll happen," I say. "But it'll take time. You know how slow everything is in Minnesota. It's true Suzuki Roshi was able to develop the Page Street Zendo and Tassajara, and he was only in America twelve years before he died. But that was California and those were the sixties. Something like that won't happen again soon, not even there. Things grow slowly here, but they put down deep roots, like oak trees. They grow tall and strong like the pines we planted on the hill up there." I gesture up toward the hill behind his cabin, where ten years ago a group of us planted little pines that now stand twice as tall as my head.

"You said we planted pines, not for ourselves, but for the future generations. Do you remember what you did when we finished planting that day?"

Roshi looks at me in quizzical surprise and shakes his head.

"You roared—roared like a mountain lion. It was loud, a tremendous roar. Everyone was shocked and just looked at each other. We all remember."

He brightens, smiling, and nods.

"I'm sorry, Roshi. I'm sorry I'm such a bad zen student. I wish I could have been better. Here I am, twenty years have gone by since we met at Sokoji Temple. I still haven't even become a lay Buddhist, let alone a priest. I guess I never will."

Roshi smiles. "That's all right, Don't worry about it." He always says this when I bring up my refusal of ordination and priesthood. I smile, too.

"Don't worry about it," he repeats.

"But you know," I say, "I'll sit forever. I'm very grateful to be here with you this week. I want to help Zen Center, if I can."

"Yes, please help us. Please go to the meeting Henry will have after the sesshin. They will discuss the building plans."

"Okay," I say, "I'll go."

I would like to say more, but I don't. I want to say I'm sorry—especially for the anger, for the hurt, for his disappointments, and for mine, too. I want to tell him how, despite the gulf between us, I honor his deep, unshakable commitment to striking the mind stone again and again and again. I know he has given absolutely everything to this, just this—and that it is this, not the chanting and incense, the robes and ceremonies, the ordination and hierarchy, that is his teaching.

But such things we don't say to each other, don't need to say. It is enough that we sit together again this week in the rough-sawn oak zendo, sit through sunrises, mornings, noons, afternoons, sundowns, evenings, day after day—seven days punctuated with bell and *han*, gong and drum.

Now, on this afternoon of the seventh day, together again, we sit in the great silence for long minutes, remembering, forgiving, forgetting each other's idiocies, the stubborn, implacable struggles we had with each other. Japanese silence, Scots-Norwegian prairie silence. We don't have to say much to know things are all right again.

Silence, silence, the deep zen silence. I feel a great peace flow out of our hearts, out through the windows and doors, flowing like waters between the trees and through buildings, carrying sounds of the zendo bell and the distant clattering of kitchen pots down through the river breaks to little Winnebago Creek, down ten miles into the Mississippi to be lost in the Gulf of Mexico, inundating coastlines, lapping the round globe itself.

The afternoon wanes. The incense stick has burned out on Roshi's small altar in this small cabin on the edge of oak and maple forest. It will soon be time for afternoon service and dinner.

I raise my hands and press the palms together. Roshi takes up his stick and holds it between his palms. Still seated, we slowly bow to each other.

I say, "Roshi, I thank you very much for all your teaching and for all these years. Thank you very much."

And he says simply, in his husky whisper, "Thank you very much."

It's over a year later. I'm visiting Roshi in the hospital. He's been very sick for months, but seems now on the mend. Tomoe-san has almost lived at the hospital.

This afternoon he gingerly eases himself out of the bed and carefully walks across the room to sit erect, upright, on the edge of a hospital easy chair.

I say, "Tomoe tells me that the doctor thinks you may have been fighting a tuberculosis infection. Is that something you might have gotten last year during your stay in Japan?"

"Oh, I think it is possible. Maybe so."

"Is it a problem in the monasteries?" I ask.

"Yes," he says grimly. "It is a big problem. They are famous for it."

It's one of two times I hear him say something critical of his Soto zen sect.

"It looked really bad," I say. "We thought you were going to die. How about you? Did you think so too?"

"Oh, yes," he says, nodding, smiling. "I was worried."

It's early spring in 1989. Tomoe-san calls and asks if I can give Roshi an occasional cup of tea in my home. As soon as the snow is off the sidewalks, she wants him to build his strength by taking walks. I'm only a few blocks from the Zen Center, a convenient stopping place.

"Of course, Tomoe, I'd be delighted. So how is Roshi feeling?"

"Oh," she says, "he's still weak. But he's getting stronger. And I think walking will help him very much."

The appointed day is clear and warm, the last drifts of snow quickly melting. I get home from teaching a little early to clean up the living room. I wish the kids would be back from school so he could see them, too, but they go till late in the afternoon. I set the pot boiling, get some cookies and English tea ready in the kitchen, and clear off the coffee table. Then I sit down to wait.

My living room bay window faces west, and beams of late afternoon sun slant in from the southwest, touching the room with an orange-pink glow. "Ah," I remember, "just like the sunset bouncing off the December lake into the Calhoun House that first day I saw it with Roshi and the Pirsigs."

Soon there's a knock on the door. Roshi wears mittens, a wool stocking cap to keep his shaved head warm, and a black cape Tomoe made to go over his priest's robes. I open the door. He's thin and appears tired, but his eyes still sparkle. We're both a little hesitant.

"Ah, Roshi, thank you very much for coming to tea," I say, ushering him into the living room.

"Oh, thank you very much, Erik. This is a very good place for me to stop in my walk."

I bring things in from the kitchen. He sits on the couch, his legs curled to one side, leaning against the armrest. He seems smaller, not much bigger than a child. We sit for a time quietly sipping tea and munching cookies.

"How are your boys?" I ask.

"Oh, very good," he says, and laughs. "Ejyo is away at college now. He studies very hard. And Yasuhiko is working. His wife has had her baby. Oh, the baby is very active, very strong." I listen, delighted in his pride in the accomplishments of these men I first met as small children in Monterey.

"And how is the Zen Center?"

"Oh," he says, not so cheerfully, "there is always some problem.

There are many questions about how to develop buildings at Hokyoji. I think the Soto sect will give us some money."

"They've been pretty generous," I say.

"Yes, that is good. They really want to help us. How are Katie and Scott?"

"Oh, they're really good," I say. "I wish they were here today for you to see. They're so big!"

And we talk on, two fathers, two friends.

It's a year later in February. I'm spending the night again with Roshi and Tomoe. He's exhausted, in terrible pain. Someone must stay over every night now to help. I'm sure it's a death watch, but Tomoe struggles to be hopeful, taking me to the kitchen to show me how to brew a traditional remedy recommended by an herbal doctor in Japan. I'm to set an alarm and give it to him at four in the morning. This will allow Tomoe a little extra sleep. "The doctor scolds me for not giving him this medicine sooner," she says. "He thinks this can help him very much."

Downstairs a sesshin is in progress. We hear the occasional tinkle of the bell, signaling the beginnings and endings of zazen and kinhin. "Oh, Tomoe-san!" I say to myself. "You had hoped one day to live with your family separate from the zendo so the boys didn't have to be so quiet during meditation. Now they are grown up."

Roshi is sitting up on the couch in the living room. He watches a taped Japanese feature film depicting an arctic dogsled expedition. I sit next to him in an easy chair. Tomoe clears up supper dishes.

The men on the screen are in trouble. There is snow blowing, and vast vacant spaces through which they urgently mush their dogs, shouting excitedly in Japanese.

Roshi takes morphine for pain. He struggles to sit upright on the edge of the couch, to attend to his guest, to be present here in the human world once more before the drug wears off and, again, pain and darkness close in. Watching the show, I talk little, try simply to be here for him.

Soon he wants to return to bed. But first he needs to visit the bathroom. I assist him in. In a few minutes, he calls me back. The morphine is fading, his pain so severe he can't walk further.

Tomoe goes downstairs and brings up Henry from the sesshin. Henry and I carry him gently in our arms from the bathroom to his bed.

We lay him carefully down. His eyes close and he quickly falls asleep. I say goodnight to Tomoe and go back to one of the boy's rooms. He's off at college, and the unused room echoes vacantly. Sadly, I throw a sleeping bag out on the floor and crawl in.

A few hours later, somewhere after midnight, Tomoe wakes me. Roshi is in agony. She's not sure how much more morphine he can have. She has called Cary, another old student, who has already come to the apartment. I follow them into his room. He looks tiny—a child. Lying on his back, he moans gently and moves his arms fitfully, searching for some position that can relieve the fierce pain. Tomoe decides he must go back to the hospital.

Cary tells me that a neighbor's car blocks one end of the long alley. The ambulance can drive forward up to the back gate, but will have to back out a hundred feet through crusty, rutted snow. She asks me to try to wake someone to move the car out of the way.

I walk out into the night, a light winter wind blowing cold across the frozen lake. In shirtsleeves, hunched against the wind, I hammer repeatedly on the neighbor's back door. A light burns dimly from somewhere inside the house, but no one answers.

Then the ambulance is here, already pulling slowly up the alley, wheels spinning, lurching into the deeper ruts. Two men hurry upstairs, and Roshi, strapped to a stretcher, is carried down and slid into the back. Tomoe and Cary, bundled up in winter coats, hurry to climb in after him. Then the ambulance is creeping backwards, red backup lights glowing on the snow, and suddenly, before I know it, he's gone.

Shivering, I slowly walk back upstairs to the empty apartment. Aimless, unable to sleep, I prowl the rooms where fifteen years ago, full of fresh dreams, so many of us rebuilt, replastered, repainted.

I enter Roshi's study and kneel at his altar. The candle is out and no incense burns in the bowl. Here is his roshi's stick—it thwacked my shoulders again and again when he caught me drowsing before sunrise in the zendo. Here a little Buddha statue, here pictures of his teachers and friends. Here little Japanese decorative items, Buddhist play pretties, that remind me of knickknacks kept by elderly aunts on their mantels.

And here his dream—an altar raised up in the heartland of America, where states are bigger than the whole of Japan, an altar from which the Buddha's peace would radiate forever.

We struggled together, Japanese water, American fire. Struggled with the bullying, brutal mind that begs you to quit, give up, roll over and hug the pillow, have just one more hour of sleep, one more, oh, one more, oh, please, just one more!

I rise and cross the room. For the first time in my life, I sit on the zafu behind his desk. So many times he sat here, me on the other side, discussing car batteries, his kids' schools, the Zen Center budget, a translation for his next lecture.

I pick up his wristwatch. It's still set an hour ahead for last summer's daylight savings time—the time before he got so terribly sick.

I see books everywhere. The bookcase across the room is covered with cloth so book titles and authors don't distract students who have come for dokusan. No student will see him in dokusan again.

Behind me in the bookshelf, bound in red leather, is the first corporate minute book of the Minnesota Zen Meditation Center. I take it down and open it. Turning the pages, I see minutes of our first meetings set down in black ink. It's a record of discussions, debates, decisions, all written out at length, first in my hand, then in others'. Ah, so much of our lives was given to this enterprise.

And Roshi, here on the desk is your own book, *Returning to Silence*. What troubles you had with your English—and how few years to enjoy this sweet triumph of your own English in print. With a pang, I think, "I didn't even ask you to sign a copy. Was it really that hard, Erik, to pull down anger and ancient pride—to be simply a friend?"

This building I helped break and rebuild, these carpets I've sat upon for hours, this room where we've tested each other, sometimes angry, sometimes laughing. Did I this night really hold you in my arms, your hands clutched with the deadly pain, your arms writhing, searching for relief—now a little old man, now a wrinkled child? Did I really see you just now carried down the stairs and away, as Tomoe, so steady, so

scared, looked on? Oh, Tomoe, how I miss the Christmas sesshins—
and your cactus, overflowing in a waterfall of silent red blossom.

How the two of you must have wondered at times, waking up in the
morning with your two little boys in a distant, foreign town in the
unimaginable North American heartland. Did you remember how we
were the enemy when you were teenagers? Was loneliness softened at
sundown, when your white-plastered rooms filled with golden light
reflecting up from the lovely, mile-wide lake?

I shiver again and look over to the casement windows on the south
and east walls. They still leak, breathing icy night air onto my feet and
ankles. Years ago I had a plan to improve their seal against the northwest winds, but the old house always had some more pressing need.
Slowly, lingering, my eye travels around the room. The altar and its
Buddha shed quiet radiance, yet everywhere paint peels, plaster cracks,
and makeshift brick-and-board bookshelves warp under the weight of
ink and paper. "Oh, Roshi," I think, "even now, after seventeen years,
your study is poised between beauty and shabbiness. Was there not
time to take root here by these shores?

"Now it all ends in stubborn battle, a battle to sit on the couch with
your spine upright for one more hour, mind whirling—one more hour
escaping the pain—just one more hour remembering how it was to be
a healthy man, relaxing, quietly watching an hour of television with
an old student. Two zen masters taken by cancer, each twenty years
before his time. You and Suzuki helped bring the dharma east. Is this
the price you paid? Were you caught between America and Japan, fire
and water, ground between the tectonic plates of East and West?"

I hear a muffled snoring from the zendo below me. In a few short
hours, just before five, the zen students will wake. They'll sit again.
They'll sit all day.

I rest my palm on Roshi's book, whispering, "You didn't fail, Roshi."
Tears start in my eyes, a lump swells in my throat. "You didn't fail.
Never think it."

He brought a gift of silence. And I owe a debt I can't repay except,
in each moment, to teach more silence.

Rubbing my eyes on my sleeves, I murmur, "I'll repay it, Roshi. I
swear, I'll repay it."

I touch fingertips to his worn tabletop. The grain in the wood flows and flows. Just so.

It's a week later. Warm afternoon sunshine thaws the late winter snow. I glance out my living room window. Katie and Scott and the girls next door play in the front yard after school, running, jumping, squishing mud, then splashing it off their boots in sidewalk puddles. I sink back onto the couch to watch, curling up against the armrest. Angling sunlight streams in the bay windows, warming my feet and hands.

The phone rings. It's Tyrone, another old student of Roshi's. "I knew you'd want to know that Roshi died last night," he says.

We talk quietly about Roshi and the long illness. "Toward the end," Tyrone says, "Roshi motioned Tomoe to come close and gently puckered his lips for a final kiss. We were so moved. It was an utterly simple act."

My throat catches, and I grip the phone, both of us silent.

Finally Tyrone says, "I know you remember his sailor's cap."

"Oh, yes, of course," I say.

"In the morning, some of us were there, and Tomoe brought it down and put it in the coffin."

The cap! His alter ego, his mischief, a mask for the little boy shy about being a strange bald Japanese in Minnesota, a boy lost somewhere before World War II in the Japanese Army and in the grim postwar monasteries.

Out in the yard, it's getting dark. Katie and Scott, ages ten and eight, come in, flinging off wet boots and mittens and jackets. They sit down on the couch next to me, one on each side. I tell them what's happened, then cover my eyes and sob.

"Why are you so sad?" Scott asks.

"He was my friend," I say. "I'll miss him."

Scott is concerned, wondering at my tears. He snuggles close, pats my shoulder, and takes my hand, just like I do when he cries. Katie, on my other side, puts her arms around me, hugs me, and gives me a kiss on my wet cheek.

The next morning I join others in the zendo who have come to sit with the body. Cold air flows over the floor through the half-opened casement windows. Meltwater from the snowy roof rattles down the downspouts. I stand, offer incense to the body, and bow.

Waves of peace, great ocean rollers, flow out and out from the coffin, out from that small motionless form. The melt from the roof falls, pattering, pattering, in puddles outside the half-opened windows. It flows down through the early spring puddles, broadening out on the land, gathering itself into the edges of the mile-wide frozen lake.

I leave the zendo and walk. Warm days and frosty nights have pulled up the maple sap. It drips from the ends of broken twigs, leaving dark, wet patches on the maple trunks. I leave the sidewalk and press the tip of my tongue onto cold, wet maple bark—so rough, oh, so sweet!

On the next Christmas Eve I bring Tomoe a gift. I've done this every year since the Katagiris arrived in Minneapolis. First I brought things to delight children, then gifts for grownups, and last year a colorful fish for a first grandchild.

Now, her first Christmas without Roshi, she is in the upstairs apartment alone. When she sees the little cheerfully wrapped package, she catches her breath and looks down and away. The tears rise to my eyes, and there's a lump in my throat.

Then, quickly looking up with a smile, she accepts the gift, saying, "Please wait." She runs inside.

She returns a few minutes later with a little package. "Please, this is for the children."

"Oh, Tomoe," I say, "it's been such a hard year."

"Yes," she says. "It has been a very hard year. But now he can rest."

13

Wash Your Cup

THE RAVEN SQUAWKS AGAIN, BRINGING ME BACK to the Crag. I look over at him. Still nonchalant, unconcerned, he stares out over the trees, his ragged feathers trembling in the wind. Beyond him, to the north above distant foothills, I see the hawks. Two specks soar into one, then apart, drifting lazily. The sun, reddening to blood, leans on a peak to the west. A joyful fatigue steals through my whole body.

So I sit. I sit here on the Crag, a stone on a stony outcrop, mind marking memories as they rise and fall. Waiting for nothing, watching for nothing, I wait, I watch. Time flows endlessly, buoys up the dusty world, pools in the expanse of my belly moving with each slow breath, in and out, in and out.

The mountains teach this in sparkling snowmelt waters that move, move without ceasing, polishing to a marbled enameling the fractured, ice-shattered rock of the basins. The mind in zazen learns that polish, a smooth softness from the eternal cut and wash of time.

Everything is mine, and nothing—this delicate, strange body I protect and cherish, the scraped skin that with an ancient wisdom of the blood now heals itself, this mind that rolls through all things. Right now I'd take a death, leave a carcass on the Crag—meat for the coyotes, pearl bones they'd gnaw and scatter while punctuating the mountain night with yips and yaps and yowls.

My mind opens to the ten thousand things, reflected, floating—the raven keeping his black watch—the hawks in sexual feint and parry soaring high above the land—the Douglas firs, lightning scarred, roots knotted into living rock, bolts bowed back from centuries of storm winds blown blustering across this crest of land—these rough black rocks, inhospitable yet warm from the afternoon sun, re-radiating that ancient radioactive fire—the great basins below me, encircled by mountains, drifting in the hazy warm distance, darkening as the sun's red orb is sliced finer and finer by a thin sawblade of distant western peaks.

All this the effortless weaving of the vast mind loom, all this floating on mind stuff—floating through the pinhole in the iris of my eye, carried on waves of vibrating energy down fibrous nerve passageways, sunlight reaching deep inside my skull.

"It's getting late," I think. "Time to get back down to the cabin." Stiff, aching, happy, I unwind my legs and gather my things into the little pack. Standing, with palms pressed together, I bow slowly to each of the four directions—first north, then east, then south, then west—softly whispering, "Thank you!" with each bow.

Then I step from rock to rock down the black pile of glacial rubble, hit open sage, and settle into hip-swinging strides that carry me fast down the steep hills, my boots taking long slides in gravel until the heels bite into hummocks of turf. The fine dust and crushed sage fill my nose as the basin darkens before me.

In an hour I'm comfortable, sitting in my folding chair in the cabin. The room is warm, the wood cookstove roars, and my dishpan of breakfast dishes sits on top, waiting to be washed. Ice tinkles in a glass of scotch I cup in my lap.

"Well," I think, "tomorrow I'll have to get after the ditch again. Installing a waste valve and pulling the line straight up is really the best way to go. I'd better get to the dump, too."

"Hold it!" says another voice. "Keep your mind on Katagiri's mat.

Zen is every minute. Remember the old story? 'Have you finished your tea? Well, wash your cup!' "

I set down my scotch, stand, and walk over to the dishpan. On the top of the pile is my white coffee cup. I rinse it with soapy water, brush it with the dish brush, then pick up a scrubber and begin to work out stubborn, dark stains at the bottom.

Out the window, in fading autumn light, the sky is darkening blue, the dying heather a glowing red.

Glossary

BARDO   Tibetan for "in-between state"; the period after death and before a new rebirth, traditionally forty-nine days. In *The Psychedelic Experience*, Timothy Leary, Richard Alpert, and Ralph Metzner suggest that the descriptions of after-death experiences in *The Tibetan Book of the Dead* (*Bardo thödol*) are also descriptions of states of consciousness experienced in meditation—and therefore important guideposts to orient psychedelic voyagers.

BODHIDHARMA   Bodhidharma, the twenty-eighth patriarch after the Buddha, brought a profound meditation practice and authentic understanding of the Buddha's teachings from India to China in the sixth century. Some consider him a mythical figure.

BODHISATTVA   Sanskrit for "awakened being." An enlightened one who, out of compassion, accepts rebirth after rebirth in order to aid myriad suffering beings.

BUDDHA   The term comes from the Sanskrit root *budh*, "to awaken." Thus a buddha is a human being who has awakened from the sleep of the ordinary dualistic mind and now fully experiences the fundamental oneness of all Being. The historical Buddha, Siddhartha Gautama (563?–483? B.C.E.), was born into a noble family in what is now Nepal. It is said that after renouncing a long, debilitating, and spiritually fruitless asceticism, he vowed to sit in meditation until he had resolved the dilemma of human suffering. After forty-nine days seated under the

Bodhi Tree, he realized perfect enlightenment. Later he would describe this liberation simply as "bliss."

CH'AN   See dhyana.

CURANDERO (masc.), CURANDERA (fem.)   Spanish for "healer"; a shaman. In Huatla de Jimenez in June of 1955, Maria Sabina was introduced to Gordon Wasson as a "curandera de primera categoria" who could guide him in the mushroom ceremony.

DHARMA   A key term in Buddhism used to denote ordinary things like chairs and trees, as well as the underlying Law of the universe. In its broadest sense, the Dharma is the ultimate reality known fully by the Buddha and expressed in his teaching.

DHYANA   Sanskrit for meditation, concentration, and mental absorption, but the term suggests more than a mere focusing of the mind. It points toward an infinite and unitive awareness. The word became *ch'an* in Chinese and *zen* in Japanese and gave a name to the schools that emphasized the Buddha's silent sitting as the path to realization.

DOAN   The title of the person who, among other duties, rings the bells that mark the beginnings and endings of meditation periods in the *zendo*.

DOGEN ZENJI (1200–1253)   The Japanese zen master who, after intense practice in China, established the Soto zen school in Japan. His writings are pregnant with poetry, philosophical insight, and enlightenment.

DOKUSAN   A private interview between zen student and zen master in which questions of zen practice are raised.

EIHEIJI   One of the two principal monasteries of the Japanese Soto Zen School, founded by Dogen in 1243.

ENLIGHTENMENT   A word commonly used to translate the Sanskrit *bodhi* (awake). The Buddha is literally "the awakened one." In this context, the term *enlightenment* has no relation to its traditional use in the West to denote rational, scientific understanding as opposed to superstition and dogma. Various Buddhist traditions countenance various types and levels of enlightenment, but the Buddha's awakening is presumed to be final and complete.

HAN   A wooden board suspended from a rope and struck with a hammer three times a day to signal dawn, dusk, and bedtime.

HEART SUTRA   A short section taken from the *Prajnaparamita Sutra* and commonly recited in the Mahayana tradition. It asserts the interdependence and ultimate oneness of form and emptiness—yet their independent existence. *Form im-*

plies the myriad objects that humans can perceive. Emptiness implies infinite unconditioned Being. This affirmation of paradox underpins the many contradictory and a-logical statements in zen koans, as well as the presumption in zen that all philosophical and theological systems (even Buddhist ones) are but verbal nets cast to catch the reflection of the moon in the water.

HOKYOJI   The country temple founded by Katagiri Roshi in southeastern Minnesota. It is presently a center for zen retreats and seminars, and has several year-round residents.

HYAKUJO   (720–814 C.E.) A great Chinese zen (ch'an) master of the T'ang dynasty. From him comes the rule "A day of no working is a day of no eating."

JOSHU   The Chinese zen master who was asked the question, "Does the dog have buddha nature?" He answered, "No!" This question is often given as a koan.

KASHYAPA BUDDHA   The Buddha of a supposed age that preceded the current one in which we now live and into which Siddhartha Gautama, the historical Buddha, was born.

KINHIN   In Soto Zen, a slow, walking meditation of five to fifteen minutes that is practiced between periods of sitting meditation.

KOAN   A paradoxical or a-logical statement given by the zen master to a disciple as a problem to solve. The disciple works with the koan in meditation and confronts the master in dokusan with possible solutions. A famous example is "What is the sound of one hand clapping?" The Zen Master Mumon Ekai said a koan is brick with which to knock at a gate so as to awaken those inside. When someone finally opens the gate, the brick can be thrown away.

LUTEFISK   Norwegian for "lye fish." A traditional Christmas dish of the nineteenth-century Norwegian immigrant communities on the Midwestern prairies, who now had no access to the sea and fresh fish. It is prepared from dried cod preserved in lye, reconstituted by soaking and then boiling. The dish has lost popularity with subsequent generations.

MAHAYANA   The Mahayana (Sanskrit for "Great Vehicle") and Hinayana (Sanskrit for "Small Vehicle") are the two major schools of Buddhism. The Mahayana is a later development, which went beyond the traditional monasticism of the Hinayana to emphasize the laity and the Bodhisattva ideal of awakening all beings.

MOKUGYO   A wooden drum, first made in the shape of a fish, now assuming a more rounded form. The drum establishes a steady beat during the chant of sutras.

NANSEN   (748–835 C.E.) Hyakujo's teacher. His is the famous saying, "The ordinary mind is the way." This ordinary mind, he explains, is "vast emptiness."

Glossary ————————————————————————————

ORYOKI   The set of nesting eating bowls with utensils, napkin, and wrapping cloth that is traditional in the zen monastery.

PRATYEKA BUDDHA   Sanskrit for "solitary awakened one." The Mahayana tradition is critical of the Pratyeka Buddha, for unlike the Bodhisattva, he enjoys his awakening selfishly, failing to help other beings to enlightenment.

RINZAI   See *Soto*.

ROHATSU SESSHIN   A sesshin held from December 1 to December 8 that commemorates the Buddha's enlightenment on the eighth day of the twelfth month.

ROSHI   Japanese for "old master," a title for a zen teacher who has had deep enlightenment experience. After some years in Minnesota, Katagiri Roshi became impatient with the corrupted uses of this term and asked students to address him as Hojo-san, a less exalted term for an elder monk or the abbot of a monastery.

SAMADHI   Sanskrit for "to place together; to make one." A state of undistracted concentration in which the mind is one-pointed. Huston Smith notes the parallel between *sam* and the Greek *syn*, and between *adhi* and the Hebrew *adonai*, suggesting the meaning "completely absorbed in God."

SENSEI   A Japanese title used for teachers and other professionals.

SESSHIN   Japanese for "gathering the mind." An intensive meditation retreat lasting one to seven days.

SOTO   Soto and Rinzai are the two principal zen schools active today in Japan. Traditionally, Rinzai emphasizes the koan in an encounter between master and disciple to push the student to awaken. Soto emphasizes awakening without words through the quiet, formless meditation of zazen.

TOZAN (807–869 C.E.)   One of the founders of the Soto school in China. While wandering as a pilgrim, he is said to have experienced a profound awakening after glimpsing his reflection in the water as he crossed a stream.

ZAFU   A round black meditation cushion stuffed with kapok, traditional in Japanese zen practice.

ZAZEN   Japanese for "sitting meditation." The form is commonly seen in statues of the Buddha sitting erect, legs crossed, hands placed one atop the other in his lap with thumb tips lightly touching, eyes cast gently down before him.

ZEN   See *dhyana*.

ZENDO   Japanese for "meditation hall."

ZORIS   Traditional straw sandals that are held on by a thong that goes between the great and the next toe.